NO STARTUP LEFT BEHIND

Learn How to Launch an Idea and Skyrocket to Startup Success

REAGAN T. POLLACK

ISBN: 978-0-578-84808-2

Edited by Jen Schuster

Cover design by Riyaz Ali Khan, Upwork®

Reagan Pollack, PO Box 22726, Carmel, CA 93922

www.reaganpollack.com

First Edition

Printed in the United States

First published in 2021 by Presidential Technology

Printed by CreateSpace

For my family.

Your support, love, and wisdom meant more than you could ever know. Thank you for always believing in my entrepreneurial dreams.

Disclaimer:

The author is not a financial advisor, attorney, accountant, or certified business planner, nor claims to be. The content in this book should be viewed as purely subjective in nature as it is based on the author's experience in his own businesses conducted years prior. Always take counsel from a professional financial advisor, attorney, accountant, or certified business planner in regard to your own business formation, management, and financial investments. There are many risks associated with starting your own business and working in a startup company, and most owners and their investors lose all of their principal capital and equity investment when the company dissolves. The content, methods, techniques, stories, and strategies outlined in the book are meant to solely provide subjective education to help founders better familiarize themselves with what might occur in some early stage ventures. All content, information, methods, techniques and strategies outlined herein are purely subjective in nature and should not be followed verbatim without first seeking professional financial, legal, and business counsel. The content should only be used for educational purposes to illustrate the author's own experiences. Examples, charts, graphs, metrics, and any recommendations contained herein are for educational, illustrative purposes only. You should always conduct your own research, make your own informed decisions, and seek counsel with a licensed professional or business advisor before proceeding with any decisions that may affect your company, shareholders, customers, suppliers, investors, or employees. To protect the privacy but retain the educational benefits of the stories within, some names have been changed.

TABLE OF CONTENTS

FOREWORD

To succeed in business, as in life, you must prepare for anything. But there comes a point, where every entrepreneur must cross the chasm, and step out from the cozy, protective womb of ideation, and into the world where opportunity awaits to be conquered. What lies ahead may include public criticism, bankruptcy, failure and self-deprecation. Startup days are like the weather — hard to predict past a few days, dark torrential storms may abound, but eventually, sunlight will emerge to light the way forward, providing that is, you last through the storm.

Over the course of your entrepreneurial journey, if you discover a willingness to fail in the pursuit of greatness, massive social change, and disruptive innovation, you will develop a confidence the likes that you have never experienced before. But you must give first, before you can get. You must plant, before you can enjoy the fruits of the harvest. You must conquer the inner, before you master the outer. This is the sacrificial contract that all entrepreneurs sign. Often the risks outweigh the returns, and when we're lucky, the return outnumbers the risk. I am not here to be your muse, that, you must discover on your own, in your own way. Nor am I here to show you any get rich quick tricks that will guarantee your financial success — as that is surely impossible. What I am here for, is to shine a beacon of light as you embark out on your entrepreneurial journey, to help you see your new adventure not with rose colored glasses, but with battle-tested x-ray vision, so that you will not only develop the what to do when, but also find the why in what you do. Let's begin.

INTRODUCTION: THE FOUNDER'S FUMBLE

When I launched my first startup at twenty, no one ever told me what to do, what to avoid, and how to get through the impending shit storm; I learned the hard way — by falling flat on my face, burning through investor capital, and failing over and over again. I told myself that if I ever figured the startup game out, I'd pay it forward, and share my secrets with the world. This is it. Your startup will not be left behind.

This is the first time I've attempted to document my startup story. The thought that reverberates in my head says, "Speak from the gut, tell the truth, don't sugarcoat the journey." So here it goes. After all, if you're really going to invest years of your life building something worthwhile, you deserve to be told what's really in store for you.

The three goals of this book are simple:

1. Move your messy idea to launch in months (not years).

2. Point out lethal startup landmines so you can avoid them.

3. Get you prepared to fail so you can unlock success on the other side.

To me, the greatest skill that I have in my life, is the ability to dream up an idea, think about all of the resources that I need to make it happen, build it, launch it, scale it, and reap the rewards. Being an entrepreneur is truly a gift.

This skill, called entrepreneurship, I was not born with. Don't worry — we can learn to master it as it is a learned skill, not given at birth. It only took me a decade to learn, countless failures, and hundreds of thousands of dollars' worth of investment between schooling, books, seminars, and multiple startups to get the hang of it. I'm going to condense over a decade into a few hundred pages of bittersweet startup reality. While I can't just give you this skill, I can show you the keys that have helped me to unlock my own potential, simplify the journey, and shown me how to persevere through failure, so that should you choose to start or grow a company, you can do it faster, easier and far cheaper than I did.

While the world may not care about your startup, I do. Your success is truly my success. Why? Because I've been there, alone with my vision, up against all of the obstacles, praying for profits but only seeing debt. I know what you're facing today, and will be facing tomorrow, and you deserve to have someone in your corner. Allow me the privilege of helping you get the most out of your startup and your journey. The world needs great companies, led by smart founders, and if I can help you get there (yes you), then I've done my part.

Now, why are you reading this book? Really, ask yourself, why? Have you had a market hunch or product idea floating around in the back of your mind for years that you just aren't confident enough to launch and risk it all for? I get it, the monthly corporate paycheck is hard to give up. Or maybe you're mesmerized by the financial independence and personal mastery of one's own life that successful founders seem to exude, and that lights you up because you want that for yourself. Or maybe, you've been through a startup failure before which cost you tens or hundreds of thousands of dollars and a lot of personal struggle or pain, but you know there's more fight in that dog inside — you just need to see the light at the end of the tunnel one more time to know that success is still waiting for you on the other side. Lastly, maybe you've been there and done that twenty-five years ago as part of a startup squad — leaped over some fires, scaled like mad to conquer a market, and reaped some of the financial fruits of a harvest. But that was a quarter century ago, and a lot has changed since that era. You still want more out of life, and you want deeper, lasting meaning in what you do today and tomorrow. Quite possibly, you want to leave a lasting legacy to provide a trans-generational business for your kids. Wherever you're coming from, I know there's concrete value in the coming chapters for you.

This book is not an instruction manual that guarantees success. Why? Because that would be total BS. There is no "Do A + Do B =

C Success" formula. There is no one-size-fits all playbook that works in every situation an entrepreneur may encounter. But, there are patterns that accelerates success, and I'll share them with you.

I've discovered that there are these repeating patterns that seem to always emerge at every stage, and there are decisions that lead us to rapid failure or growth — the choice is ours. By being able to recognize these signs, and by being able to see ahead of our journey before we even begin, we gain an arsenal of tools that can unlock insights to lead us to create value faster for our customers, push us to overcome obstacles when they overwhelm us, and help us define success personally, so that we don't get lured off course by sensationalized stories of "Overnight Entrepreneur", "From Idea to IPO", or "How to Become a Billionaire".

We will traverse from the inner mental and emotional challenges you face today (and will face shortly), to the external challenges you will face from every angle — from messy market hunches to unique insight discovery, from financial discombobulation to seeing the KPIs (key performing indicators) that matter most, I'll walk you through market research, product development, launch, failure and scale. I'll be your tour guide into what really happens in entrepreneurship — not what you hope happens.

I only ask one thing in return from you — when you become your version of successful, create the business that gives you what you desire out of life, and master your understanding of your own entrepreneurial journey — I want you to pass this valuable torch onto others, so that they too, can rise to their greatest potential. So, we got a deal?

To help you jump right in, I've tried to front load the content so that you get right into what matters when you're just starting up. We'll journey from business planning (or lack thereof), through product pricing, understanding markets and behavioral psychology of the consumer, to marketing campaign development, competitor analysis, mastering sales, financial planning, and scaling. The final chapters highlight my first two startups, and more specifically the absolute total shit storm decade that we faced and shows how I fell on my butt and failed dozens of times before ultimately finding startup success. By the end of the book, you will be able to spot avoidable landmines before they crop up, and be able to ideate, plan, launch, scale and/or leap over failure. Let's jump in!

CHAPTER 1
FAIL FIRST, THEN SUCCEED

"You see things; you say, 'Why?' But I dream things that never were;
and I say 'Why not?'"
—George Bernard Shaw

"I fucking failed." The words fell from my lips in exhaustion. I was tired of trying to hide it from the world. Our startup had burned through $123,000 of investor capital, our lead web developer had just dumped us for another company and a six-figure salary, and we were left with a website full of unfixed bugs, and 3,500 hopeful subscribers who still believed we could help them succeed in the music business. It was 2008, in the height of the worst global financial recession since the Great Depression, the record industry had imploded trying to protect their lucrative CD, as the shift to digital was in full force. Early-stage Venture Capital funding had evaporated overnight. I was twenty-one, my business card read CEO, but I was holding on for dear life. It was heading right towards us, and there was nothing I could do — every decision had led us to this moment — failure.

Two years prior, my entrepreneurial inquisition had beckoned me back east to Babson College, the #1 ranked entrepreneurial business school, then back to California post-graduation, to run my first dot com, WorldMusicLink — a LinkedIn® meets Match® web platform aimed at connecting unsigned talent with companies in the music industry. As a musician myself, I knew the industry was painfully fragmented — only a select few became rich winners, and the rest struggled to survive. The industry yearned for a digital system to increase the odds of success, amplify talent discovery, and bring pros into the twenty-first century. Our team of seven account executives, two investors, and one developer were counting on me to lead them through the financial nightmare, but I had to face the music — without an infusion of VC funding, we couldn't pay our staff, rent, or advertising, let alone scale our subscriber base beyond our buggy Beta. We were broke, emotionally depleted, and headed to the rocky shores of dissolution. Even with a top business degree in my hand and Silicon Valley at my door, we had little chance of survival.

On the surface, the situation felt eerily familiar, as I had read about this before — startup failure — during my time at Babson in the copious Harvard Business School® case studies we read in our entrepreneurship classes. Back then however, I always had the right answer for the professor, "Why doesn't the CEO just go out and raise another round of financing and partner with that Fortune 500 company to sell his product B2B instead of B2C where margins are higher? That should increase sales by $10 million in Q3 and add $20 million to the balance sheet in a Series B giving them an 18-month runway. It'll all work out just fine…" I would proclaim confidently from the front row, leaning back in my chair, arms tucked casually behind my head as if I were relaxing on some Bahamian beach like a multi-millionaire entrepreneur who had been there and done that. But I hadn't. I didn't even have one clue as to what running a startup was all about — but I could convince you otherwise. Aside from a handful of business books I'd read, my twenty-year-old entrepreneurial ego overshadowed my lack of any concrete founder experience — as they say, I was all bull and no cattle.

But this time, I needed a real answer for WML, but had none.

There was no professor prodding me along, there was no letter grade that would validate my ideas and help me escape the shit storm; this was real life. Ten staffers and thousands of subscribers were depending on me to figure it out. "I'm a failure…" I told myself under my shallowed breath. Tomorrow's newspaper headline flashed in front of my eyes — Twenty-One-Year-Old Music Startup Founder Plays Final Tune — Dies from Panic Attack in 600 sq. ft. Office Cubicle.

The pressure mounted in my chest. My pulse beat like a kick drum inside both temples. The world was looking for WorldMusicLink to thrive, die, or get off of the stage. I wasn't prepared for this to be my final tune. Mentally, emotionally and physically, there was no way I was going to become that — a failed founder.

As I sat in my faded, used blue telescopic chair in front of my laptop, I stared out of my office window at the oversized clocktower hanging high ahead of the building. Time stood still — the daily adrenaline high of the startup I had come to rely on to keep me going, suddenly faded away. I was out of ideas. All I could think of was "Where the hell did I go wrong? I wish I could be an overnight success like Branson or Bezos. I would never become a failure…"

I had always dreamed of being an overnight entrepreneur, the one who fearlessly takes an idea to market and IPO in a wild flash by making all of the right decisions along the way to the top of the mountain; leapfrogging competitors, launching at just the right time, building just the right features that millions yearn for but had been denied. There he goes, our entrepreneurial hero, flying across the midnight sky, saving us from the shackles of life's ghastly problems, with the perfect alchemy to solve our tumultuous pain, boredom and frustrations. His products seem to just get us from first blush — they speak to us without ever saying a word. How could we not love our entrepreneurial hero and praise him for blasting away all of life's shortcomings?

A decade later, postmortem, I revisit that tiny 600 sq. ft. office, and look up at the same clocktower hanging high above. Time moves a little faster now. I think back on some of the most famous founders of our modern era — Richard Branson, Jeff Bezos, Jack Ma, Elon Musk — and think to myself, "What would they have done differently than I did back then?" Pausing for some great insight, I hear nothing, only a seagull screeching as it flies high above, oblivious to my gaze.

After so much time distancing myself from the painful emotions of my first startup's dissolution, I gain a wave of objectivity; a clarity that I didn't have at twenty-one. No longer am I craving the avoidance of failure — the superhuman ability to leapfrog over everything, and instantly become my very own overnight success story without experiencing any of the challenges, disappointments, and failures required to earn my right of entrepreneurial passage. No longer am I leaning in with my inflated ego but stepping back with a big dose of ruthless reality. In this detached moment, I realize something simplistically profound that I didn't then — becoming an overnight success is one of the greatest lies I bought into. The term 'overnight' lured me into believing that it was more than just possible, it was the goal. Overnight meant that failure along the way was simply not part of the equation. How delightful that would have been!

But sadly, I am not the only one who plays the overnight record to himself; most entrepreneurs believe that if they just play all of their cards right, that they will reach tomorrow's stardom. How could we not? We look up and visions of Elon Musk rocketing into orbit on a SpaceX® Falcon 9 flash across the midnight sky. We play a song, and memories of Steve Jobs in his black turtleneck sweater on stage at his Apple® keynote reverberates in our ears with his phrase, "Here's 1,000 songs in your pocket." We post a picture and recall Zuck sitting in his dorm room at Harvard one minute, and the next, bringing billions together to share their lives in real-time across the globe. Remarkable feats of entrepreneurial heroism that all end in incredible wealth, power, and adorned accomplishment.

The success of these entrepreneurial ventures are intoxicating elixirs that make us too, dream, that we could create the next billion-dollar empire. The enviable stardom of these apparently 'overnight' entrepreneurs fills our souls with a desire to risk it all, in the pursuit of fame and fortune at the end of the rainbow. As we prepare to set sail in the calm waters of ideation bay, we are never quite prepared for the tumultuous storms that await in the choppy markets offshore, no matter our educational pedigrees or diligent preparations. So, we entrepreneurs have a choice — to stay in the safe haven harbors where our ideas make hypothetical millions, or, set sail to discover unchartered lands and face the startup storm head on.

Before setting sail, we delude ourselves into believing two fatal truths, the first being that when we launch, the world will miraculously come beating down a path with wallets in tow to buy our products and make us rich, and secondly, that failure is simply not part of the equation— we're going to succeed unscathed with our original big idea materialized in the market.

Through sheer dogged determinism we will reach the promised land where IPOs, mega yachts, and Ferraris await, we tell ourselves. So, we do everything in our power to avoid failure at all cost — we never change our startup's course, we never pivot our product to adjust to evolving market needs, and we never swap out bad hires even when they are killing our momentum. We tell ourselves we have one shot for glory. This is it. We can't make a mistake, otherwise we'll fail.

But here's the truth folks — in one of life's most ironical paradoxes, the compass that leads us to success actually forces us to sail through both the bay of customer apathy and along the rocky shores of failure. If you escape both, your startup might make it out alive.

It took ten years to crystallize this — the world doesn't care about your startup — but it's your job to make them. Oh, and if you're not failing, you're not actually taking the creative risk required to build something that can endure.

So, you're telling me that all I need to do is fail and then succeed? Sorry, it's not that simple. In a modernized world oversaturated with startup ideas, products, platforms and services vying for our daily clicks, dollars, and attention, following the traditional rulebook doesn't even get us noticed. The traditional model of a perfect business plan, a jargon filled investor slide deck, and vanilla branding does little to help us launch, learn and earn. Being a little different simply doesn't cut through the cacophony of absolute crap that overwhelms us all on a never-ending basis.

For decades the BS business buffet that we've been fed is as follows — turn your passion into your startup, perfect your business plan, hire the best people, and build a perfect product — the four go-to rules of entrepreneurship. Do all four, and you'll succeed.

While that might have worked in the 80s and early 90s when we didn't have the Internet in everyone's pocket, hyper competition crawling out of every crevice of the world, and virtually little barrier to block our brand from the advertising melee that plagues every size screen. Simply put, playing by the old rule book gets us no closer to rapidly winning a market, moving customer's dollars into our pockets, and becoming profitable before we burn through all of our own cash, or that of our investors. The traditional startup playbook is simply failing founders left and right — not the market, not your motivation, not even your product.

As I stood there looking up at the clocktower, an image of my younger self, fresh out of college, a newly minted entrepreneur crossing through a burning doorway flashed through my mind. *"Through"* failure, I said once more under my breath. "That's it! *Through"*. That's the first entrepreneurial secret that gets us to door one of success, but who the hell wants to fail first, and then succeed later? Everything started to make sense in that very moment. How could I have arrived at success if I wasn't willing to totally crash and burn first?

Call it bad market timing, exhaustive spending, poor product market fit, disruption from the outside, implosion from the inside; the rationale for why we fail can go on and on into the wee hours of the morning. They all end the same way — coulda, woulda, shoulda, dissolved.

According to a 2018 SBA (Small Business Administration) report[1] on startups and their longevity, one out of every five businesses (20%) started between 1994-2013 failed within the first twelve months, while half (50%) failed within five years. You heard that right — so pitch me 5,000,000 startup ideas, 1,000,000 will fail before your next birthday, with more en route to the dissolution graveyard thereafter. It's not a game of which idea wins, it's a game of absolute survival at all cost. Startups are downright risky; most new ventures are statistically guaranteed for the idea graveyard. So why even try? How can we stack the odds in our startup's favor?

As I dug deeper into failure, I discovered most breakout entrepreneurs — Reid Hoffman, Jack Ma, Jeff Bezos, even Thomas Edison — developed an unfair competitive advantage that helped them succeed over everyone else. It turns out, through failed ventures, and a willingness to repeatedly start over again, that the burning ember for success is eventually lit.

Successful entrepreneurs share similar DNA; the ability to overcome past failure, persevere, and forge ahead to find the next opportunity.

Before founding LinkedIn®, and ultimately selling it to Microsoft® for $26.2 billion, Reid Hoffman created SocialNet, an online dating and social networking site that ultimately closed up shop, but as he credits, led to the preparation for LinkedIn. Before Jeff Bezos founded Amazon®, one of the most powerful e-commerce platforms in existence, and became the world's wealthiest billionaire, he created an online auction site that morphed into zShops, a brand that eventually met its demise. And while entrepreneur and venture capitalist Peter Thiel is well heralded throughout Silicon Valley for launching PayPal®, Palantir®, and being one of the early angel investors in Facebook®, he experienced a 90 percent loss of $7 billion dollars in assets in his hedge fund, Clarium Capital®[2]. There are countless examples of failure to triumph stories; this is America after all. But maybe Thomas Edison eloquently put failure best into entrepreneurial context for us, "I have not failed. I've just found 10,000 ways that won't work."

We can all agree that failure at anything is painful. But why? Is it because the common approach is a one and done strategy; an all or nothing mentality? We put all of our eggs in one basket, and when they break, we're done, and don't go searching for anymore eggs. Therefore, when we fail at achieving an intended result, we automatically internalize the result as a failure of ourselves, and not on the experiment at hand. One of the most overlooked distinctions, yet it has profound implications on our psyche, our lives, and the success of our companies. How naïve it is for a green-thumbed entrepreneur, like I was once, to think that their first company will become their best performing company. Startups require practice, and practice comes from repetition, and progress comes through failure.

Entrepreneurs I advise today fall into two main categories when facing a challenge — those who try something once, and when they hit a roadblock, they give up, never try again, and return to mediocrity (aka corporate cubicle life). And then there are those who try, hit the same roadblock, go back to the drawing board, and find a new way to drive over the damn roadblock!

In the startup world, the best founders are obsessively thinking about ways to better serve their customers, approaches to create better systems, strategies to build better products, and are relentlessly curious as to how and why things evolve over time and succeed. They see entrepreneurship as the most effective way to create an impact in the world, invest their time, and leave a lasting legacy for those they care about. However, even great founders have their own limitations, but they take steps to address them. To counter personal deficiencies, they are masterful at attracting the resources that they lack to move their projects ahead, no matter their lack of resources.

There's no one model for a great founder — but there are similar elements — tenacity, an insatiable hunger to learn and grow, and a dogged grit to overcome every, single failure. The elite entrepreneurs are consistently re-investing in themselves, to move their next bold idea to market, despite prior failed attempts at glory. Every day is a new opportunity to practice and improve their business.

Nobody Cares About Your Startup:

So, here's the cold hard truth about startups — nobody cares when you launch, and nobody cares when you fail (unless they lost money over it). It's your job as CEO to make them want to care.

Our modern-day world is completely oversaturated with new products popping up on our radar screen on a daily basis with offers, trial coupons, app download requests, new registration forms, and betas out of every corner of our inboxes. By effect, it has created a de-facto impulse to ignore it all, and simply not care until it becomes a household name. While the traditional startup founder focuses on a competitive matrix, fearing some adjacent rival may eventually launch a competitive widget to compete against his, the biggest competitor of them all doesn't come from a matrix my friends.

The scariest and most pernicious competitor is simply — apathy.

From the apathetic small local retailer to the Fortune 500 category manager, the last thing buyers want to do is review and take on an unproven new product. Investors listen to pitch after pitch after pitch that all start to sound the same by Friday. The last thing they want to hear is, you guessed it, another vanilla pitch with a hockey stick chart that says they're the next Uber® of Ubers, a platform for the last platform, and a disruptive, game changing, revolutionary, scalable version of bullshit. Users have more profiles and trial accounts spread across the web that are forgotten about on virtually every website you can think of. From maxed out credit cards to mile high student loan debt, consumers are running out of places to put all of the crap that they bought at the discount store. But here you come along asking them for just one more swipe — pass, delete, and mark as spam is the new knee-jerk reaction from Gen-Z through Generation Geriatric.

But here's the flip side — without new ideas, the world falls flat. The world picks a small handful of winners out of a sea of ideas, and the chosen ones move humanity, the markets, and our personal lives exponentially forward. I'm not saying we should all give up on our ideas, rather, I'm saying entrepreneurs have to be brutally honest about today's bloated business world, and smart enough to choose the right idea to build, launch, scale and focus on.

But how do you know what the right idea is to launch?

It's hard to say. Most great companies don't start out with the original idea they launched. They evolve over time, but most founders give up when their original idea hits the first wave of chop offshore.

It pains me to see so many talented, ambitious founders of every age, nationality, gender, and market give up after just one swing of the startup bat. The world is in dire need of visionary leaders solving problems that ameliorate lives both locally and globally. Greatness shouldn't have one chance. Even the best home run hitters get at least three to four at bats every game to hit one out of the park. The feeling of even hitting a business single seems to unlock something within us and lights the way to connect bigger on the next at-bat. It has for me. But when we swing once and strike out, we feel nothing, and often return to the bench dejected and fearful to strike out again next time.

While technology and consumer demands adapt at an exponential and alarming pace, the startup land minds, phases, founder requirements, and human-centered behaviors of customers remain almost unmoved; they appear to be stuck in time. But who reads instructions before assembling a startup, right? We don't have time for that, we're entrepreneurs on a time crunch trying to change the world!

So, tell me this, how come millions of founders fail every year, and return to cubicle mediocrity? Is it because of the reality of life's growing bills and student loan debt that creeps back in and urges us to find financial security in a corporate job when our startup just isn't getting any traction? Is it because once we finally launch the darn thing, no one actually gave two cents about our new product offering? How could that be, our projections projected millions in year one!

As entrepreneurs, we see the glass as half-full, not half-empty, otherwise we would never take the leap of faith to launch, right? As Steve Jobs famously said, "Here's to the crazy ones, the misfits, the rebels, the troublemakers, the round pegs in the square holes, the ones who see things differently…because the ones who are crazy enough to think that they can change the world, are the ones who do."

Then why don't we study and learn from the crazy fallen soldiers, their startups, and codify their mistakes? Because we'd rather take the jump, be the "wild and crazy ones" and slap CEO on our business card. I should know, that was me when I was twenty, starting my first web company out of my dorm room. Certainly, it's more convenient to ignore the millions of failures while we are starting our own company. Our startup will be different we tell ourselves! We won't fail! God, we're so hopped up on the startup sauce to see reality.

By facing the walk of startup shame to see what really happens when we're building, launching, and selling our hearts out to indifferent buyers, customers and investors, we can learn more about how to overcome the hardest phases of the journey. Moreover, by studying startup failure at an uncomfortable and microscopic level over the coming chapters, you will uncover the unique insights that ultimately led to my own entrepreneurial success — believe me, I won't sugarcoat an ounce of it — I have fallen smack on my face, been turned down by hundreds of indifferent buyers and investors, and also found ways to sell millions of dollars' worth of product by slugging through it all. If I can do it, so can you too.

By the end of this book, my goal is to impart an understanding that through the startup storm and countless failures, you can find success. Let's stop applauding the handful of over-hyped entrepreneurs we keep hearing about and trying to emulate their journeys — we will never know what they truly went through to get where they are today. We will never know all of the mistakes they made because we only read about the mega fundraising rounds, the instant IPO, and the global land grab that jettisons them into the entrepreneurial hall of fame.

No Startup Left Behind is a breath of fresh air in the coddled, avoid-failure-at-all-cost world of traditional entrepreneurship that aims to wait until passion strikes to even launch, please every customer at any cost, and over promise but underwhelm every market. I'll simplify the startup journey for you, from your messy hunch through ideation, customer journey mapping to uncover unique insights, fundraising, launch, scale and profitability generation. Additionally, I'll provide a roadmap for tackling the biggest competitor of them all — apathy — and provide time-tested tools backed by entertaining personal anecdotes that will help you, our illustrious founder, break through the endless wall of "Noes" from corporate buyers trained to pass, unconvinced customers, and investors waiting to poke holes in every line of your elevator pitch. Believe me, they're all waiting for you. Will you be ready?

No Startup Left Behind might not be the book you want to read to feel good about your startup, it's the book you need to face to prep for the battles ahead. A long overdue dose of no BS rules and key takeaways, filled with entertaining stories that draw us inside of the startup trenches. Get ready for a refreshing slap in the face for newbie founders and veteran business owners alike to wake you up to what really matters, and for whom at every stage of the entrepreneurial journey.

We'll throw out the conventional business book, as I guide you through the keys from inside the trenches of ideation, development, launch, scale and harvest. We'll look at failure from both within the startup, and outside. Whether you're launching a new food truck in San Francisco, a trendy new retail boutique in London, or the next web platform in Beijing aimed at disrupting an incumbent dinosaur and ameliorating the lives of millions of users, it's my hope, that with my hard lessons fought and un-sugarcoated anecdotes, you will be able to leap over avoidable land minds, and fear failure nevermore. And should you fail, you'll stop crying about it, get back up and try again — your success is waiting for you on the other side. Mine was.

CHAPTER 2:
LET'S GET STARTED

Forget Passion. Focus on Profit.

Is there a difference between founders who know how to make money, and founders who know how to build a business? You bet there is! The art of building a business can be taught — entity formation, financial projections, product development, distribution, accounting, hiring, and managerial best practices — but the art of making money, must be experienced more so than taught.

Just look at eight-year-old hustlers with their lemonade stands. Do they have the fundamentals for a business? Yes — raw materials, a retail space, an employee or two, and the gall to launch. But, have they spent six months setting up their legal structure, hiring a staff, setting up employee payroll, stock option plans, and board meetings? Nope.

When you launch your product or service, you figure out really quickly how to make money when you ask people to open up their wallets and buy from you. They will either accept and pay you, will reject and provide a reason (price, lack of features, amenities, location, speed of service, etc.), or will just walk or click away. So many entrepreneurs I meet with spend too much time building all the extraneous elements of their business, and not enough time on simply asking customers to buy today (monetization). I should know! I did this with my first startup, WorldMusicLink (WML).

Think about how that eight-year-old runs her lemonade stand — she sets it up, gets the materials, puts up a sign, and starts yelling for dollars all within the same day. She runs to the actual part that matters most: monetization. She doesn't care if she makes $10 or $100 that day. She just wants to launch, learn and earn baby.

Kudos to our lemonade gal! However, the art of growing revenue and profits in a corporation, over time, requires more. It derives from you becoming the ultimate tester. By setting up dozens and dozens of hypotheses (educated guesses) and quantifiable tests to measure those against to determine the outcomes, you get increasingly better monetary results over time. Nobody nails that out of the gate — so don't beat yourself up over it. As you launch, you'll be forced to test your price point(s), your marketing campaigns, your website imagery, essentially everything until you find the right combination(s) for your chosen market(s). Sometimes, from day one, you hit the right combination — woo-hoo! 99% of the time though, you need months to sort it out, a tenacity to keep fighting to find the right combinations, and capital to keep you afloat until you do. Most folks just get lazy, try a few experiments, get some mediocre results, and throw in the towel at the first sniff of rejection. Cue the violins. Sound familiar?

Becoming the Great Experimenter:

The sooner you realize that your business is one giant experiment, and you are the head lab researcher, the faster you can take control of the levers to adjust your experiment to reach profitability. The key is to find a lab that is cheap to tweak and adjust your model, product or service to the needs of paying customers. If you're at the mercy of an expensive web programmer for every edit of code (as I was with WML), or want to pivot to try something new, you will either need a war chest of cash, or will need to get him to work for sweat equity. More on this topic later.

I once asked one of my entrepreneurship professors, and former Board of Advisor, Bob Caspe, "So Bob, how do I figure out what price to charge customers?" His answer was so simple and effective, I want to share with you what he said. He goes, "Reagan, just keep raising the price until they complain, or stop buying, then lower it just under that, and you've reached the right price." Oh Bob, absolute pearl of wisdom. Remind me why I took finance courses when I had Bob's masterclass of financial street-smart wizardry?

Many people, without business school or finance backgrounds, make money, and a lot of it. How? Well, they truly listen and solve consumer pain points. They understand a simple fact — we're all human, and you're never just selling a product or service, you're selling a person an end result. Think about that for a minute — why do you buy anything? Are you buying a hairdryer, or are you buying the end result of perfectly dried hair? What's the last thing you bought? There are countless examples, but the point is, know what solution (end result) the customer is ultimately going to get from your product or service, and then sell that.

Waiting for Passion to Strike:

Most folks want to feel passion in their work, and don't want to necessarily own or run a big business with thousands of employee headaches, board meetings, earnings calls and compliance requirements. They don't want the endless hiring, the gut-wrenching firing, the page after page HR paperwork, or the "How the hell am I going to pay for this?" financial obligations from borrowing outside capital from debtors just to hopefully scale and cash out. The average small business owner wants cash in her pocket every day. She wants a simple, effective business that works for her, rather than her working for it. She wants the freedom from having to wake up early to open the shop or stay up late to serve the last order. She wants endless upward growth opportunity, not fixed success. The Web today enables her to build a business cheaply, test ideas on the fly, eliminate the crap that doesn't work, and focus on the ones that make real dollars every day. There's less hand holding with the Internet as consumers today are savvy and want simple tools to make the buying decision themselves.

If someone asked me if I am day in and day out passionate about the product or service I am selling, I'd say no — let me explain. I am passionate about ensuring that customers get great value from their orders. I am passionate about helping my customers make the best decision possible, so that I can get out of their way, and they can get on with their lives and focus on more important things after buying from me. I am passionate about ensuring that I make money every day. I am passionate about simplifying my life, so that I can work less, make more, and enjoy my ephemeral time on Earth. Will you always be passionate about the product you are selling? It may come in waves — one day you feel totally into the business, and other days, you question the entire thing. That's normal. Get comfortable with the ebb and flow of passion and learn to replace it by focusing on 1% daily improvements. For me, progress drives passion. Passion hasn't always driven progress, as there are many uninspiring days in the life of an entrepreneur.

Personally, I love the overall entrepreneurial journey, and I love growing any business I am involved with, which fills me with excitement every day to do something better, faster, easier than the day before. I don't view my work as work; I view it as a fun, creative challenge. A lot of people I talk to have endless business ideas, but they are waiting to be 100% impassioned to start a business. They are trying to create the perfect business that makes them feel 100% satisfied every night when they go to bed, and then somehow wake up with millions of dollars in their bank account from their big idea. They are waiting for that perfect idea, that perfect opportunity, that perfect time to start the business. I don't know about you, but there is no perfect in life. There is only right now.

Do you need to "find your passion" before you launch your startup? Contrary to what most business gurus tell you, no, you don't.

Is it helpful to find an area that you understand better than most and that you enjoy? Yes. For those folks that do find passion, I applaud you, as that will surely help get you through the growing pains you will face in your startup journey. But lack of 100% passion should never keep you from trying something out. Who knows? You may just find out that you love actually owning a business that works well and pays you handsomely? One caveat — unique insights and knowledge in a space, over passion, however, will save you time and money figuring out how it works, and how to win in that space (more on this in a later chapter).

I think there is a difference between being passionate about something (derived from emotions), making money (derived from your business model), and starting a business (derived from knowledge). Ask yourself, are you the kind of person that has to be 100% passionate about a product to sell it? Are you the kind of founder who has to have everything perfect before you jump, or can you accept that some days you will feel it and others you may not, and acknowledge that nothing is ever perfect? If you're the latter, then you're ready to take the leap of entrepreneurial faith, because let me tell you, after having multiple startups, I found more passion in the overall (imperfect) journey than the actual day-to-day tasking. If you're waiting for passion and perfection, I'm sorry to say, but you need to sit this startup game out.

Here's where we might all agree passion really should belong. Have passion for creating a better tomorrow for yourself and somebody else. Have passion for making something out of nothing. Have passion for leaving your old life behind, proving to yourself that you can become the best possible version of yourself. Have passion for proving to the naysayers who doubted your dreams. Have passion for leaving a legacy that someone can look up to, one day. That's passion I can believe in. Not the Virtual Reality space, not a Bitcoin movement, not a scooter with a mobile app. These are products and services — these are not emotional pillars that never fade with time. Products, services and spaces are fleeting — they ebb, change, evolve and flow into something new. If you were passionate about the CD industry, you would be quickly unimpassioned when the MP3 arrived. If you were passionate about using Uber®, you'd be unimpassioned when a self-driving car picks you up in a few years thereafter.

What if, instead of passion striking before you started, it grew over time? Would this change your outlook on everything? For me, that's how it works. The more I get involved with a project, the more I learn. The more I learn, the better the results get. The better the results get, the more excited I get to keep forging ahead. As I forge ahead, I get more impassioned to grow, serve, and enjoy the journey.

Passion is a by-product of my actions, not a prerequisite to start.

The Business Plan – Build with the End in Mind:

At most B-Schools, they used to teach you to write a business plan and try to predict it all. Let me tell you, life doesn't happen like that. I wrote a fifty-page business plan for my first venture, which included ten pages of five-year projections, burn rates (how much cash you would go through in the first twenty-four months), hiring head count build ups, cash flows, profit & loss statements, and a stock offering sheet for an investor. It was beautiful (insert tear)! We were a semi-finalist in the school's business plan competition, a feat that I am very proud of, however within one year, that business plan was re-worked, tweaked and re-read by me hundreds of times. None of it ever came to reality.

Save yourself the trouble of writing that 50-page plan over months, and instead write a 3-to-5-page Turnkey plan in days.

The Turnkey Business Plan:

The first page should include:

• **The Challenge**: What is the true pain you are solving and for whom? How can you clearly define or quantify this pain?

• **The Solution**: How will you really solve it? Can you prove the outcome? If so, how? If not, think twice about picking this challenge to solve.

• **The Opportunity**: How realistically big is this market, and who cares so deeply about it that they have to have it?

• **Total Addressable Market (TAM)**: Don't say, "If we can only get 1% of a 100-million-dollar market we will make a million bucks!" Rather say, "What does it take in time and money to build up to acquire each customer?" Multiply that out for the month or year and that will be more accurate.

Example: You make forty cold-calls per day. 5% convert (that's two orders at $200 each totaling $400 in total sales per day). It takes you 6 hours (5 mins per call plus a few mins of research/prep time). Perform this five days per week and project $2,000/week in sales ($8,000/month or $96,000/year 1). That's bottom-up, not top-down projections.

• **Team**: Who is helping you, guiding you, or who will you need to solve this issue? When you start a company, you get a lot of advice, but what you need is real, roll-up-your-sleeves action. Do you require a Technical Co-Founder? Do you need a Financial Maven? Do you need a Head Chef? No need to fill in all of the roles just yet, just the key ones to scale you to one year out.

• **Financials**: Limit this to a basic start-up cost guide for the first 6-12 months. Whatever you project, add 25%-50% to your costs to be more conservative and accurate. No need for a five-year pro-forma statement here folks.

• **Unit Economics**: Break down what you're selling, how much it costs, what are you selling it for, and what the gross margin is in percentage and dollar amount.

Gross Margin is Sales Price minus (Cost/Sales Price) x 100 (to create the percentage). For example, you buy something for $50, sell it for $100, and $50 is profit (50% gross margin). In month one, you sell 50 units, or $5,000 in sales. Month two, 100 units, $10,000 in sales, etc.

Business Model: Business-to-Business (B-2-B)? Business-to-Consumer (B-2-C)? Business-to-Business-to-Consumer (B-2-B-2-C)? Flesh out your wholesale price to businesses, or your Manufacturer's Suggested Retail Price (MSRP) to consumers.

For example:

XYZ Corp is a wholesale B-2-B company, that sells its line of women's shoes through wholesale distributors, who service retailers. Our MSRP averages $100 per shoe, and we wholesale them for $50 per pair. We operate on a 50% gross margin basis, or $25 per pair in gross profit. We sell through West Coast US Distributors and have expansionary plans to scale to the Midwest and East Coast via additional retail channel partners, by partnering with the following Distributors as we are a value-add to their product ranges in the following ways. Etc.

• **Milestones**: Milestones are specific deliverables that you must meet to advance the business. They help you see a roadmap for actionable items that you need to accomplish to reach the next tier of growth.

Examples might include:

• Week 1: Research domain name online with domain provider.

• Week 1: Buy domain name, add hosting plan, set up DNS setting.

• Week 1: Set up our first corporate e-mail addresses.

● Week 2: Design logo (there are freelancers on UpWork® or a Logo Maker tool online for example)

● Week 3: Incorporate business (example: Use a reputable business attorney or possibly LegalZoom®)

● Week 4: Choose a website building platform such as Shopify®, Wordpress®, SquareSpace®, or WIX®.

● Weeks 5-9: Create About Us Page, Shop (Catalog), Shipping Information Page, and Returns Page.

● Week 10: Meet with first 25 prospective buyers and gain feedback on initial web store, product range, and price points. Integrate feedback into next week's build.

● Week 11: Integrate feedback from Week 10 user sit downs.

● Week 12: Soft launch to friends, family, and alpha users.

Make sure to hold yourself accountable to meeting these deliverables on time. You will be building momentum, and that will help you get to launch faster.

Okay, so I want you to just step back and understand that your goal is get all the startup high level stuff out of the way quickly, so you can get to testing and seeing if folks even want what you're offering, as cheaply as possible. It's better to invest five-hundred bucks in thirty days, and see no results, than take one year and one-hundred thousand dollars with a perfect business plan that never materializes. Become the rapid deployment (launch) entrepreneur — not the ten-year researcher.

Pick Your Flavor of Failure:

A common fallacy among first-time founders is that they believe that failure happens at the end of a startup — the culmination of a series of compounding bad decisions that leads to a singular outcome — namely dissolution. That's not true. Failure happens at virtually every stage of a company, and frankly speaking, failure continues to occur well into the lifespan of every successful company that has been around for decades. If you ain't failing, you ain't sailing.

Failure strikes at different times for different teams, and I can prove this to you with the following. Below is the typical journey of 99% of startups, regardless of industry, product, service, or geography — they all experience at least a few of these failures:

Stage 1: Problem/Pain Identification

The entrepreneur experiences or witnesses a pain point in the market, notes it, and thinks to herself, "There really needs to be an X solution to solve Y."

Failure at Stage 1: Fear of Launching

She recognizes the pain but fails to launch anything. We all have friends or zany uncles who boast about their one brilliant idea that's someday going to be worth a million bucks. Reality is, they failed to do anything about it. Ideas are cheap, execution is hard.

Stage 2: Ideation/Testing/Market Feedback/Solution 1.0

This type of entrepreneur has identified the pain point and taken action to see if their initial hunches and ideas for solutions have legs with a specific user group.

Failure at Stage 2: Not Building What People Need

Here, the entrepreneur takes it upon herself to go down the solution road to build what she wants, and not what the market is really showing her what they need.

Stage 3: Building the Product/Team

Here, the entrepreneur has assembled a small team to build out the product or service aimed at solving a specific problem. They've done the hard work of starting up, building a 1.0 product, and attracting talent and are moving ahead.

Failure at Stage 3: Inability to Work Well with Others

Call it personality differences or hyper controlling tendencies, many entrepreneurs fail at this phase when they simply can't lead others well, or work at a rapid pace with others to get to market without being a damn perfectionist. Perfectionism kills startups — plain and simple. It is antithetical to what's required to get to market on time.

Stage 4: Launch/Dealing with Problems/Bottlenecks

With a product in the market, the problems begin to pile up from every direction, as you skate from launch to building an actual profitable business that serves customers consistently well. Operational, Emotional, Financial and Intellectual bottlenecks can stymie growth at this stage. When the going gets tough, the tough don't just get going, they get smarter, faster, and nimbler.

Failure at Stage 4: Failure to Overcome the Daily Grind

Let's face it, when you create something from nothing, by very definition, the entire experience is both new for your company and for your users, thus, failure is baked into the equation because you both are in un-chartered territory. Many entrepreneurs fail to overcome the daily grind that ranges from user problems, product glitches, hiring issues, operational hurdles, cash flow problems and more.

Stage 5: Sales/Marketing/Advertising

In the transition from building to selling, entrepreneurs and their teams must change their attention to sales, marketing, and customer interactions, which, often times, leads to early disappointment and requires months of slugging through rejection to find their way out.

Failure at Stage 5: Fear of Rejection

You've built it, now you've got to change hats and go sell the world. Oh shit! Many entrepreneurs are great builders, but terrible salesman and marketers. Salesmanship takes 99 "Noes" to hear 1 "Yes" — this takes time to get used to, and frankly, no one likes to be rejected. Human niceties have conditioned us to seek approval and win hearts and minds everywhere we go since we were little kids. Breaking that habit to win wallets requires hundreds of "Noes" which builds the salesmanship callus that's required to scale. Many entrepreneurs fail here because they just can't handle rejection, and the fear of future rejections stunts them back into either procrastination or staying stuck in product build-mode forever where it's cozy and warm. In business, everything starts and ends with sales. If you've got gold, but no one knows, you're going nowhere fast.

Stage 6: Building Traction

Whether this means increasing user figures, driving higher levels of revenue, or amplifying the distribution of your product, it all sums to one word — traction.

Failure at Stage 6: Gaining Objectivity

A common group who gets to this point can't grow out of the one-to-three-person team in a garage to a business with $100K-$1M in revenue. A lot of this boils down to an inability to focus on the things that matter in the business and amplifying them, as opposed to continuing to launch more features or expand the product range horizontally with new additions that simply strip the focus away from the one or two products or services that contribute the most margin and momentum for growth. This is actually a failure of analytical skills — the ability to be truly, emotionally detached and objective about what's blocking the business from accelerating up to the next tier.

Stage 7: Raising Capital

If your business is intent on growing fast, you will at some point need outside capital. That can come in the form of a bank loan, a line of credit, an investment from an angel investor, a venture capital round of financing, a private equity round, or a strategic investment from a partner company.

Failure at Stage 7: Inability to Persuade

Traction, as you will see, drives most funding. Moreover, the inability to convince others of the attractiveness and urgency of your investment is at the core of this failure. This could mean that you are approaching the wrong investors, it could be your lack of traction or inability to articulate your path towards growth or profitability, or, this could be due to your inability to highlight key differentiating factors and the competitive moat you've built around your product and model.

Stage 8: Hiring/Scaling/Partnering

This phase is all about amplification of your company. The focus of leadership is to hire talented people with the right skillsets to magnify the results to drive faster outcomes. Partnerships with other companies also come into the forefront here.

Failure at Stage 8: Breaking Out of the Comfort Zone

Hiring takes guts – it requires the ability to remove the tendency to micro-manage and control all elements of your startup. Partnering with other companies also requires, by very nature, a release of control over the outcome of your product or service. When you sign a new distributor on to represent your line to help you expand into a new territory, it forces you to relinquish control of a portion of the engagement with customers, marketing experience, and point of sale. Whether you're expanding your retail operations to new cities, or launching your new product overseas, once the experience is out of your hands, you have to trust the process, and this, requires faith. Many entrepreneurs simply fail to scale for fear of losing control — of the office, people, process, product design, sales programs, of customer engagement, etc.

Stage 9: Monetization

While I could list this earlier on in the typical startup process, often times, companies are so intent on getting to market and building traction with free users, that they delay monetization until later. Monetization doesn't just refer to going from not charging to charging, on the contrary, it could also mean raising prices for your product line or to a specific customer.

Failure at Stage 9: Not Knowing Your True Worth

This goes without saying that a business cannot survive forever if it never turns a profit. Even investor capital at some point dries up, so there becomes a return to monetization at some point. Some companies can strategically delay monetization by raising larger and larger rounds of financing, but profit procrastination eventually comes due, and often delaying it until later can metastasize into larger, more systemic financial problems.

Many entrepreneurs launch a free product, build traction, and then when faced with the decision to starve and die (close up shop) or charge (and possibly flourish), they fear charging their users and thus, die from financial asphyxiation. Conversely, some companies, even ones who have been around for decades, hold their pricing to the market for years upon years, and over time, are faced with rising costs from every corner and a declining gross margin that swallows them alive. These entrepreneurs fail because they never raise prices for fear of losing customers that they fought hard to win years ago. In trying to feed the world, we end up starving ourselves — ironically tragic.

Stage 10: Exiting

At some point, you either sell the business (via an acquisition), hire a replacement and then retire, or file to go public with an IPO (initial public offering). All of these in some sense of the word, is an exit experience. Additionally, dissolving a business falls into the category of exits.

Failure at Stage 10: Letting Go

When you've climbed from the bottom all the way up to the top of the mountain, you simply have nowhere else to go. Letting go leads to a tremendous number of failures — from deciding to sell the company to another firm or individual, the fear of letting someone else run or ruin your baby casts a long shadow on your legacy, and to many, just isn't worth the upside. Alternatively, should you be lucky enough to go public, it means that you are giving up both equity and control in your company and the strategic direction to the public markets — this represents fear for many, even though the upside usually comes with a large payday and global expansionary opportunity.

Lastly, the one that plagues most founders, is the fear to let go of a dead business. It is the culmination of all of your hard work, your napkin sketches come to life, your own hard-earned dollars invested over the years, and the sleepless nights you'll never get back. However, even for entrepreneurs like myself, saying goodbye to our baby is harder than it looks. The pain that we feel is a combination of one-part remorse mixed with one-part hope, that we could give it one more go to try to figure it all out. Tomorrow always seems brighter than the past. Failure to let go is, in my opinion, the hardest one of all to get through.

As you have read above, failure is not a singular event. It's usually not even a one-time decision that led you to fail. Rather, all ten stages come with ten different types of entrepreneurial failure types. If you recognized any of the aforementioned, don't worry, you're not alone. I have experienced all ten types personally over the past decade. Am I a failure? You bet I am. If you're going to win, you need to learn how to lose.

Failures are not terminal (unless you define them as such) — failures are part of an endless journey that moves us uncomfortably around the next blind corner, through the labyrinth, towards success.

Playing the Movie Backwards:

Most entrepreneurs visualize starting with a napkin sketch and moving it through startup to some grandiose version of success. Scratch that thinking — we've got to go the other way. Think of the type of business you want to run (end in mind first). Truly imagine it as already being built. No more business plans, no more user testing, no more awkward conversations with new hires about equity compensation. The product is built, the office lease is signed, and you've got money rolling in. It's working! Stop, take a minute, and visualize it all humming. What does it look and feel like?

Now, what does your role look like? Are you busy hopping from meeting to meeting, dashing on a plane to meet with a buyer at a major retail chain, or are you sipping on a cup of coffee lakeside checking e-mails on your phone while your team of twelve handles it all for you back home? You see, everyone has a different vision for what success looks like in their mind. By leapfrogging into year two, you can get a sense for what your business might actually look, feel and operate like. Instead of starting at month one and only looking ahead at the next quarter, you take a magical leap forward to see your future — if you can't see it my friend, you can't build it. Get comfortable with zooming ahead to the future and back to the present to build the dream today. It's easy to get caught up in all of the minutia of building a company and forget why you started on the quest in the first place.

While traditional business plans were designed to get you to think five years out into the future, in theory they are a great exercise to help construct a framework and visual of what your idea could materialize into, while in practicality, they become obsolete once they are printed to paper. While I encourage the practice of writing down specific milestones and architecting the design and build-out of year one of your startup, in this context I am more so imploring you to harness your imaginary and intuitive abilities to feel what it feels like to have it all come together and be finished. By closing our eyes and getting into the daily or weekly habit of visualizing the laborious steps being done and having a business that finally is working well for us, we build the emotional connective tissues with a future reality that pulls us towards manifesting that physical moment, and not solely getting lost in the brick-laying process of startup formation.

Even if we are first time founders who have never experienced corporate success before, we can still visualize a future reality that connects the dots between what we're building today, and the destination that we're going to get to. The journey between the beginning and the vision's end will very much be different than you imagine, but you alone have to define what the feeling will feel like once you arrive where you're wanting to go. If you want to feel empowered, running a multi-national corporation, visualize jet setting across the globe dashing from power lunch to ringing the NYSE closing bell. If you want to see the smiling faces of your customers when you open up your small retail shop, paint the picture of their warm embraces in your mind, and how proud you feel to be a part of their lives. By playing the movie backwards, we remove a lot of the doubt, fear, and limiting beliefs in our ability today to create a successful tomorrow for ourselves. Every founder's vision for what success looks like for herself varies from person to person, and you must decide where this journey will take you before you begin. In all reality, we never will know exactly where it will take us, but we can create a magnetic future reality that pulls us to get through the startup storm to enjoy the sunny days ahead. Whenever you become burdened by your startup's challenges, I encourage you to go back to playing the movie backwards and connecting with that future successful founder, proudly looking back on the journey. For me, this has helped me navigate many unfathomable, challenging days, and has given me the entrepreneurial juice to build faster and smarter so I can meet my future self on the other side.

CHAPTER 3:
THE ROLE OF THE FOUNDER

Stories Sell. Features Don't.

There is a distinctive difference between a company that symbolizes something greater than the sum of its parts, and a company that just sells parts to people for a buck. Call it a mission, a vision, a narrative, or even a North Star — some businesses craft meaning from day one, making it a priority from launch, while others stumble upon their crafted meaning later in life. The third group, simply never makes meaning at all, just relies on selling x to y based on market demand z. Sure, you can be successful running just about any business, with or without a North Star, but to attract the most passionate people to your company as employees, customers and partners, I firmly believe you must make and convey deep meaning to the world. Why should your startup exist, and why should it endure beyond you?

Companies that set their compass on a powerful heading not only reach their destination quicker, but also build unwavering loyalists along the way.

I asked Eric Yuan, Founder & CEO of Zoom®, a leading enterprise video conferencing platform with a market capitalization at time of writing of $116 billion, "What is your North Star?" His answer:

> It's a hyper-competitive business world, the need to create positive and powerful differentiation in a given market has never been so important. For Zoom, this meant going well beyond creating a great product — We set out to build a culture which was humble and hardworking, authentically empathetic to our customers' experience and passionately customer-focused. We empowered each and every employee to go above-and-beyond to Deliver Happiness. When I see customer sentiments which show Zoom has transcended a

simple commercial exchange and is truly happy to work with us — that's powerful, and that's what delivering happiness looks like to me.

As Mr. Yuan's mission to "Deliver Happiness" continued to resonate deeply with customers, employees, and Wall Street investors, Zoom has continued to garner the top ranked spot in positive reviews across Gartner Peer Insights, Trust Radius and G2 Crowd since their successful 2019 Initial Public Offering (IPO).

Some companies start their business by pledging to donate a portion of proceeds to charity, while others aim their product or service at ameliorating the lives of those affected by a disease or the less fortunate. They both have a built-in mission that drives meaning that all stakeholders can believe in and champion.

If you don't have meaning beyond being another coffee shop, another retail brand, another e-commerce site, you should stop and consider what your customers, employees, suppliers and investors might deeply care about. Ask yourself, why does your startup exist beyond offering customers what it builds?

Our corporate slogan for my first dot com, WorldMusicLink, was *Connecting the Music Industry*. Our internal narrative was to "eliminate the struggling artist, forever." We felt the music business was, and still is actually, disconnected, fragmented, and seems to favor the few — leaving millions of talented hopefuls offstage. The model, which still exists today, is akin to a pyramid, with millions of aspiring musicians at the bottom, and a handful of financially backed celebrities who make it to the top. Our goal, was to flip the pyramid of power, bridge the gap between the heard and un-heard, and lay the foundation for deep, career accelerating relationships that would spark careers, and bring a broken industry into the digital Millennium. Lofty? Yes. But we crafted meaning beyond our digital platform, and into the lives and careers for an underserved population of artists.

Listen to the words that we used to define our narrative — eliminate the struggling artist, bridge the fragmented industry, flip the power paradigm — these are words with meaning, passion and purpose behind them, all pointing towards creating a higher standard. When we believed in our North Star, others could believe in it too.

Can your company be the vehicle through which they are able to find meaning, help others, and feel good in the process? Don't let that opportunity pass you by. Find meaning and make it a deeply rooted, integral part of your business. It can be something simple like choosing to only source local produce for your restaurant and support local farmers, or partnering with diverse suppliers (woman-owned, family owned, LGBT, veterans, etc.), or donating your product to someone in need when your customers buy one from you (the Toms® shoe model). Find your meaning!

While we often craft external facing narratives, internal facing ones matter too. There is a growing movement of employees, particularly among Millennials and Gen-Zs, that seek deep-rooted meaning and purpose over compensation. Meaning matters — plain and simple. Compensation and our ability to work on projects that meet our skillsets might make us show up to work, but what makes us deeply want to stay there? The feeling that your work matters, that it has an impact on the world, and that in some small way, it's leaving a lasting legacy to make the world just a little better than you found it.

Remember, when your employees go out on weekends, or talk with family and friends, and are asked, "So where are you working these days?" they want to be proud of where they work. They want meaning behind their paycheck. They want to be confident in saying that they love their job, and what they love most, is the ability to impact the lives of others with their brand, product, or service; that they are making a difference by just showing up to work to open the doors. It's not just another job — another paycheck, another 9-to-5 at a big software firm selling enterprise grade software to mid-level IT managers — it is a deep-rooted mission for change; to change the world.

Partnerships – Think Them First to Win

There was a time, when I received a cold e-mail request out of left field. It read something like this, "Hi Reagan, pardon the cold e-mail, but I'd like to discuss a technology that has been developed with you, that will solve the issue of royalties for artists (or lack thereof). Would you make yourself available to discuss?" I replied "Sure, could you tell me a bit more about what you are doing, and your relationship to the product?" He went on to explain the technology a bit, and I offered to talk on the phone with him. During our call, for ten minutes straight, I let him talk about the startup he was advising, their technology, their lack of product market fit and capital, and his lack of connections in the Music Business. After hearing him out, I asked him point blank, "So, how can I help you?" He explained that he had no connections in the space and wanted to tap me for introductions to specific music executives he had in mind that I had worked with in the past, who are powerful players in the space. I had a revelation mid call. My thought was, this guy doesn't even know me, cold e-mails me, calls me, and now he wants me to do all the heavy lifting for his benefit, start introducing him and recommend his company (of which I know virtually nothing about), to my contacts — executives with whom took me years of relationship building to establish from scratch — as if I'm his new employee? You've got to be kidding. He failed to understand how an equitable business relationship should work.

Perhaps if he had started his pitch by asking me thoughtful questions, getting to know me, instead of just starting with his elevator pitch without any dialogue, he would understand more of my experience in the music industry, my viewpoint on where it is at today, and give me some time to ponder which individuals in my network might actually be open to helping him get to the next level. He was asking me to go out on a limb for him, vouch for his startup (of which I didn't know any of the employees), and after just a ten-minute phone call! I got to hand it to him for being courageous, but the approach could be refined.

I do believe in equitable relationships — one in which both parties benefit mutually. I'm not talking about financial compensation, so don't get the wrong impression. What I am talking about is, maybe this was a technology that I could've wanted to be a big part of and an advocate for. Maybe I might have wanted to review some literature prior to introducing him to my network. Maybe I might have even wanted to become an investor, instead of just passing the referral along without first right of refusal at the deal.

By jumping in to ask people for things without offering something in return, denotes a lack of an equitable mindset. Conversely, in offering people an opportunity to be a part of your journey, you build relationships, not transactions.

When I started WML, I was twenty, I remember asking older successful executives to help me, and in return would give them a Board of Advisor seat, a future option to buy stock in our startup, and public recognition. I would feature their name, biography, and photo on our website, and put them in a press release giving them notoriety in the community and to thousands of our users. I granted them with the opportunity to impact a young CEO and shape the company's strategic vision to help forge the future of the Music Industry. I thanked each advisor from my heart after meeting with them, and after every call, and I would personally hand write them a thank you letter or e-mail. At Christmas time, I bought all of our Advisors small gifts as a token of my appreciation and had them shipped to their homes.

Now, I may have gone above and beyond what most founders do, but I believe in equitable partnerships. I believe in giving before I take, in sharing in success together, and thanking people along the way. I never paid any Advisor as we didn't have the capital to spare, but they would all take my phone call and help me out because they felt that I truly valued our relationship and their mentorship, which I did. I had full intention of paying them once we started making money, but from the beginning I always thought partner together to win, despite our lack of financial resources. That equitable partnership mindset is the reason why many of my former advisors are still some of my friends over a decade later.

I encourage you to put yourself in the mindset of the person you are about to talk with and ask yourself how you can help them win first, instead of the all too common — ask, take and Irish goodbye. Think about building relationships that will endure ten, twenty, thirty years, not a five-minute pump and information dump. Not all people are motivated by money. A heartfelt thank you goes miles in most people's book. The opportunity to be part of a worthwhile movement. The ability to share one's personal advice, be listened to, and have someone demonstrate true gratefulness. These are the building blocks that create long-term, equitable relationships that matter. Think them first — I promise you will get further faster and build a truly valuable network of friends in the process.

Being CEO – The Flame Thrower & Fire Extinguisher

As a founder, you have two key roles - A Fire Starter and a Fire Extinguisher. What do I mean? Let's start with existing fires. I define a fire as something that happens that you either:

a) Didn't plan for, but can have catastrophic results for your customers, employees or business if it isn't extinguished.

or

b) Something that you could have planned for, but now are faced with a dire situation, and must react quickly to put out the brushfire before it grows into a full-fledged forest fire.

Knowing which fires to put out first, and why, will be a key driver of success as you journey through the startup process. There are simply too many fires to put out at one time, in exhaustive fashion, then one can hope to accomplish in any week or month. That is why you will need to find ways to keep the kindling process of your business to a manageable amount — one that is within your budget, and capabilities, so that you do not get into a situation where you have completely overextended yourself or your business financially or operationally.

When I was starting my first business, I wanted to do everything at once. From logo creation, to product design, to website building, to raising capital, to hiring and opening an office space, to incorporating, it was all required, but too much and all at once. I created too many fires for myself to manage. Even for a small team of three co-founders, it was too much work all at once. I urge you to take baby steps in the beginning, to start a mini project (e.g., logo design), and try to complete it as best as possible within a manageable amount of time, then once that is done, move on to the next phase.

Startups are not 30-yard dashes; they're 26-mile marathons.

Now, to the other side of the equation — starting fires. It is imperative that you keep the creative pilot light lit inside of your entrepreneurial venture, so that you always have quick access to launching the next mini project, task, idea, or program. You can't put out so many fires and be so far removed from the fire-starting process, that you end up snuffing out your own idea generating startup flame.

The level at which you will become a Fire Starter and Fire Extinguisher, will be unique to the nature and intensity of the type of business that you start. For some, the go-to-market strategy must be executed very quickly to meet consumer demand or an ephemeral market opportunity that's here today and gone tomorrow.

A great way to stay organized with respect to this process, is to structure your day in two parts — bifurcating one to putting out fires that crop up, and the other to starting new ones that fuel growth. I like to split the two up so that I put on my fireman hat in the morning, after the issues of last evening have cropped up, and then put on my firestarter hat in the afternoon when things settle down, and I am able to work on new marketing and sales campaigns, partnerships, hiring, etc. Over time, when situations arise, you will be able to identify them quickly as one that needs to be put out or have fuel poured on. This ability will set you apart on a mental level, and better prepare you to tackle anything, that happens throughout the day.

Case in point might be the following scenario on a Monday. A customer calls you irate, complaining that their product didn't arrive on time and that they are demanding a return and a full refund. At the same time, you get an e-mail from your bank charging you an overdraft fee as your daily balance has gone negative as your credit card company auto swept their monthly payment a few days earlier than you anticipated. As you're dealing with these two issues, your lead developer asks you if they should start working on the next sprint build for your application or should they complete a persistent bug fix that's been lasting for months. You're ten minutes late already for your marketing meeting with your team to discuss a new social media campaign that you're about to launch for Spring. What fire do you put out first?

While the fires that crop up may differ, this is a typical, daily occurrence inside the trenches of most startups — four or five things going off the rails and hitting you all at once. My recommendation is to snuff out the things today that will burn your startup the fastest.

In the above example, you need to replenish your checking account before you can issue a refund to the customer, otherwise your overdraft will continue to grow. If a bug has been on the docket for months, there's a reason it hasn't been fixed yet, so it can wait one more day. But the bigger question you should be asking yourself from a development standpoint is should we be building more features if the existing ones still don't work right? Who is authorizing more features? Is it the engineering lead? You might need to set a new company standard that says nothing ships until the last bug is fixed. After replenishing your bank's balance, you should issue a refund to the customer and give them a heartfelt apology for the delay (even though it wasn't your fault but the shipping company's) — it's harder to acquire a new customer than to retain an existing one. If you've hired smart, driven marketing people, they will start the meeting without you and will be just fine — you can always get caught up later on. If, however, you've hired people who wait on you just to act, then you've hired the wrong types of people for a startup. You might even consider empowering anyone at your company to respond to a customer complaint and issue a refund without your authorization if it is under $200, as this could free you up from being the only person who can handle financial transactions.

Automating the Fire Extinguishing Process

By hiring smart, autonomous, responsible team members, you free up bandwidth for yourself as a CEO so you don't have to put out every fire that crops up. Even smarter, is to create fire extinguishing systems and procedures that prevent recurring issues from starting in the first place. Examples could include building self-service customer tools like pre-paid return labels so customers can issue their own returns within a 30-day window online in their account without calling or e-mailing your team to request it, a no questions asked return policy for orders under $50 to eliminate management approval, auto replenishing features to ensure checking accounts never overdraft or other critical services such as hosting are never turned off unknowingly on you that might impact your company's services.

Often times the same types of problems crop up repeatedly, and our job as a smart entrepreneur is to recognize when problems are the same sort but varying flavors. This way, we can create the systems that empower our team and our customers to put out their own fires should they crop up and frees your time up to focus on more important elements that drive your startup further, faster. We must have objectivity of the problems, categorize them into types to recognize them more clearly, define why they cropped up in the first place, and then build solutions that prevent them from happening again. There's a reason why fire crews spend many weeks a year bulldozing fire break lines in the forests and along highways – they recognize past situations that threatened the population, and have taken action to build defensible, self-servicing barriers that prevent future fires from burning out of control.

CHAPTER 4:
THE WORLD WITHIN

In·sight - the power or act of seeing into a situation; the act or result of apprehending the inner nature of things or of seeing intuitively. Moreover, insight, is the capacity to gain an accurate and deep intuitive understanding of a person, thing or situation.[3]

En·tre·pre·neur - one who organizes, manages, and assumes the risks of a business or enterprise.[4]

I have come to learn, over the past decade of being heavily involved in and around startups and the entrepreneurial community, that the most successful entrepreneurs possess a unique insight into one or more of the following four areas. I call this type of deeply tuned-in founder, an Insightrepreneur.

Insightrepreneurs are able to zero in on one, or more, of the following four areas when developing their new ventures. These unique insights provide a competitive barrier, a runway of time against competitors, and a stronger product-model-market fit that others just lack. With sufficient identification and rapid execution, this typically yields faster traction, exponential (cheaper) growth, and extremely loyal customers who evangelize a brand earlier in the startup lifecycle.

The Four Magical Insights:

1. An undiscovered or overlooked (un-attractive) market.

2. An ignored, shared human experience that others gloss over.

3. An emerging trend (or soon to be shared behavior/economy).

4. A deep situational or acute, circumstantial insight.

Typically, startups focus on just one of the above insights, and usually a small echelon of majorly successful ones, overlap and combine these elements to craft a unique solution to a problem that gains global dominance in what appears like an overnight success.

The Four Magical Insights are not mutually exclusive; they are combinatorial. If aggregated, they can become powerful.

To be an Insightrepreneur, first, remove the burden that you must take money from the user and identify deeply with their situation. Really put yourself in their shoes for a moment, as hard as that may be to do. With practice, great entrepreneurs can develop an almost sixth sense, to dreaming up solutions to problems that they witness in the marketplace. It takes time, but you will be able to listen more effectively and deeply without casting prejudgment (biases) or forcing solutions, but rather letting solutions emerge from your intuition, as you listen to user stories, identify common themes among personas, and continually ask "Why?", "What's making them say this?", and "What if something could solve that pain – how might they respond?"

Call it entrepreneurial enlightenment, but I have witnessed some of the most successful companies of my day - Tesla®, Airbnb®, Uber®, DropBox®, Square®, Snap®, Facebook®, Instagram® - reach record user growth, virality, and market adoption, without forcing their brands down consumers throats to win hearts and wallets.

Insightrepreneurs intuitively know what users experience when they are researching for a product, when they are struggling with an antiquated solution in the market, or when they are continually facing the same problem over and over again in their day-to-day lives. They transform their own hunches into data supported user feedback loops, that provide them with critical, deep insights into specific sets of situations, areas, workflows, and user archetypes that drive innovation, deliver solutions that people absolutely fall in love with, because they either rapidly increase life's pleasure, or rapidly decrease life's pain.

How to Discover New Market Opportunities:

Step 1: Listen, observe, ask.

Listen, Observe, Ask. Only focus on a user's intended outcome and current problems (pain) in achieving that outcome.

- Where are they failing today?

- Why are they failing?

- Are they really failing, or are you projecting because you're so hungry to force a new piece of technology or solution into that market just because you want to operate in that space?

We have to really get honest with ourselves here about the severity of the user's friction, and more importantly, not exaggerate a market problem just to slap technology and a startup label on it. You are not the startup in shining armor (just yet), you are the intimate researcher. Listen for clues, observe behaviors, recognize friction.

Step 2: Hit pause on the revenue button.

Hit the pause button on revenue generation (how you win). Focus entirely on value creation (how they win). There are usually multiple ways to solve a problem — ones that require a low level of innovation, to ones that require a very high level of technology, infrastructure, and capital to pull it all off. Sticking a stake in the ground to build your startup around one solution isn't the right choice. The right choice will emerge later from testing. Map out all potential solutions first — from the simplest ones to the most complex, expensive, or hardest to pull off.

Step 3: Be honest. What can you realistically build today?

Determine what's realistically feasible to create/offer to solve the pain today (or within a reasonable time frame and budget with what you have). Choosing a solution that may take three years to get to market may not be the right choice and choosing a solution that has no barriers of defensibility against competitors leaves you open to others too quickly.

For example, if you observe a customer shopping at a grocery store trying to reach up high to grab a product from the top shelf, your first reaction might be to launch a robotic lift system with AI motion detection that automatically knows when a user is reaching for something and it grabs that item and brings it down to them. This is the Silicon Valley problem — technology is always the answer. But in reality, maybe not. Maybe, the cheapest and fastest solution to build might be a basic arm extension reacher, or maybe a plastic step ladder, or maybe a movable shelf, or how about a simple call button to page the tall store clerk to that location to reach for the item. There are usually a full range of solutions — from crude, rudimentary to highly sophisticated, technologically advanced ones — our goal as the entrepreneur, is to map out all of the possible solutions, rank their time to market, capital required, market opportunity, and competitive defensibility to determine what works best for the user, and what can you truly build a long-standing business around. Why spend one year and spend $1,500,000 building an AI prototype if you can buy a step ladder for $15, sell it for $30, clear $15 in profit, and scale that solution to 50,000 other retail stores around the US? I love high tech, but tech doesn't solve every problem. Sometimes thinking of the absolute simplest way to solve a problem helps you prove or disprove the demand for a market over a costly, time intensive, technological solution.

Step 4: Get underneath the problem to understand what's driving it.

Talk with potential users. Re-frame the pain they are experiencing, and ask qualifying questions like:

"So, what I'm really hearing is that the current solution to this problem is A, but the underlying issue that really perplexes you is this (B). What if, a solution that solves B were to exist? Would solving B also help you solve A?"

By getting users to explain the why under the what, you'll unravel a deeper insight into the underlying motivation behind their issue. This is where innovative solutions emerge that connect emotionally with users. Go there!

Step 5: Experiment with potential solutions, solicit feedback & rank them.

Experiment with users by having them draw pictures of their pain points, current solutions, and show you what their intended outcomes may be. Present varying options back to them in the form of a collaborative dialogue that brings them into the innovation process and rank them in order (1-10) of importance of solving pain today. Avoid the "nice haves" to solve pain. This helps you to see what they see, from their perspective — not yours — to deliver deep lasting value. We must always see from our user's eyes, not ours. Don't innovate just to innovate.

Focus on delivering acute value, because value delivered, becomes invaluable to the customer.

In exchange, the customer is willing to provide you with a deeper level of engagement or a higher monetary return, as they will feel you truly get them and feel connected to your brand, product experience, and company. The greatest brands of all time aim to deliver more than a utility, a commodity, an experience, or a platform — they deliver a relationship built on understanding and trust.

One tool I use to get into the insight zone is to take a notebook or smartphone out with me everywhere I go. I watch people carefully, and when I see them get frustrated, express happiness, or exhibit a process, I stop and ask myself what was their intended goal, what was their need, where were their roadblocks, and how might they be improved? You can try this yourself. The key is to avoid thinking about a market, a business model, how the idea might actually fly, how it might make money, or even if you could pull it off. Just go from insight to ideation and write it all down. You can later go back to refine the solutions to a few that might be prototype-able. Here is the design process encapsulated in a nutshell:

1.   Gather Insights

2.   Ideate Solutions

3.   Get User Buy-In

4.   Build Prototype(s)

5.   Deploy, Test Solutions, Measure Results

Let's deep dive into a few of these insights further:

An Undiscovered, Overlooked Market:

There are "attractive" markets, and frankly, there are "un-attractive" markets. "Attractive" markets often have a lot of media buzz and/or hype around them. If there's an acronym for it — AI, VR, AR, ML, NLP, WEB 3.0, D-AAPS, CRYPTO — then you can bet those are being heralded as "attractive" markets. For example, becoming the next Uber® for on-demand hiring sounds pretty compelling. Becoming the next Uber® for plumbers might not. However, I implore you to not discount un-attractive markets. Imagine being able to open an app and order a plumber on-demand whenever you have a backed-up toilet instead of waiting two days for the guy to hopefully show up. It may not be the slickest demo pitch, but I can guarantee you that other entrepreneurs are not running up that creek with or without a paddle anytime soon. Plus, there's no acronym for that market. Wait, there is one, BS! Plumbers crack and backed-up toilets aside, there could be a pot of gold waiting for you in these types of un-attractive, overlooked markets. Think making PDF file storage easy is cool? Nope. DropBox® built it into a $10 billion valuation with a $1 billion 2017 revenue run-rate[5] though. Un-attractive markets are often undervalued and highly overlooked. Don't make this mistake. Anytime there are a mass of potential users experiencing a recurring problem, inefficiency, bottleneck, or poor experience, there's the potential for a multi-million or potentially, a billion-dollar business.

But, it's hard to fall in love with an un-attractive market, as we want so desperately to brag about our "hot" space and show it off to the world. Call it the trophy startup, it's a fool's errand to solely focus on the obvious consumer facing spaces. Typically, there's a lot of competition down there by the low hanging fruit — consumer product goods, apps, restaurants, creative industries (music, arts, etc.), food, beverages, clothing, retail shops, etc. But as you go up the idea ladder, to higher, harder and often times "un-attractive" problems, the air gets thinner, and the entrepreneurial competition lowers exponentially. Sometimes it's because these spaces seem boring or historically insignificant to today's society, but they can be very lucrative. However, sometimes there's good reason why no one has ventured into a specific space — as the amount of ambition, resources, capital, and time required to implement them are too challenging to garner and deploy.

The Musk Test:

To illustrate an entrepreneur that continually seeks to solve the world's hardest "un-attractive" challenges, enter Elon Musk. My Elon Musk test can be used to gauge your concept against what Elon might do. You see, Elon doesn't launch the next Italian restaurant, the next dog walking app, or even the next software company — he builds his *own* markets — electricity — from cars to solar panels, Tesla's goal is not to just take market share away from GM® or Ford®, it's to build an entirely new, off-the-grid electrical distribution network that's powered from a renewable resource, the Sun. Take The Boring Co® — a subterranean, earth moving transportation network of lightning fast tunnels that will change mass transportation forever once adopted, and thus, reduce millions of tons of atmospheric pollution causing traffic jams that plague our most trafficked cities and suck countless commuting days from our lives every year. With SpaceX®, he's literally launching us out of Earth's orbit, to build the world's first reusable rocket deployment and re-entry system, which reduces hundreds of millions of dollars, if not billions, and in the process, opens up an entirely new ecosystem for space exploration and new opportunities that leverage his reusable rockets.

Elon solves fundamental, but really hard problems, with out-of-the-box solutions. Electrical innovation, tunneling, and rocket reusability might not be the "attractive" spaces for most, but they impact billions of people's lives globally. The competitive air is thinner in some of these arenas, as no clear-cut winner, model, or price point exists yet. You don't have to follow Elon, but it is a helpful exercise to practice when you're thinking about what your business will look like in five to ten years at scale, if successful. Will the market be flooded with copy-cats? Will the market dominance that you have today be overshadowed by other players who drive the price point down to zero? Could your company create an entirely new industry instead of just being another player in a saturated market of many?

Changing Up the Business Model:

So, how can we innovate within an area that maybe isn't so extraterrestrial? When there is a lot of competition in a space, often companies all operate with similar business models — by simply flipping the business model without changing the actual product/ service, you can create an entirely new category that you can be a new leader in.

Case in point, restaurant food to-go orders — you used to have to call the restaurant, put your name in, and drive down to park, go inside to pick it up, then pay, and drive all the way back home. Just re-engineer the delivery part, and you've got a massive new opportunity — GrubHub®, Amazon Fresh®, DoorDash®, UberEats®, Postmates®, Delivery.com®, Seamless®, etc. Same Product (Food). Different Model (Mobile Delivery). During COVID-19, when cities began shutting down indoor dining and hundreds of millions of people around the globe were stuck at home, mobile food delivery picked up incredible momentum. While a pandemic might not be part of your business plan's original market tailwind, these companies realized before COVID-19, that mobile connectivity and changing consumer behavior was occurring that would fuel a new ecosystem that connected hundreds of thousands of restaurants with a new market opportunity in a convenient, turn-key system. The pandemic has accelerated the adoption of these mobile food delivery apps, but the smart entrepreneurs behind them recognized the market and technological conditions were in place for mobile food delivery to springboard off of. In this instance, technology was used to connect the digital dots between established industries and hungry consumers. The only piece that was needed to solve that challenge was simplifying the online ordering and delivery elements. It became a win for consumers to receive the convenience of delicious meals while in the comfort of their homes and apartments, and it was a win for restaurants to amplify their marketing reach and thus, their recurring revenue potential. For drivers, it provides a tertiary piece of value, on-demand income generation that helped put extra dollars in their pockets when they needed it. A win-win-win that connected a new product, with an existing market, with a new business model in a cohesive way.

A Shared Human Experience:

Markets are nothing more than a concentrated collection of humans, that share alignment towards achieving a similar set of goals. They can be of a certain age, location, educational, or occupational pedigree. When I say shared human experience, I am referring to finding a deeper, internal type of connection — one that is emotional or humanistic if you will, not quantifiable as in where you went to school, what you bought recently, or where you currently live — these are demographic benchmark data points that you can buy from industry report services. An emotion, that drives user-generated content on websites like Facebook®, can emerge from a wide range of emotional drivers like the need to fulfill one's ego, the compulsory need to share, the innate desire to express oneself, the lifelong quest to learn more than one has ever known, or the more primal, need to bond and build relationships that endure. Websites, products, services and online communities that tap into these types of deeper emotions, often connect with their user-base on a more profound level, that pierces the vail of promotional branding, market positioning, and disrupts incumbent players. Moreover, they create a lasting bond that takes the user to a new place, a higher experience, and a more substantial connection with life in new and exciting ways.

Snap®, for example, enables users to share in real-time mini stories that are as ephemeral as life is — they disappear once seen (or within 24 hours) — just enough time to share in the experience with the other person, connect on a more fun, romantic, or plutonic level. Facebook®, Instagram®, and Twitter®, empower you to rise above the crowd and be recognized, heard, and find meaning. Instead of sharing your pictures, videos, and thoughts with just a few friends or family members, you now have access to thousands of connections and the wider public world, if you so choose. That tremendous megaphone emblazons the heart to share, and keep on sharing, as the cathartic, instantaneous feedback delivers a sticky feedback loop, that keeps you checking, and re-checking how many likes, followers and comments you receive. Views and likes prove to us that our opinions matter, that we belong, and that we can connect to something greater.

Uber®, positions you with instant car service at the push of a button. Frankly, it could be described as the freedom app, that lets you explore new areas of your city without the need to rent a car, the app that unlocks travel to places far and wide, all without the responsibility and financial burden of owning or renting a car. With UberPool®, you're instantaneously, and sometimes serendipitously, able to share a ride with strangers that can become your next date, connection, or business partner. The days of waiting for a cab with the questionable bullet-proof middle divider, scruffy beard and Jersey accent are long gone. "Where to, Toots?"

These are just a few of the newly minted companies that have scaled dramatically in the last few years, but under the hood, they are more than just good apps or sites, they are companies that have bridged the gap between commerce and a deep emotional customer experience. They have tapped into a deeper echelon of shared humanity that doesn't show up on a demographic pie chart or a market positioning matrix. Humans use products that they like once in a while, and use products that they fall in love with on a routine, if not obsessive, basis. These products have become more than a collection of utilities; they are an emotional extension of our shared human experience and quest to unlock more.

Be insightful, create products that swoon customers over, and create an unbreakable bond that taps into emotion that won't fade away quickly.

Evolving, Rapidly Expansive Trends:

If fads come and go, then trends are powerful upwellings that raise tides and moves mountains. Trends disrupt incumbent large cap companies that fail to innovate (think Amazon® vs Borders®, Apple's App Store® vs Tower Records®, iPod® vs Sony® Walkman®, Netflix® vs. Blockbuster®, the list goes on). The companies behind these massive successes identified micro and structural trends before they were known to the world and threw their product out in front of the trend so that when it hit, they were first to market or better yet, first in the consumer's mind.

Spotting a trend coming is like surfing — the world's best surfers, in the heat of competition, are able to spot 'outsiders' — the waves that are far away, hard to see, but if they break, they will be very big opportunities. If you want to ride the big wave, you've got to spot the outsiders. You can't just drop in on the one that's peaking right in front of you as it's already in decline and will likely crush you.

The shift from vinyl records to recordings on CDs, to digital MP3 downloads, to music streaming has been well documented. But only a few companies had been able to successfully navigate that evolutionary tale. The shift from gas powered cars, to fuel efficient hybrids, to electric vehicles, to auto-charging solar powered vehicles, will be recorded as another disruptive change that shattered existing players who didn't spot the trend, and didn't position their companies ahead of the curve. Be ready to spot the next wave, and get out in front to ride it, so that you have a real shot to surf it all the way in.

Deep Situational or Circumstantial Insights:

These arise from day-to-day experiences, or, from unique outlier situations, that you go through. Sometimes I find myself having the best ideas when I am traveling, observing new cultures, geographies, businesses, and ways of doing things. Other times, I am doing the same old thing that I did the day before, but this time, I stop and really observe what is going on around me, and step back to ask myself, "Why is this happening the way it is happening?", "Why is he or she struggling with that, this way, so many times?", "How come they are following this or that, and ignoring that?", "Is this the best way to accomplish x, y, or z?"

In the course of life, you can sometimes identify a unique insight in doing something a certain way, that no one else has explored yet. This gold mine can often lead you to create a new path for thousands if not millions of people like you, to follow in your footsteps. You will know you are onto this, when you have a deep understanding of a problem and have discovered a solution, or when the problem is experienced by everyone else except you, as your approach to the normal problem yielded a new solution that you just "saw" before anyone else did. Write these experiences down in a journal, or on your smartphone, and keep track of your emotions as you experience this. Did it make you feel relieved or alive when you found the solution, and when you shared it with others, did they light up and get excited to see it from your new perspective? These are important moments that if properly identified, by an Insightrepreneur, can yield big payoffs.

For example, maybe you color code your sticky notes to rank them in order of increasing importance for "things to do". This ultimately leads to other people at your office copying your prioritization system, which then leads you to develop and market a product of color-coded sticky notes for engineering teams in the Bay Area. From there, you build a companion mobile app that bridges the digital divide and takes the concept online, where laptops, mobile phones and PCs can all create color coded sticky notes online to stay visually organized and accomplish more, faster.

Vision – Why Mind Control Wins:

There's been much written on the topic of the Law of Attraction. From <u>The Secret</u> by Rhonda Byrne[6], to <u>Think and Grow Rich</u>[7] by Napoleon Hill, virtually every guru at some point or another has pontificated about the power of attracting what you spend your time focusing on. I am not here to reiterate what has been said, but I want to speak to you from my own experiences, as I agree that what you focus on materializes.

When you start a company, you are essentially telling the Universe that your kernel of an idea deserves space in this world. It is your bargain deal with the Universe, that the more you are willing to contribute to the advancement of said idea, the more you believe it should return success, adoration, and ultimately riches back to you and your family and friends. Right? Well, sort of. Many people start a business with the dream of getting rich and getting rich quicker rather than later. But very few people spend the time to clearly think about how much rich means to them. Is it a specific number? A specific object that you will be able to afford or have bestowed upon you when you achieve said results? How concrete and exacting can you be if you really tried to, to define what this success would look, feel, sound or be like? Here's where you take 1 minute and stop reading, to really do this exercise…

Figure 4.1

Figure 4.2

To me, being "rich" means the following: (be as <u>specific</u> as possible):

____

____ .

What did you come up with? Was it a giant 120 ft. yacht sitting in the glistening Mediterranean Sea with fresh seafood platters, champagne, and fun music playing?

So, with a small search, that yacht is actually $4,286,285 — a 2006 Pershing 115ft yacht, slightly used, and her name is Ginger. Here she is (figure 4.1)[8].

To put a price tag on it, makes it real. We need this to define "rich" or "successful", otherwise we live in a state of delusion.

The point is, rich is not a number. Wealth is not a thing; it is an overall generality. In startups, we live and die with specificity. We need concrete numbers, because they bring it into the forefront of our radar screen. Whether you go browsing on Pinterest® and make a private wish list or vision board with cutouts of what amazing things your new business will bring you, it doesn't matter, unless we are specific.

Or maybe when you closed your eyes, you envisioned a beautiful townhome in Jackson Hole, Wyoming, complete with a modern kitchen with open floor plan, nestled in the foothills of outdoor country activities year-round? Perfect for you and that special someone, and possibly a little one. That's on sale for only $369,900. Don't believe me? Here you go (figure 4.2)[9].

Let me put this another way. Let's say you are my sales manager, and up until now, I, as your boss, have always just accepted your sales figures each month as it is what it is, and never questioned it. Now, all of a sudden, I tell you that we need to increase our sales for Q4. What's the first thing you are going to ask me? "By how much boss?" So, he is asking for an increase in output, and he needs to know how fast you want to run the machine to yield that output. Same is true with our goals.

We need unambiguous clarity when it comes to what we want.

If you start a business just to have something nice to do, or something to stay busy with, or something that will pay the bills, you will end up with exactly that. But usually, plus that headache of managing something that is barely treading water to survive itself.

Same goes with operational goals. It is not good enough to just do better than you did last month. You need to have a number, a target. Even the best bow and arrow will only hit its target if it is aimed at the right target. Otherwise, that perfect archer will hit everything else.

**Always pick a specific target. This ensures everyone and
everything is aimed at hitting the mark.**

Now, here's the secret that Tony Robbins® wonderfully helped to develop, that I would like to share with you: As you get close to reaching that target, before you reach that target, you need to set a higher target. If you wait until you reach that target, you will lose momentum, and can easily regress back to lower metrics and standards than the previous goal. You see this all the time with athletes, as they gain momentum and are about to reach the Championship, they don't set their next goals and then are like, "Wow, we won...now what?" And they are lost and unsatisfied, and ultimately will resort to things that give them the same rush as going after their goals but often with negative consequences. If you would like to learn more from Mr. Robbins on goal setting and achieving your dreams, I highly suggest attending one of his seminars as I did, like Unleash the Power Within® or reading his books like <u>Awaken the Giant Within</u>[10]. - I promise, he won't disappoint!

We need personal goals that are private, we also need company goals that are public, and I would stress even further to work with every person in your company to ask them what their goals really are. This creates higher standards so that everyone can reach even further than what they thought possible before.

Wouldn't it be interesting if you knew what your sales manager really dreamed of earning, versus what he settles to accept? How might he become more motivated if he felt that you supported his personal dream of earning that, and that you would do everything in your power to set him up for success so that he could achieve that personal dream by way of your company? How might that deeper level of transparency, mutualistic support radically disrupt the standard modus operandi of most corporations in existence today? I would argue that it would lead to a level of unbounded trust, love, and adoration between employer and employee, and would fundamentally change the purpose of the team's mission and quite possibly, the trajectory of the company's future results.

Getting back to magnetism, if we can become concrete with our personal and corporate (shared) goals, we can then visualize what we want to accomplish and by what date and can hold ourselves accountable to that. If we succeed, great. If we miss the mark, we can then evaluate how we might have adjusted our approach to gain more traction faster.

Without clarity and singularity of focus on individual and shared goals, we will surely not attract what we want, and will attract whatever the world, our competitors, our unhappy customers, or our partners throw at us. These forces are always available if we just let them drift into our minds, hearts and offices. If, however, we take the opposite approach, we are setting ourselves up for success and a culture that thrives on visualization, progress and applauds continuous achievement towards specificity, not generality — targeted clarity yields undeniably more accurate results.

I want to make one last point on this topic. If we were to take this approach one step further and be more honest now about our company's goals with our suppliers and partners, accountants and lawyers too, we may just gain a greater level of excitement in their buy-in to achieve our goals. Many times, focused excitement and progress towards our goals is contagious, and everyone enjoys supporting people on their quest to reach victory. How might the relationship with your supplier change if he knew that your goal was to double your purchases from his firm by the end of the year? Would he be more willing to extend you credit, more favorable product selection and customization, lowered transactional fees, or faster delivery of your merchandise? If we just randomly buy from him and never let him know why we are doing what we are doing and show him how he is a trusted partner in our shared growth, he may never feel like he is part of our journey. Let him in on your goals, and he'll feel he wins when you win.

Humans enjoy mutual progress, and deeply appreciate the unexpected phone call that does the opposite of what everyone else does. Call your supplier and thank him for his fantastic service, and let him know about your ambitious goals, and tell him that when you succeed, so will he. I guarantee you that no one will ever talk to him like that, and he will feel more inspired by your journey and will support you through thick and thin. Same goes with your Accountant, Lawyer, Service Providers, Consultants, etc. View them as trusted partners in achieving shared growth together, not just transactional providers.

Remember, they are human beings that go home at the end of the day to greet their spouses, eat dinner, and have conversations about their work. They want to feel inspired; they want diverse stories, they want to feel that their work has meaning and impact, and that they are valued deeply for their commitment to your success.

And the best part is, you will be telling the truth, because deep down, this is really how you should feel. For me, it has meant the difference in many situations throughout my business career. It has helped me get more support, in more ways, than I can even begin to describe. I hope this provides the same value for you, and draws the best of everything, closer to you, and faster.

Gaining Speed – Why Time is Priceless

The proverbial expression, "Time is money" from Benjamin Franklin is often connected to images of wealthy Wall Street investors who realize the opportunity cost that ephemeral time has on their personal net worths. However, for an entrepreneur, time is the single most important metric that you should keep track of. I will explain this in further detail, as you were probably thinking that money or your product's features, or even your customers were. Wrong!

Time to market launch accounts for a large number of failed startup ideas, that either took too long perfecting a product before launching, or too long in testing or researching before actually delivering anything of value.

If you think you will spend three months building a product, and it actually takes you twelve months, the market opportunity may have come and gone. Often another startup or an incumbent, larger company will launch a similar idea, as the market will be providing them with similar metrics and feedback on what to launch. Your initial hunch will have only had a few months before it expires, and thus, awards the other company with that clever insight into the changing dynamics of the market or consumer that you thought was your "secret sauce".

The faster you launch, the better you stack the cards in your favor for creating market awareness of your solution and brand as the category leader. If you wait too long, then you will be the second or third in the category, and will be fighting for attention, and will have to compete against other entrants on feature sets, pricing, service levels, and other factors that all either cost you more time and money, or will position you as a runner-up offering. It's better to be first in a market and be wrong about the solution, than be fourth and have to fight for market share.

When you raise capital, you're buying time – survival time.

Sure, money gets your branding, employees, office space, and product features built, but it really gets you more time to play. When you have time on your side, you have the luxury to experiment longer with product copy, features, distribution channels, cohorts and more. You have time to experiment with marketing to position wider or deeper with alternative messaging, and to attract better caliber team members because of your traction. Lastly, more time means more gestation periods with consumers to win their minds. Many entrepreneurs spend too much time trying to raise money, often 6-12 months, when in effect, they would be better off spending that precious time improving their product, talking to customers, and increasing their brand than trying to raise capital. Even with a war chest of cash, say $20 million from a Series-A round, you can't reverse 6-12 months of traction from other companies. You'll end up spending 2x-3x more than you should have just to catch up to where they are at with their product development, team, publicity, and customer engagement.

In the beginning of a startup, there is a flow — of ideas, of conversations with prospective users, a progressive movement from ideation to materialization. When you take breaks and stop working, you stunt the flow and cause entrepreneurial regression whereby you begin to lose momentum towards achieving your milestones. Nothing is more impressive to customers than when a new solution emerges out of Beta, to a product without bugs that solves their pain, in a short period of weeks, not months. That lightning-fast turnaround time from buggy Beta to polished v1.0, sets a gold standard with your early adopter consumers that you care about creating a best-in-class outcome and that you will work tirelessly to solve it until it is right.

If you pitch a solution to a problem, and a prospective consumer or business shows initial interest, and it takes you six months to build it, then you show it to them, and they report bugs that prevent them from achieving the "eureka" moment of a solution from your product, and then it takes you another three months to fix the bugs, and then they have to be re-pitched on the value proposition, you will lose all of your momentum. Fast startups have mojo — a 6th gear that propels them to the next milestone on the entrepreneurial journey.

Startups with mojo see problems, build solutions quickly, pivot to get them right, and scale like mad. If you're not part of this flow, you're toast, as your competitors are closer than they appear.

Time is also vital when it comes to publicity. When you get offered an opportunity to be featured in a notable business journal or industry trade publication, you are the Rockstar of the hour. The sizzle of that publicity will last about 30-90 days. After that, it's over. If you can't keep up the sizzle, you fade out. So, when planning a PR roadshow, think about how you can keep the sizzle up for the next 6-12 months. Don't be a flash in the pan, be a burning ember that ignites into a roaring fire then an unstoppable force. Leverage your media exposure in one publication to attract more media attention in others. Use your customer testimonials in January to get more customers to sign on in February. No one wants to hear about a customer that came aboard nine months ago when the product was totally different. They may still not be your on-going customer, right? Everyone wants what is hot and growing today. You need to plan for this and use that momentum to keep it going.

Time is also important when it comes to hiring. When you can tell that amazing engineer — who is currently working for a big tech firm — that you just got two other talented engineers from another big company to sign on to your backend development team last week, that adds a F.O.M.O (fear of missing out) halo effect to your startup. That's a great halo effect to have. It will help you negotiate for more favorable terms and will help you attract better quality talent that may just need a little excitement to goose them into making the jump to join your startup adventure.

How to Close a Fundraising Round – Why Timing Matters

Investors like to invest just before a startup has a breakout moment. This ensures they can still get in for cheap on the equity but realize some immediate up-side potential. Savvy investors know that publicity doesn't guarantee success down the road for startups, but rather customer or user traction is usually the biggest indicator of sustainable, progressive, upward growth.

A few highlights of timing that can interest investors, employees and new customers are:

• Fresh PR in a major media journal, TV, podcast or trade outlet.

• A new partnership deal you just struck with a strategic player.

• A new round of financing you got commitment for.

• A hotshot employee from a major firm you attracted to your team.

• A business plan competition you just won.

• An important milestone you just checked off (or will very soon).

• A new office lease or partnership with a key supplier you inked.

You must realize every day that time is the enemy.

Time is fleeting, and the market opportunity may be growing, but it may also be floating away. Even the best products and services have their moments in the sun. Remember the cupcake retail shop era? How about the MP3 player explosion? Or who can forget the social networking eruption in the MySpace®, Friendster®, and Facebook® days?

The best way to get ahead is to plan the most vital elements that strip you of your time but move your business ahead the fastest for early in the life of your startup. If that's customer research, get chatting. If that's product development, launch that prototype. If that's customer adoption, start dialing for dollars. If that's fleshing out the team, get to recruiting that A player. If that's raising money, start networking and building your slide-deck. The goal should be to set a cadence that helps you stay on track of your goals and keeps you day after day tackling the biggest issues first.

I can tell you firsthand that I made early mistakes with timing with my first startup. I spent four months building our first business plan while in school, then another six months refining it and re-writing it. I spent six months building a series of hand drawn wireframes in both black and white and full color with colorful buttons, pages, icons and whistles. I simultaneously spent nine months trying to hire my ideal Web Developer. I also spent about eighteen months trying to raise capital, one by way of an equity round of seed financing, another by way of a Series-A round of financing, and a third by way of a convertible note. I probably also spent about two months working on the logo. The logo!

How to Get One Month Ahead of the Competition:

Have you ever felt like you just don't have enough time in a day to do all of the things you have been meaning to do? Write that letter, e-mail that investor, re-build that website, get to the gym, the list goes on and on.

So, here's a hack that I learned in 2018 and it has changed my life forever. Every day, we only get twenty-four hours to make it all happen. However, for 1/3 of the day, or eight hours, we are sleeping. So, we really get sixteen hours a day to make it all happen. From Bezos to Edison, Hoffman to Musk - each entrepreneur got the exact same number of hours as you get today. How did they accomplish so much?

Now, of those sixteen hours, most people routinely wake up at 7:30 am, and go to bed by 11:30 pm. Subtract the average digital screen time of two to six hours, and we only have ten hours of our lives to accomplish anything substantial or new. If we can just set our alarms to wake up by 5:30 am, every day we get an extra two hours to accomplish more. Now here's the amazing part. Just two little hours extra a day, compounded over the year is one extra month every year! You're not reading that wrong. Imagine that, from just two little hours — not texting people, not scrolling through your phone, not watching negative news and playing videogames, you name it. At 5:30 am, everyone is sleeping, the house is quiet, no one expects you to respond to e-mails until 8 or 9 am — this is your time to crush it.

In the beginning I'll admit, for the first week, it's a drag. It's dark outside, and no one wants to leave the cozy comfort of a warm bed. But if you could live for the next fifty years and continue waking up just two hours earlier every day, you would gain an extra four plus years of life more. I'm not asking you to eat a bowl of Kale or get your ass out onto the cold beach for some bootcamp class. I am asking you to carve out two little hours just for you and your startup, every day. If you can't commit just two little hours every day to your own future, then who is going to commit to you? Really, ask yourself the question, wouldn't you rather wake up two hours earlier, accomplish a ton, and be a month closer to seizing a market opportunity at the end of the year than all of your competitors? You'll be a startup warrior who seizes your time on Earth each and every day. If you don't find the hustle to commit two extra hours each day to your startup, then you will always find an excuse to give up, not start, not move ahead, and return to cubicle mediocrity. You deserve more from your life, don't you? I'm not even asking you to do this forever, that's up to you and until your startup is running at full steam. For me, I'm no longer scared of getting up at 5:30 am. I just tell myself that I need to crank out a few more hours tomorrow morning, set the alarm, make my coffee, and hit the ground running. How do you think I finished this book? Hundreds of 5:30 am days. I'm not tired, I'm proud of the pages that I am delivering to you today. You, yes you reading this now, were my goal every morning at 5:30 am — finish the book so that I could help you succeed faster!

CHAPTER 5:
PREPPING FOR LAUNCH

Something that I didn't understand when I launched my first startup in 2007, was how expensive it would ultimately be to just flip the Open for Business sign. I guess if they really told you that, most people wouldn't even try. A burn rate is entrepreneur for how much cash you burn monthly. Here's an approximate of what I spent on my first company, WML. Was this the right decision? Maybe. But, now it's so much cheaper to start a company than back then.

General Legal Fees: $10,000

- Incorporation
- Terms of Use for Website
- Independent Contractor Agreement
- Employee Share Option Program (ESOP)
- Stock Certificates
- Term Sheets
- Cap Tables
- Various Counsel Communication

Trademark Fees: $5,000 - $7,500

- Consultation
- New Trademark Search
- Application Fees
- Renewals
- Counsel Communication

Delaware Registered Agent Fees: $400 per year
State of California Fees: $900 per year (minimum franchise tax and state of information annual filing fee)

Tax Filing Fees: $400 per year

Logo Design/Graphic Designer: $250

Office Rent: $18,000 per year ($1,500 per month)

Office Leasehold Improvements: $3,000

Business Cards: $350

Domain Setup/Server Hosting/E-mail Plan: $250 per month

Company Logo Printed T-Shirts: $500

Employee One (Student Developer for Alpha Site): $1,500 total

Employee Two (Lead Developer for Beta Site): $50,000 per year

- I decided to run an Ad on Dice.com® an IT employment website focused on top talent. We got one reply. I hired him. He was about the age of my grandfather, but he was experienced and just wanted a job to stay busy with. I negotiated to get him for $35 per hour, and he was happy with that. We outlined the wire frames for the site design which I spent six months creating and perfecting all the pages and workflows. He was an Independent Contractor, and not a full-time employee, so he was free to come and go when he pleased and would work on his own laptop. He paid his own taxes and we sent him a 1099-MISC form for that. We didn't have to pay payroll taxes to hire him and pay him, and we had no complex employment plans or benefits for him as he was an Independent Contractor. This saved us money, but it also did not guarantee that he would stay with us for the long haul. He ended up working with us for a year and did a great job. The coding was slow, and it had bugs like all software Betas, but it was a working Beta, and it enabled us to launch and start taking subscribers in. We were making money. Unfortunately, he got offered a six-figure paying job with the government so he ended up taking that job, before we could get all the bugs out and launch our version 1.0 product.

Unforeseen Expenses:

- There were other expenses from online advertising on MySpace® ads, Facebook® ads, Skype® phone plans, meals with potential investors (who never invested), oh and yeah, our bank at the time Silicon Valley Bank® would charge us $15/mo. just to keep money in their business checking account. We never could keep the balance above their required limit to not charge us those fees, but that's part of the startup journey.

That totals to approximately $95,000 in startup costs! That was before we had a chance to launch or market version 1.0 of our product and really make any money. I don't know about you, but if I told you in Chapter 1 to give me $95,000 to have the opportunity to start up, you'd laugh and shut this book. Right? If you recall, we raised $123,000 in initial seed capital, so the actual start-up costs only left us with $28,000 in the bank — far too little to make many product tweaks, test marketing channels, and hire additional staff.

I almost forgot, when I closed the business down, we had to pay "Death Taxes" as I call it. The state of Delaware wanted their $300 for taxes (minimum franchise tax) for the current year, and then $250 for the certificate to dissolve the company, and the State of California wanted $8 to file the paperwork to revoke the ability to transact business in California. That's $558 just to say goodbye.

So, here's the truth — if you start up the way we did, you need capital. You need money to make money, right? Well, maybe not as much anymore. We did things a certain way, a way in which I was advised by business school and by professionals to which I talked to, and the point of showing you this, is to help you find ways to create money in a cheaper way. We wanted to do everything the right way, the professional way, but you don't have to follow what we did. I actually implore you to get as far along as you can, as cheaply as possible, until you have proven your product or service sells, and is making money.

Today's times are a bit different; you can incorporate and file for trademarks with LegalZoom® for a few hundred bucks, you can build a powerful website with content management systems like SquareSpace®, Wordpress®, Joomla®, Drupal®, Shopify® and more without coding knowledge. You can design a logo online and buy it for under $50 on a site like LogoMaker.com®. You can do some test marketing online for a couple hundred bucks to see how many clicks you can obtain and track conversion data for free with Google Analytics®. You can create social media pages for free and get even more traffic and build customer relationships without spending money on traditional advertising for starters. You can make YouTube® Videos to better educate consumers on your new store or product, you can find sales reps (on UpWork®) and only pay them commissions on sales they create and not pay them a salary until they prove themselves. There are many cheap ways to grow. I encourage you to explore them all.

The secret to a successful launch is to understand that there usually aren't very many successful launches. Sorry to burst your entrepreneurial bubble, but most launches produce mediocre results, and while emotionally disappointing to the first-time founder to experience this, for the second or third-time founder, a launch is the beginning of real-world tests. Launching is not the end, it is the beginning. To win the marathon we can't expect to win once the starting gun goes off, we must pace ourselves to establish a cadence that prepares our startup to learn as fast as possible, adjust the product, market and model aggressively as needed, and dig deep to commit to the enduring challenge.

Some of the founders I have advised, have worked tirelessly for a year to then launch and expect millions to come pouring in. I advise that the real work begins at the launch. You transition from building a product or service, to marketing and selling – while on paper this sounds easy to do, for many, it is far more challenging than it appears. The goal of a launch should be to close the gap from startup theory to delivering concrete value as fast as possible for users.

CHAPTER 6:
PRICE BY DESIGN

Think about the last purchase you made. What was the price, and what did you buy? Did the price end in .99, .95, .88, .00, .50? Did it even have cents at the end? Or was it a whole number?

Pricing plays a role in everything we purchase, and more importantly, in the things that we decide *not* to purchase. There's an old expression that says, "Everyone has their price". Let's think about this for a moment and change that expression to "Everything has its price". Imagine for a moment, if you will, a horizontal line. On the left-hand side, it reads $0.00, and on the other side, it reads $1,000. If we were to take say a book, there is a point at which that book would fall between $0.00 and $1,000. If the book was written by let's say a fifth grader (no offense to them, many are brilliant), you might think it could retail for around $5 a copy. That might be, in your mind, a reasonable range in which to price that product to a given market. If, however, the book was the new JK Rowling (author of the best-selling <u>Harry Potter</u> series), you might move that up-market to a price point that falls within say $15 — $35 (paperback to a hard cover). So, at what point exactly does something become, in our minds, overpriced? At what point does the *perceived* value of a product, service or experience tip the scale and pass over the affordability crest and down to the bottomless pit towards Ripoffville?

What if I were to tell you that the same JK Rowling book that I previously alluded to was now priced at $1,000 per copy, at first blush you might balk at it, and say, "That's ridiculous dear boy!" (do use your best British accent). So, I would then be forced to substantiate the extremely high price point (as compared to the standard market price) by showing you additional value propositions. I could say it was the first printed copy, or it was the personal copy used by JK Rowling to read to the children of Prince William and Kate, or I could say that it includes a handwritten signature addressed to you! Whatever I say, it needs to resonate with you at a point where the higher price point justifies the value you *perceive* to receive.

The higher you go up-market with pricing, the more gross margin you can conquer, however, the more pressure you put on your brand to convey the *perception* of value received.

Pricing is one of the most important elements of becoming a successful startup (or not). Before we even delve into markets, consumer behavior, hiring and more, we need to address the very tenant of a transaction, and price is right smack in the middle of your widget and your customer's wallets.

At time of this writing, I did a test on one of my e-commerce sites I run. I noticed that one of our products was priced at prices ending in .00 ($10.00). So, I changed the pricing to end in .95 (like $9.95) and we started to sell more. Why? The difference was only $0.05 cents, relatively small enough no one would ever notice losing under a car seat, but why was it more effective? It's because that little $0.95 denotes more value. 5's, 7's, and 9's equate to a bargain. Most people buying this item don't really need them, they just like them for event décor; it's not like water, food, paying your rent, etc. So, changing the price to be $9.95, versus $10.00 helped us increase our sales by 2X in that category. I encourage you to never write your prices in stone, rather experiment, and don't get attached to them. Always ensure you're making money but try different scenarios out and monitor the results. Often times, a marginal change in pricing can yield huge results.

So, what's *your* pricing strategy? Is it to study the competitive landscape, track other price points, and then set your prices at just a fraction underneath? How original — you and everyone else is on the rat race to the bottom. It's very rare that startups set out to create a premium priced good within a market that is known for extremely high competition and price sensitivity (e.g. Software). Traditionally, software was priced high because the cost to develop the software was high. As the cost to produce the nth copy went down dramatically, and eventually as costs went to the cloud, marginal costs fell to nearly nothing. However, I still see companies launch their pricing strategy aimed at being $5 per month cheaper than the next SaaS (software-as-a-service) player, only to realize a year or two later that they burned through all of their investor's capital as they under-priced their product, and they can't, all of a sudden, jack up the pricing for existing customers by 25% just to get back to profitability.

Virtually every market has four types of players:

1.   The Low-Cost Leader
2.   The Premium Player
3.   The Customizing Specialist
4.   The Superb Value Creator

1. The Low-Cost Leader:

Think Walmart® — a nearly omnipresent retailer that offers the lowest prices across essentially all of the consumer categories from paper cups to cosmetics to toys. Their goal is to optimize everything by buying in bulk, negotiating with suppliers to offer the lowest prices, and having the most attuned mass distribution channels possible, all in an effort to pass on the lowest price points. From Walla Walla to Tuscaloosa, low-cost leaders aim for mass appeal. They also come with a no questions asked return policy — wouldn't want to argue over a $1.98 beer koozie — if you didn't go to college, that's a foam holder to keep your beer cold, not your hands. You really missed out — we loved our koozies!

2. The Premium Player:

Think Gucci® — luxury meets fashion meets exclusivity all wrapped around a brand built on status, top craftsmanship, and aspiration. Think extremely high price points for the category that they play in — clothes, shoes, handbags, accessories — plus a totally exclusive shopping experience that delights you at every step with a personalized shopper there to wait on your every request. Hello London, New York, Tokyo, LA. This type of end-to-end experience handles everything from design, to manufacturing, to distribution to retail exparience and unique décor. They treat their brands as living, breathing pieces of artwork, and by buying from them, you've joined the cool, elite club of the rich and famous.

3. The Customizing Specialist:

Want lime green shoes with a pearlescent tongue and bright orange soles that read "CoolCatOnCampus"? Companies like NIKE® have pushed away from being exclusively mass-market retailers, to catering to the custom-minded consumer. These consumers demand quality, function, and unique design appeal — all a challenge to produce, but they're happy to wait for delivery. I once ordered a pair of custom NIKE shoes — it took nearly two months to arrive, but when they did, boy did I look like the coolest kid on campus. The Customizing Specialist understands that their customers want to use products to express themselves, differentiate themselves from everyone else, and above all — have a story to tell others. Emotions drive consumption of customized goods, not just the price point or speed of delivery.

4. The Superb Value Creator:

This is a strategically positioned company, given that they have studied the market, and have found a unique insight that helps offset one of the main cost factors that other competitors just have to eat. Think e-commerce companies like Amazon®, by removing the traditional Brick-And-Mortar retail stores and the massive up-front CapEx (capital expense) and on-going OpEx (operating expense) costs to maintain and run them, e-commerce companies can offer the same quality products, for a reduced cost, up to 40% less. The challenging task, historically speaking for e-commerce companies, was both market adoption (built on trust), high-speed mobile connectivity (which we now have), and rapid delivery systems (drop-shippers and trucking companies are perfectly aligned to deliver nationally within days, not weeks). When these factors all merged, it created a ton of new winners within either oligopolistic or monopolistic markets.

Your Pricing Might Be Flawed:

A very common approach to SMB (Small-to-Medium Size Business) pricing is to sum all of your costs: A+B+C+D+E = Total Costs of ABCDE — and then add a percentage mark-up on top, say 20%-100%, depending on how you *feel* the market will accept or reject it. For example, if all of your costs to make a pizza add up to

$5.00, then you would just multiple that by two to sell it for $10.00 yielding a markup of 100%.

We are not talking about Gross Margin. Remember a 50% markup yields a 33% gross margin. A 100% markup yields a 50% margin.

Gross Margin:

Step 1: Selling Price - COGS (cost of goods sold) = Gross Profit

Step 2: Take Gross Profit and divide it over your Sales Price to yield Gross Margin.

E.g.: $10 item - $5 costs = $5 profit (then $5/$10) = 50% gross margin.

Gross margin shows how much money you keep as profit from each unit sold.

Mark-Up:

Step 1: Selling Price - COGS (cost of goods sold) = Gross Profit

Step 2: Take Gross Profit and divide it over COGS to yield Mark-up.

E.g.: $10 item - $5 costs = $5 profit (then $5/$5) = 100% mark-up.

Mark-up shows how much more your selling price is over your costs. It does not show you how much profit you actually get to keep for selling each unit. An important distinction when establishing price points for your product or service.

So now that we just did a refresher on Gross Margin vs Mark-up, let me get back to our very common SMB pricing problem. Remember, the average business owner just randomly adds up all of his direct costs and then slaps a markup on top, puts it out for sale, and calls it a day. This model is supremely flawed, because it essentially is a cost-based pricing strategy, hoping for a sale based on a randomized mark-up. Why is it flawed? It doesn't pick a specific quadrant to play in, based on the pricing matrix that matches the merchant's product or service with the perceived value it creates in the consumer's mind. Welcome to No Man's Land Pricing.

All Roads Lead to the Median:

Median is the mid-point of a series of numbers for all of you Rockstars who slept through high school math. When we launched WML, remember we were giving a free basic profile away to both a Musician and a Music Industry Professional/Company, and then if they elected, they could upgrade to our PRO plan and select either a monthly, quarterly or annual plan. We offered a leading music royalty organization's members a special discount if they paid by the quarter, and a larger discount if they paid up-front for the year. When we launched, the pricing was $13.45/month for the Monthly, $11.65/month for the Quarterly ($34.95/3 months), and $8.95/month for the Annual ($107.40/12 months).

While we thought that pricing the PRO subscription lower was more attractive for the user, it actually turned out to not be. Pricing perception is a funny thing — price your product too low and customers think there's either a gimmick or it's a piece of junk, otherwise why are you charging such a low price? Price it too high, and you're ripping them off, therefore discouraging sales.

When we launched the PRO Subscription with the aforementioned pricing tiers, we had weak sales. We decided to change up the pricing of the PRO Subscription and tested it by tripling our annual plan to $299.95. You heard that right — we literally 3Xed our pricing for no reason other than to test it out. This put us in a higher price point to what some of our competitors were charging. Our sales jumped almost immediately! Most customers decided to go with the median (quarterly price point). Lesson learned — price too low and go broke trying to convince people of the value of your product.

When in doubt, never launch just one price, as that gives the customer a binary choice – yes or no to buy it – which in turns gives your company a 50% shot of them buying or not. If you launch just two tiers, they often start out with the cheaper one to see if it lives up to the hype you claim it does.

But, when you offer three price tiers, it stakes the value threshold of your product in the consumer's mind at an upper limit for your highest price point, so in our example, $299.95 was the *perceived* value of the item on an annual basis. By raising the highest price, you are able to also raise the lowest price and it will appear as if it is a bargain as it will be the cheapest of the three. Even Houdini would be amazed at that pricing trick.

Most customers return to the median price and choose the middle tier. Why? The median denotes a hybrid where the best of the features meets the most affordable price point (aka value).

So, what are you selling and who are you selling it to? Are you the Low-Cost Leader, aimed at the bargain hunting masses looking to sell on volume? Or are you a high priced, exclusive, luxury, deluxe, Premium Player aimed at selling fewer units at higher prices but making larger profits by servicing that exclusive group?

Purposefully pick your market quadrant and price it to win.

CHAPTER 7:
SALES

At its most rudimentary level, sales is about connecting the dots between a customer's pain and your proposed solution. The more effective you are at establishing that connection with the right audience, the faster sales will materialize, and the easier you'll make it on your startup to grow at an accelerated rate. Failure to do so, results in poor sales, marginalized traction, and ultimately, dissolution. No other element of a company's long-term vitality is more important than its ability to generate sales. There's an old adage that says, "Nothing moves until you have sales".

However, many tech-centric founders I advise, fall in love with their beautiful code, their app's intricate features, the glimmering bells and the harmonized whistles. They've convinced themselves that better tech ultimately wins category leadership. Remember, products and services are a means to an end, not an end to a means – they are the connective tissue that removes the pain from a customer's life or business, and delivers a solution that increases their happiness, income, or saves them time so they can focus on other priorities that matter more to them and their constituents. In selling a product or service, your job is not defined in the customer's mind by selling the product or service, that's in your mind and on your financial statements. In their mind, it's when your product or service actually does what it claims (or suggests) it does.

When a customer buys from you, it's the beginning of their relationship with your company. Your job, to exceed their expectations, is just being put to the first test.

Most first-time founders focus on building a better product, while second-time founders focus on gaining greater distribution, and third-time founders focus on faster profitability. How do I know? Because I've been all three. Which startup do you think goes out of business the fastest?

Don't sell features. Sell results.

Here are a few examples where I tried to sell features and failed miserably. With WorldMusicLink, I'd sit down with musicians and bands, and start off by presuming that I knew what they wanted (first red flag) — to be discovered by a big record label and become millionaires. For many, that was true. I'd start my pitch by claiming that our platform connected them to some of the top Record Labels that were seeking independent (unsigned) music talent. All they needed to do, was sign up, fill out a profile, and reach out to them with the platform. The deal would surely find them eventually, right? Problem was, I couldn't guarantee the result. So why would any band believe me? It wasn't up to my platform to guarantee an outcome, actually contrary to that, when bands did reach out to labels, the labels might respond, but most didn't — essentially digitally mimicking their real-life personas — avoiding dealing with new talent until the exact moment where they are about to become a star anyway.

So, with WML, I pitched the feature set instead of showing how 'x' number of bands just got offered recording contracts (the desired result). Out of insecurity to admit that I couldn't guarantee a deal, I'd backpedal, and started pitching features like there was no tomorrow. "Wait, you get to upload 1 music track with the basic version, but, once you upgrade, you can upload three full albums with ten tracks each," I'd tell the band leader. "Plus, you can also now upload your music videos, docs, calendar events, and have unlimited messaging between your band, any other musician, and any music industry professional or company online, pretty cool right?" They'd look at me and nod in agreement that the features were cool, but I could sense I wasn't striking the right chord to their wallet. The destination was lacking. I was selling features, and not results.

By selling features, I was hoping that they would connect the dots to the site's intended value. But in reality, I was failing the customer. I was selling the sizzle but without the steak. Buyers can only see so far in front of them. When they're seeking to arrive at a destination (solution), and you're talking about the new reclining seats on the airplane and endless potato chips — they realize that those things are nice, but they won't *guarantee* their arrival on time at the desired city.

So, this goes back to my earlier point about feature overload. If you have so many features to explain, not only will it have cost you a bunch of time and capital building them out, it will also cost you more time that it's worth explaining how they work. In a sales pitch, you don't sell features, you sell results. Repeat after me once more, you don't sell features, you sell results.

For my second example, at LaDolceDeal (a group buying website), when I'd sit down with merchants, I'd pitch them to supply us with a deal to their establishment. While the model of couponing is straight forward, I could never guarantee them an outcome (new sales). While they were looking for 'x' number of tables to fill up at their restaurant, or 'x' number of new bookings at their spa, or 'x' number of gross merchandise sales for their new boutique — I was essentially telling them that I would feature it to our 4,000 subscribers, and we would wait and see how many would either buy the deal or download the coupon and bring it in — both of which, had no guarantee behind them. If I could have proven, or guaranteed, that 5% minimum always bought our deals, then I could translate that figure to transactional sales, say 5% of 4,000 subscribers at $50 each is $10,000 in new sales. But I couldn't. So, again, I'd backpedal and talk about how easy it was to upload the offer online, add in photos and video, and we'd do the rest. I'd walk them through an example deal and show how the PayPal® checkout works for the consumer, and how they print out the offer or pull it up on their mobile smartphone with a scannable QR code. I'd go on and on about that, never delivering the customer to the final destination, but rather being a tour guide highlighting all the sites along the way.

Don't be the tour guide. Be the cab driver. Get them home!

Rejection 101:

From the ever popular, yet unoriginally benign "I think I'm going to pass for now", "Thanks, but no thanks", "This just isn't a fit for us right now", and "I think we are all set", to the soul crushing "NO!", "Not interested, please stop calling", and "This is spam, remove me from your e-mail list pal" — rejection comes in 31 deliciously, repulsive flavors that leave you feeling like crap.

There's a big difference between listening to someone tell you about what a "No" sounds like, versus experiencing a "No" firsthand. The feeling of rejection literally can cut to the core of an entrepreneur. It feels as if your very dream, your life's purpose, your words, actions, investment, your baby, and hard work have all been put on display and shot down, leaving you to feel vulnerable, dejected, and remorseful for even attempting in the first place.

Rejection burns, but what's worse, is self-deprecation.

However, there's a silver lining! When you get rejected outright by others, they are essentially voting yay or nay on your business model, your price, your product, or your service – they are *not* rejecting you personally (most often). Customers, investors, and team members are not rejecting you, but it can surely feel that way. You must come to understand this stark difference, gain a distanced level of objectivity, otherwise, you will always feel personally attacked, and will be plagued by fear of rejection from others — forever.

This simple, yet key distinction took me years to accept. I have come to realize that there is no other human on this planet that can make me feel like I am less than. When I create something, even if it is just a start, an idea, a prototype, a sales pitch — I took the extremely bold step of trying. Kudos to me! My idea may surely have flaws, but I am not being personally attacked, only the validity of a business around this idea may be. Don't get suckered into thinking that you and your idea are one in of the same. They're not.

You are the creator of the idea, you are the farmer of the idea — you water it, it may (or may not) grow — but you are not the seed or the plant. Your job, as an entrepreneur is to identify a problem, create a viable solution, provide all the required nutrients for the idea to grow and flourish, and then get out of its way.

Building a "No" Callus to Get to your first "Yes!"

When you start to hear enough "Noes" you should be starting to have fun. What? Yes, you should be actually relishing in the process of being rejected. Believe me, it will become a game — the perfect opportunity to learn from and press on. But, the problem is that people confuse personal rejection with rejection of an idea, a process, or an offer, and immediately block out all of the amazing feedback that comes the moment the rejection siren blasts — letting their fragile emotions take center stage and blind them from the golden nuggets of truth. This is the exact time you need to counter with deeper, probing questions to get to the core of the "No". Stop crying, stop loathing in self-pity — start probing and listening so you can defeat rejection #43 and move on with prospect #44 you're going to talk to in an hour.

The more "Noes" you hear, the stronger you become. You will be able to laugh at rejection, and every time you pitch your idea, you will get smarter, faster, and nimbler in conversation, and will reach your intended goals quicker.

There was a time, during the WML and LaDolceDeal days, where I would start to recite rejections out loud before the customer even had a chance to think them up and say them! You should have seen the look on their faces — total bewilderment. I would say, "I bet you're wondering how much this subscription is going to cost your band, right?" They nod. "$14.95/month, now hold on one second, that may seem high." They would retort, "How did you know I was going to say that?" I continued, "But, that's actually cheaper than a six-pack and pizza your band was going to blow through tonight at rehearsal, am I right?" He nods again. "Isn't the success of your band worth a few beers and Dominos®?" I would just smile, knowing that they're the twenty-fifth band today to hear my pitch, and I already knew the next objection point that was around the bend.

It wasn't always that smooth. I used to stumble out of the gate, get rejected at every sentence, and keep pressing for the sale and never actually listen. Listening enables you to adjust the flavor of your pitch. Everyone prefers a different flavor. A one-size-fits-all sales pitch is a prefix menu — only a few suckers bite and pay the overpriced fee. If you win the few, your business never grows, only your ego.

You will predict, with practice, the exact time when your audience will object and question something you've just said, and when they agree, you will be able to create any outcome from your presentations because you will have anticipated all of the red flags — the objections, the lack of features, the questions related to pricing, the doubt due to your inexperience, the lack of a team, the lack of funding, etc. Knowing objections puts you in the driver's seat. Learn them!

Practice makes you perfect. Rejection makes you profitable.

The more you practice pitching, the more the same issues crop up. It's your job to learn the 25 most repeated objections, craft a rebuttal for each, and steer the conversation down the road so everyone wins. Don't fight objections, rather listen, and write them down. The next time you pitch your product to a customer or business to an investor, you will have most of the potential issues laid out for them to see, and you will have an answer for all of them. For winning investors over, acknowledging venture risk up-front and potential problems down the road you may face, builds trust, which in turn garners respect. Your foresight will be interpreted as the experience needed to do the job well, and thus, you will get to a "Yes" faster and more often. For winning customers, showing *both* the plusses and minuses of buying from you builds trust, and trust builds sales.

The best pitches aren't pitches — they are fluid conversations that build trust and get both sides to take the next steps towards a deal.

Today, because of all of the rejection I have persevered through, I am very confident in myself, and have the ability to think fast on my feet. I can often have a great conversation about any topic with just about anyone. I can bond over a burger and a beer, or at a black-tie affair. I can handle objections from a customer over a $50 order, and of a Fortune 500 buyer over a million-dollar deal. People are just people, regardless of what their objections look like.

There will be many times in your life that you will need confidence on-demand, where you will suddenly face a barrage of objection points from others, and you will need to speak with clarity and true conviction that compels. You will need to have a crystal-clear vision and remove any sense of doubt. These moments define us and draw on our past experiences by demanding leadership. How will you fare, if you have nothing to draw back on? Objections give us a foundation from which to build strength, to discover our value.

Rejection builds success through failure.

So, what is the fastest way to build a rejection-proof corporate callus? I urge you to go out and get rejected today. Get rejected and get rejected often! Let your business, which is essentially a working experiment anyway, be critiqued by as many people as you can find.

Let your pricing be rejected. Let your product be ripped apart. Let your ideas for the future be challenged. Why would you want to have everyone just nod in agreement, and then you fail later on because you weren't able to refine things to be the best possible outcome they could become? You wouldn't. You would want to refine it all to get to the core of brilliance. You want your pitch to go from a 15-minute stumbling, boring monologue, to a 30-second Steve Jobs silver bullet that solves a problem and excites people to want to join the ride. You want your product to be understood within seconds, not how, after a 30-minute sales call, the prospect finally quasi understands what the heck it does and how it may help them. You want your pricing to be the rationale of value received, not price paid.

Rejection solves most problems, if you learn from it. You can't just buy rejection or learn it in a book, you have to go out, face it, and earn the rewards of success waiting for you just on the other side.

When I first started as an Independent Sales Rep for my family's business, I was only paid 5% commission on the sales I generated. Let me tell you, this was tough. I thought it would be easy — I'd make a few phone calls, spiel off a few lines about the history of our company, and they would open up and give me a fat purchase order. Boy, was I wrong.

I would start my calls by jumping into my pitches without giving them an opportunity to breathe and get a word in edgewise. I would talk for about three minutes straight, and then ask them if I could send them samples. Samples! Some buyers would say, "Sure, why not kid?" and others would reject me outright. Of the ones that would reject me, I would go back into a longer 3–5-minute pitch on how we were different, and how they would be making a mistake by not buying from us. When they would accept my free sample offer (from being completely worn out from hearing this kid sell hot air), I would then have to spend time packing up samples, making labels, writing a cover letter, include my business card, and walk over to the post office to mail the items. I would follow up a week later to inquire if they received the samples (which I knew they had because I had tracked it online, and it said it was signed for) and then I would ask if they wanted to buy. Most would say "No", some would say "Maybe" (then would lead me on for a few months to later say "No"), and others would ghost me — simply avoid and never respond to my follow-up calls or e-mails.

The typical No-Maybe-Ignore Buyer loop continued until I learned how to pitch smarter. I learned later on that a key to ask before you even pitch a prospective customer is "Are you the right person who handles buying for this category?" This is a qualifier — if they answered "No", I would ask for an intro to the right person. If they said "Yes", I would then ask (after I briefly explained our company and what we were seeking) "Are you open to hearing about this opportunity?" Most people don't want to be closed, and don't want to reject an opportunity that could potentially make them more money or help them get a raise once the boss sees how much they just saved the company on this item from a new vendor.

In sales, as in life — what you ask for, you often get.

Many salesman and entrepreneurs present something, but never ask for the sale! I used to ask for the ability to send them samples. Samples! That was my thing. I was the sample kid. I was scared to ask for a sale believe it or not. I felt samples would get me in the door and they would come back blowing up my phone to buy once they got them. It's actually embarrassing that I have to point this out, but I fell prey to this. I got so caught up in the product, the pitch of our company, our vision, how we were different, that I never asked for the sale.

When you ask, you have a 50/50 chance of getting what you want. Ask yourself, what is the goal of this call? If I could establish two goals of this call, my primary goal (the sale), and my secondary goal (fallback goal) (a request for samples, pricing or a follow-up call), then I have accomplished my job with every lead. A failure might be no reply, or no interest — but I could then at least update my CRM and move onto the next prospect. Always have an outcome in mind before you start. Don't just wing it.

Flip the Script – How to Get Customers to Sell You:

How you ask is also worth pointing out. I used to ask for the order, but many buyers are averse to just saying "Yes" outright and giving in to an order. It's not even their money, but they act like they are doing you a favor by buying from you (no matter the amount). They feel like somehow, they lost if they're sold, but if they buy (and drive a hard bargain), they win. Call it psychology, or just living up to your title of Head Buyer. When I was seeking orders from customers in other countries, naturally I wanted a big fat 40 ft. container order, but buyers don't want to just give you money — they want to feel as if they made a buying decision, not that you sold them.

What I learned they wanted, was an opportunity that other companies in their market don't have access to yet. Something unique that would help them grow faster. They themselves want to win; they want exclusivity to the new gold mine. They want something that makes their company differentiated, where they can beat their competition. To solve this, I found out that by asking a potential distributor the following, they were more apt to ask for samples, review pricing, and actually order, than before, when I would just pitch and pray for an order.

The Five "W's" to Winning a Sale:

1. <u>Who</u> are we? — this sets the foundation for credibility.

2. <u>What</u> do we sell? — this sets the tone for relevancy today.

3. <u>Which</u> companies do we supply? — this creates instant social-proof and success by association (if you work with the big boys, then you must be worth my time).

4. <u>What</u> are we seeking? — this establishes the request for a reliable partner.

5. <u>Would</u> you be open to this opportunity? — this creates a time-sensitive opportunity for exploration that might pass them by should they decide to pass.

The 5 W's create a foundation for sales success — they establish credibility when you don't have it and sets the stage for the ask/get opportunity. After explaining the 5 W's, I would say:

> We're seeking a reliable distributor in your country (reliable is the key word - no one wants to be unreliable, it's bad for business), who has the capabilities to effectively market our products (this questions their skills) and handle the demand that we have received from your market. We're unsure if you're the right company for us to partner with yet (this creates doubt), but we are hopeful that you could prove to be that company that could handle this big opportunity (we believe in them, now go and prove it to us). Would you be open to exploring this?

Now, what I am saying above is 100% honest. I was seeking a reliable distributor, someone to handle demand in that market, but did we have folks beating down our door in that market just yet? Yes, we had some inquiries, but not lines around the block. It didn't matter. Demand, even small amounts of it, is the building block that matches future supply.

Did we need someone with huge capabilities to effectively market our products? Yeah, that would be nice, but we know most distributors don't effectively market any one item as they have thousands that they stock. What I wanted was an opening order, and a 5% commission check (remember I had no salary and was working on commission and had to eat). I was twenty-two years old. Distributors want to appear capable, reliable and effective. They want to live up to the challenge, even if it is a tiny company questioning a big distributor if they could handle this opportunity. I was essentially flipping the sales pitch, and now asking them to prove it to me that they could service our customers, sell our items, and exceed our expectations.

It's funny, my father used to tell me, "Ask a bank for money when you need it, and they won't give it to you. When you don't need the money, they want to throw it at you!" He always reminded me to "Sell from strength." The above example shows how I did just that. I asked bigger, more successful companies to prove it to me, show me how big they really are by giving us a shot to handle the demand in their market for our line. By giving me an opening order that shows me how serious we should be taking them to give their company an opportunity to represent our product line, I was flipping the script. I stopped begging for the sale. I stopped hoping for the break-out order. It was now their turn to sell me. By flipping the script, they felt compelled to prove that they could meet our expectations. In so doing, they would be in alignment with my expectations of their corporate identity — a reliable, capable distributor who could service a market supremely well for a supplier. The days of hearing "we're all set right now, but no thanks" began to quickly fade away.

And sure enough, after a few months of selling, they re-ordered, and re-ordered some more. They didn't realize in the beginning how much our products were going to help improve the sales of their other items, their "proven" sellers, but we needed a way in the door.

Sure, there's objection in every arena, but you need to go through the objections to find your formula for success. Whether you're pitching investors for a Series-A round for $10 million, or you're asking your customer to open up their wallet to hand over ten bucks, you should *want* objection, so that you can focus in and start winning more frequently.

My Rule of 100 Rejections:

For newbie entrepreneurs, I want you to grab your investor deck, your sales pitch, or your product, and go out and pitch 100 people so that you can get rejected as fast as possible. I'm not kidding, if you don't get rejected now, how will you ever understand what leads people to buy later?

Getting rejection out of the way early is an incredibly telling blessing — it will save you years of struggle. All it takes is one "Yes", one check, and one deal to make all of the difference for your momentum. That one, will open up many new doors, but you've got to check all the doors to see which ones are unlocked first.

Staying organized in the messy sea of sales:

I've now taught you what worked for me — to flip the script, sell from strength, and learn to walk away from the buyers who just won't budge. Treating each sale as one of many, not one and done, sets you up for emotional detachment, which helps you stay cool under pressure, and shows you which leads are actually more apt to convert in your funnel. But, it's hard to stay organized if you yourself are not an organized person. And, even if you are, by nature, organized, having a management system that helps you see the top, middle and bottom (goal) of the sales funnel is paramount to allocating the correct ratio of time, money and effort on the nth prospective customer or user. To help you stay on track, I want to share a few tips that have helped me.

I like to keep track of my leads, prospective customers, quotes, negotiations, and repeat customers in either an Excel® Spreadsheet or better yet, a CRM (customer relationship management system) like SugarCRM®, Salesforce®, Zoho® CRM, PipeDrive® or another of your choice. Beyond just tracking your leads, this truly helps you detach from the emotionality of each lead you call by seeing each as a piece of a flowchart, that lets you better understand where they are at any stage. Breaking the sales process down into stages (Kanban style) is helpful so you don't feel like it's just an all or nothing sales pitch — there is a flow, a step-by-step process that they are going through that helps them better understand who you are, what the offer is, where the value might be for them, and how they can redeem that value. Also, this helps you track your progress as you can see the percentage of won sales and the percentage of lost sales so you can benchmark your efforts. Selling takes a lot of practice, and "Noes" are a required part of getting to "Yes". At the end of the day, we want to gain detached objectivity of the entire sales process. We do not want to get lost in the maze of quotes, conversations, POs and "Noes".

My Sales Rule of 10%:

Make it a goal to increase your sales closing ratio by 10% every week. While small, 10% compounds at an extremely high rate on a week-over-week basis. If you convert 10 leads out of 100 this week, next week when you quote the next batch of 100, try to convert 11 (a 10% higher rate). After just three months of increasingly higher, compounded closing rates, your company goes from closing 10 leads a week to closing 28, a 180% increase in paying customers. In total, you'll have 210 total paying customers (providing no churn), or an increase of 90 more paying customers, versus the 120 in total you'd have if you just chugged along at the same rate as before. Let's say each customer paid you $100 for your service a month — that's a revenue lift of $21,000 - $12,000 = $9,000 per month extra all from my sales rule of 10% (see figure below):

- Week 1: 10 Conversions out of 100 Leads (10% closing rate)
- Week 2: 11 Conversions out of 100 Leads (11% closing rate)
- Week 3: 12 Conversions out of 100 Leads (12.1% closing rate)
- Week 4: 13 Conversions out of 100 Leads (13.3% closing rate)
- Week 5: 14 Conversions out of 100 Leads (14.6% closing rate)
- Week 6: 16 Conversions out of 100 Leads (16.1% closing rate)
- Week 7: 17 Conversions out of 100 Leads (17.7% closing rate)
- Week 8: 19 Conversions out of 100 Leads (19.5% closing rate)
- Week 9: 21 Conversions out of 100 Leads (21.4% closing rate)
- Week 10: 23 Conversions out of 100 Leads (23.6% closing rate)
- Week 11: 26 Conversions out of 100 Leads (25.9% closing rate)
- Week 12: 28 Conversions out of 100 Leads (28.5% closing rate)

Total: 210 Closed Leads out of 1,200 = 17.5% new closing rate

CHAPTER 8:
MARKETING

When I was in B-School, we often talked about companies that seemed to create instant, overnight success. They went from a napkin sketch, to a multinational corporation employing thousands, changing the world, and creating billions in the process. As we covered in the beginning of the book, that's not exactly what happens. That's like the few you hear about winning the lotto who cash out from buying just one ticket. Even today across Silicon Valley, people throw out the names of Airbnb®, Uber®, Facebook® and Google® as if all companies should start, scale and exit the way these few have. There are millions who have failed along the journey from startup idea to go-to-market launch, but most actually fail post-launch in the Startup Valley of Notice Me Death.

In today's hyper connected world, there's just too many ways in which to reach your audiences and spend millions in the process advertising to steal eyeballs and win over customers. So how do you choose to spend your ad dollars when all you've got is a small budget? Do you buy more traditional advertising mediums like print, newspapers, radio, T.V. spots, post cards, flyers, banners, billboards, direct marketing, sales reps, etc.? Or do you go to the other extreme with grass roots marketing now called "Growth Hacking" to gain early (cheap) market share? Either way, it all costs some level of investment capital and time, so let's show you how to measure what's what, so you can double down on the channels that drive early-stage growth.

Getting the Best Marketing ROI:

There's a simple way to effectively compare various ad tests that you deploy for your brand that I learned from my former Board of Advisor and business mentor, Bob Caspe. Back in 2007, Bob referred to it then as Media Ratio, and today, it's akin to ROAS (return on ad spend).

For example, let's say you've opened up a new coffee shop. You sell coffee, cookies, espressos, etc. You just opened up shop, and you've got the random traffic that stumbles upon your store on the block. But you want more business, naturally. You have $5,000 to spend on marketing, and just aren't sure where to invest it for the best ROAS. You have a few options, take out an ad in the local newspaper advertising your new coffee shop and offer locals a special for $1.00 off any cup of coffee. That ad runs for thirty days and costs $500.00. You also are considering doing a mailing of a postcard to local residents in the neighborhood using the USPS (Every Door® program). Cost to design and print the 1,000 post cards plus postage is $1,000. And then you're considering a targeted Facebook Ad that costs you $200 to reach the locals in your town and a few cities nearby. How do you know which one is best for you in the long run?

STEP 1: You do a small, budgeted test and try all three.

Ad 1. Newspaper Ad (ad + coupon):
Cost: $500 (100 people redeem)
Sales: $8 per person (avg.) = $800 (profit is $400)
Gross Profit (after ad spend): -$100 (Loss)

Ad 2. Local Mailing (postcard + coupon)
Cost: $1000 (50 people redeem)
Sales: $10 per person (avg.) = $500 (profit is $250)
Gross Profit (after ad spend): -$750 (Loss)

Ad 3. Facebook® Ad (ad + coupon targeting locals)
Cost: $200 (150 people redeem)
Sales: $7 per person (avg.) = $1050 (profit is $525.00)
Gross Profit (after ad spend): $325.00 (Gain)

ROAS Formula = Profit/Cost of Advertising

I like to use profit instead of revenue for ROAS as it tells me how profitable my ads truly are performing. If you use revenue, you get a higher ROAS, but could still be unprofitable as you aren't factoring in the true cost of goods sold.

<u>ROAS Results from our Marketing Test:</u>

Ad 1.   -0.20% (Newspaper Ad + Coupon)
Ad 2.   -0.75% (Local Postcard Mailing + Coupon)
Ad 3.   1.63% (Facebook Ad + Coupon)

Ad #3 is your best choice as it is greater than the others and yields a positive gross profit.

What's a Good ROAS?

A ROAS of 1 is break-even, as it yields what it makes, and any ad that has a much higher ratio (over 1) performs even better and should be one you consider as one of your initial drivers of growth.

STEP 2: Run the ROAS with a new test of the winner and new variables.

With our above example, we will want to then repeat the test but this time, try out two more new Facebook Ads and coupons (possibly changing the targeted demographics, radius of reach, or the coupon offer itself) against our last winning ad, so that we can then re-run the ratios to determine which of those three yields the best result.

With a ROAS analysis, you can first compare various campaigns to each other despite being completely different advertising mediums, reaching potential customers. Then, you can drill down on the one channel that worked initially and run a multi-variable test to determine an additional level of statistical certainty. Now you can have a greater level of confidence in amplifying your marketing budget towards one particular medium over another instead of guessing.

ROAS in the Long Run:

While in our example test, ad number three was our winner, over a longer study period, say one year, this may not continue to be the case. Let's say that your coupon was a re-usable coupon, and not a one-time use coupon (the customer got to keep it after using and it expired at the end of the year, nearly twelve months later). Over the course of a one-year test period, the same customer who used the coupon from ad 1 (newspaper), may in fact come back to your coffee shop over and over again, reusing the same coupon offer. If you had only looked at the study for a 2 to 4-week period, you would have written off ad 1, however, by studying it over a longer period, you find that many of the newspaper customers are actually highly frequent return visitors. So, while the short-term gross profit margin was -$100 for ad 1, the 12-month adjusted Gross Profit may be $500 per customer — outranking the Facebook ad (#3).

Here's the takeaway — every ad you conduct deserves a long enough test period to see immediate (short term) and extended (long term) results, before a financial conclusion is drawn. If you can set up your ads so that they both yield short term financial profits when you need quick profits, and other ads that drive a blend of longer-term lifetime value customers — then you've got both elements working for you at one time. Sometimes you need immediate cash, other times you need sustained growth. Knowing what ads, marketing mediums, and channels drive what, at any given time, is critical to your survival as a startup and growing enterprise. Most small businesses build and launch a new product, try a few marketing channels, determine within a few weeks what works and what doesn't, and then go with their gut and some back of the napkin financials. Be smarter than that. Test for the short and long-term customer, know what levers drive what results, and more accurately predict your marketing results.

A/B Testing:

Another variant to the above is A/B Testing. You can keep this simple, or make it more complex, but just so I don't confuse you, A/B Testing essentially takes one group of customers and changes one variable so that you can narrow in the focus of a particular campaign and improve the results. Think of this like a science lab running an experiment with a variable and a control element to measure it against. By making mini tests and monitoring the results, an entrepreneur can continually integrate the mini winners into the overall product, ads, and customer experience to create the best possible product.

An example using the above, could be to compare two different Facebook ads, now that you know they provide better short-term ROI for your coffee shop. Companies like CrazyEgg®,

Optimizely®, Google Analytics®, UserTesting®, and UnBounce® have great packages that can help transform your site to A/B tests in under an hour with just a little bit of code added to your website header.

One Facebook ad might include an offer for $1 off any cookie when you buy a coffee, and another ad might include $1 off any coffee. When you compare the coupons that come in and the net profit to the transactions that day (or month) to each other, you will be able to tell which appeals to your consumers more and can then increase your ad budget more for that particular campaign using that offer.

Marketers A/B test continuously, and 99% of the time us consumers don't even know that we are being tested while we shop. When you click on a website's homepage it may appear to be in red, white and blue and have a certain 10% off offer on the top. When your brother in another city clicks on the same page, he sees a different color scheme and a $15 off offer and photo on the same page. Depending on what goals that company is trying to achieve (time on site, conversion rate to provide your contact details as a new lead for them, a sale of an item, etc.) they aggregate the data and determine with numbers, not guessing, which works best for their markets. Companies like Facebook® and Amazon® are constantly A/B optimizing for the outcomes they want — profitability, time on site, user engagement, content creation, new service adoption by a trial, etc.

In the old days, we'd have to just wing our marketing, wait, and feel our way to a workable end result that yielded some profit (we hoped). Many startups went broke this way. Today's startups, regardless if they are a mobile web app, a coffee shop, or a one-woman consultancy, can A/B test their way to conversions, repeat customers, and ultimately profitability.

If you're interested in learning more about A/B user testing, there is a ton of research and tutorials out there online on how to effectively implement it. Google even offers the ability to have your ads lead the same clicks from users to different versions of your website for you, you just set it up and they track all the data and show you the reports. You can set up various goals to optimize what they call funnels. Example: User sees your ad, reads it, likes it, and clicks on your site. They find the item they were searching for, adds it to the cart, and checks out. That is a completed funnel from lead to sale. Others may click the ad, read info, and then leave (that's called bounce-rate). If they add the item to their cart and then decide to leave, that's called cart abandonment. You can set this all up with Google Analytics®. You just add the code to your website header (it's a little snippet of JavaScript code that goes in the HTML of the page). Your web designer can do this once for you and you should be all set. Then you can manage all of your goals, funnels, reporting, etc., in the Analytics dashboard on Google Analytics®. It's free too, so if you're not using this, you're losing out to competitors who are. Do it.

As you develop your online store or site, try A/B Testing to see what elements drive what results. As you learn more of how potential users are reviewing, using, and engaging with your service, you can try different changes to improve the funnel flow and conversions.

Now, let's say you're a Real Estate agent. You don't have a coffee shop or an e-commerce website. So how the heck does this apply to you, and how can you use it to benefit yourself and make more money? As an agent, you're always looking for leads and that's why you're out and about talking in the community, attending conferences and events, handing out your card, etc. So now you set up your website, and feature some of the homes that you are currently listing. The key for you is to find out where potential leads are coming from (this will tell you where you should be paying closer attention to) and get as many in-bound visitors to enter their contact info on your "Send Me Info" page as possible. The law of large numbers suggests that a percentage of a large number should convert to a sale, so your goal should be to get as many qualified leads as possible to give you contact info. Then, you can add them to your lead list and send them an e-mail news blast when new listings come up that they might be interested in. Be sure to ask new leads to check off "how did you hear about us?" — this will help you figure out how they initially heard about you. They might check off a Google Ad, Referred by Friend, Saw Local Newspaper Ad, etc. The more you understand where your qualified leads are coming from and which channel yielded the highest percentage of conversions, the faster you can double down on your marketing spend in that area to accelerate growth.

So now I've shown you how to set up mini marketing tests, compare ad results with ROAS, determine your best marketing mediums for your money, and track various usability and conversion data. Don't you just feel like a Marketing Guru without having the need to go get your MBA?

CHAPTER 9:
THE CUSTOMER EXPERIENCE

Have you ever been given a free sample outside of at a restaurant, to then realize an hour later that you decided to order a whole meal, wine, and dessert? Restaurants in New York City are notorious for bird calling with complimentary samples, to get more customers to check out the menu and come on in to eat. It works. Why? Because of the feeling of indebtedness. Without evening knowing it, once you are given a complimentary sample, you subconsciously feel you owe the restaurant for their benevolence and decide to order. The amount of the free sample isn't the main reason why you order a whole meal, nor is the dollar amount of the free sample, although it certainly helps when the perceived value is greater than what might be expected.

Online companies do this as well. Why? Because competition is fierce to both capture eyeballs and wallets, and the customer acquisition cost (CAC) and operational on-boarding process for a new user is typically higher than one might expect, therefore, the hardest and most expensive part of the process is the initial sign-up, transaction, or first time go through the cycle.

Below is a list of common give/get scenarios companies offer:

- **30, 60, 90-day risk free trial** (mattresses, autos, websites, retail)
- **No seller fees until you sell your 1st item** (marketplaces/apps)
- **Free setup/design/proof** (creative industries, printed goods)
- **Free shipping** (per order over a specific amount or by a date)
- **Free or Rush shipping** (retail, wholesale, subscriptions)
- **3X reward points on 1st order** (airlines, credit cards, websites, retailers, clothing brands, travel cards, wholesale club cards, etc.)
- **Free gift with every order** (retailers, brands, restaurants, etc.)
- **Free gift with qualifying order** (spend $10 and get a free gift)
- **Refer a friend or new client, and get something waived** (websites, auto, banks, etc.)
- **BOGO (Buy one, get one free)** (retailers, websites, restaurants)

• **Free basic profile + 50 messages** (dating sites, websites, apps)
• **Free consultation, evaluation, expert review, or 2nd opinion** (legal, accounting, financing planning, audits, tax prep, appraisal, etc.)

I urge startup founders to consider giving away a trial, gift, free shipping or even a sample. It doesn't matter what it is, what the value is, or how you do it — just do it. Why? It works. Savvy entrepreneurs deliver an overabundant amount of value for the user/customer on their initial touchpoint with their brand — filling up emotional debt, spurring goodwill, and subsequent transactional reciprocity.

A Cook, A Song, and a Baklava:

I recently ran into a successful Restauranteur, named Bashar. Both Bashar and his business partner Faisel, are immigrants to the United States. Bashar hails from Syria, and Faisel from Jordan, and both are the epitome of immigrant turned wildly successful entrepreneur story. These stories fill our hearts with satisfaction, as they show us the true power when entrepreneurship is realized — American alchemy at its best. My father, the son of a Russian immigrant, would often remark on the topic of the American Dream, "It happens when success meets applied individualism". Bashar and Faisel have worked tirelessly to create a following for their three flagship restaurants. The duo started with just one restaurant about ten years ago, and since, have scaled to half a dozen and are on the verge of developing a potential national franchise of a quick service concept of their marquee establishment.

Now what Bashar and Faisel have perfected, is not *just* a fast moving, systematically timed restaurant. Rather, they have mastered both the art of the gift, and the art of the surprise. When they launched, they would greet patrons at the door with a smile and then give customers a free Hummus and Pita platter — a delightfully simple, yet grandiose gesture for first time patrons. Enter, the gift.

During the dinner, the duo would literally pause food service, and emerge from the back of the restaurant, with a Tar (Persian guitar) in hand, and let the eclectic inspired music play over the surround system. With microphone in hand, suddenly, the dishwasher would pop out from behind the kitchen and start singing "Besa Me", the famous Spanish song to everyone's surprise! And to make it even more delightful, the singer had a perfect voice! Enter, the surprise.

Bashar and Faisel encouraged everyone to sing along, "Besa me, besa me mucho!" People would stand up and dance, couples would clap along at their tables, while the surprise party played on and on for about ten minutes. Little did everyone realize that they had purchased tickets to dinner and a free concert! After the meal, they would gift every table with a free Baklava dessert. Enter, gift number two.

Patrons had such a fun time at their restaurants, felt like family, and often hugged the owners at the end of the meal like soon to be departed family members. Bashar and Faisel had taken the ordinary and made it surprisingly extraordinary.

Brian Chesky, Co-Founder and CEO of Airbnb®, recalls on Reid Hoffman's podcast *Masters of Scale*[11], that he implores the team at Airbnb, and thus their supplier hosts (homeowners, apartment owners, condo owners), to design the customer experience to be a 6-star experience, not a 5-star experience. He says that many companies aim to provide a 5-star experience, to really wow the customer, but end up delivering a less than stellar experience, because they haven't fully understood what's beyond a 5-star experience. To craft a truly memorable, 6-star experience, you must capture the element of surprise, wonder and delight. He has an exercise that he teaches his teams, that walks through what a 1, 2, 3, 4, 5-star experience might be. He then pushes them to use their imaginations to design a fictional 6, 7, 8, or 9-star experience that is metaphorically out of this world and usually highly improbable to deliver. The goal, however, is to then scale the impossible 9-star experience back, and in so doing, discover that crafting a 6-star experience is actually not as unachievable as the team may have initially thought possible.

Bashar and Faisel too delivered a 6-star experience, by mastering the art of the gift, and the art of the surprise. Their 6-star experience spread worldwide across social media — Facebook, Twitter, Instagram, YouTube, Snap, Yelp, OpenTable, on Blogs and more. Tourists visiting the area relied solely on the power of the crowd to steer them in the trusted direction of the best restaurant, using up-votes from the crowd online to pick out the top restaurants to spend money at over a weekend. Their restaurants were always top of mind.

The local following grew, the reviews and content poured in, and the reservations continued to flood the books. Today, their Yelp rating has thousands of positive 5-star reviews (there is no 6-star available), deliciously curated food photos, videos of people dancing and singing "Besa Me!", wonderful comments and anecdotal stories posted of jubilation and surprise. Patrons routinely remark, "We can't wait to come back! That was incredible! What a memory."

Other competing restaurants never saw them coming, nor did they ever stand a chance. The duo persevered, tirelessly working days and nights rotating shifts at their sister restaurants, all the while competitors struggled to keep up. The owners designed for both the gift and the surprise. They realized early on that they needed to differentiate the user experience and transition the tourist or local into a fantasy world where the kitchen comes to life! A place where the owners suddenly transform into the star music act right before your eyes! And, lastly, an experience that one would remember for the rest of one's life and want to share with others.

Design surprises that make the experience uniquely memorable.

Light at the End of the Funnel:

A trend today with content marketers and bloggers is to build a customer acquisition funnel that attracts a high volume of visitors and converts a sizable number to paying customers. The key to their success lies in leveraging social media — Instagram®, Twitter®, Linkedin®, Facebook® and others — to attract leads and get users to enter their virtual funnel to submit your e-mail address and opt-in. They then auto-feed them a series of tailored videos and "exclusive" web series where they peripherally talk about their topic, but never give away the key secrets. Then, they do the limited time only offer, whereby you must accept to join their program, buy their e-book, download their system, etc; otherwise, it's gone forever. You're forced to make a buying decision then and there, and pull the credit card trigger, or else you're left outside in the content cold.

The funnel's primary purpose is to give away just enough free content to build-up customer demand, and then offer leads a time sensitive opportunity to join the program and convert today.

The 5 Keys to an Effective Customer Acquisition Funnel:

Effective funnels have similar patterns which include the following:

1. **Targeted Leads** – Finding the right pool of prospective candidates who are in search for a potential solution to their problem is critical to building a high producing funnel program.

2. **Teaser Content** – Be willing to offer a sufficient amount of great content, expertise, or technical know-how to prove to the lead that your solution/program/product can back up its claims.

3. **Credibility** – In order to move from lead to purchase path, prospects often need to see quotes, user testimonials, logos from past clients, or data that lowers the risk premium for them to buy.

4. **Guarantee** – Buyer's remorse can be real. To counter this, many funnels offer a money-back guarantee, extended return window, or other promise. In so doing, they instill deeper trust post-purchase to mitigate returns and reduce poor reviews.

5. **Urgency of the Call-to-Action** – Without a firm deadline, it's hard to create enough emotional momentum to get a lead to want to convert today. Urgency forces prospects to make a decision otherwise they will miss out. A 24-hour to 1-week deadline is sufficient to move most leads into the final phase – conversion.

Funneling can be highly effective when deployed correctly, but if you do deploy a sales funnel strategy, please serve customers well and provide them with outstanding content, experiences or products once they do buy. To create your funnel experience, you can set up the phases yourself as outlined, or use templated funnels or automation kits such as ClickFunnels®, Kartra®, ConvertKit®, Kajabi®, or Drip.com®.

You always owe it to your customers to *exceed* their expectations. Once you do, they will become your unpaid sales team, promoting your business to others for years to come.

Mistakes are the Norm:

When you run a business, you are bound to make many, many mistakes. Mistakes in my mind, are tests that yield results. They help you narrow your focus, discard extraneous motions, remove markets and customers that are more effort than warranted, and erroneous people that you've hired, partnered with, or appointed, that don't align with your mission.

I've made plenty of mistakes over my entrepreneurial career. There are two types — monumental and non-monumental mistakes — and understanding the difference is critical to allowing yourself and your team to fail gracefully when taking calculated risks. By preparing for both, we learn to leap over the hundreds of minute failures along our journey that appear potentially life threatening at first blush, but in retrospect, are simply minor setbacks on our road to success.

It is imperative as a CEO to step back when faced with a decision and ask the question, "Could the outcome of this be a tectonic shifting one that could kill us, or will this just be an expensive lesson?" In so doing, we frame *both* the upside, and downside risk of every decision.

For example, a non-monumental lapse in financial judgement might be electing to give away free shipping on all orders in the beginning of your business, to later realize that you're losing money on the freight that results in a loss for a sizable portion of the orders. However, what you may not realize, is that by virtue of giving away free shipping, you've amassed a sizable number of customers that helped to validate your business and provide a launching pad from which to scale. The loss of profit in the beginning is temporary, not a permanent derailment. This is a non-monumental failure, a good lesson. We can alter the shipping rate tomorrow if need be.

Conversely, a monumental failure in decision making might be hiring the wrong individual as your start-up Co-founder and giving away 50% equity before they have proven themselves as a valuable asset to the team. Now you're stuck with dead weight — a partner that complains, stifles your growth, and has a voting right to corporate decisions and strategy that ultimately leads to future problems.

Another example might be not listening to early customers reactions to your product, and thereby, leading you to continue to sell what *you* want, and not what the market is demanding. In this instance, you have served yourself — your wishes, your ideas, and your needs — not the needs of your users. Many businesses do this, oftentimes they are mom and pop retail shops, bakeries that only sell what the owners like, apparel shops that only sell what designs the owner would wear, and restaurants that only offer meals that the chefs enjoy themselves; all not what customers truly want.

Learn from every mistake — listen more, speak less — and commit to adapting quickly if something isn't working. Non-monumental mistakes in decision making unlocks growth. Monumental mistakes kill your startup.

Dealing with the Un-Happy Camper:

My father used to tell me, "The customer is not *always* right, but they're not *always* wrong. We're all buyers and sellers of goods and services – buyer beware, seller beware". When put into that context, we realize the importance of serving customers the way we want to be treated. Sometimes things happen that piss customers off. Your job as CEO, is to make it right – no questions asked.

An example that I experienced in one of my businesses, is that when we took an order, and the customer received the order late because the carrier delayed the arrival of the package by one day and thus missed the customer's event, we would get an irate phone call to hear the customer scream at us for the delay. In actuality, the carrier and their delay were completely out of our control! Typically, small businesses, ours included, would tell the customer that "I'm sorry, but it wasn't *our* fault, it was the carrier. We can't do anything about it! We don't allow returns on items for mistakes that were not our issue." This only makes the customer madder, makes them want to then seek revenge and issue a chargeback with their credit card company, and then go rip you and your business a new one with a bad review.

In today's world, we must be vigilant when defusing angry customers and seek to immediately de-escalate the situation, regardless if the issue emanated from our company or not. In the long run, does one order really matter more than your company's reputation? When in doubt, a sincere apology and a full refund goes miles.

Let them win the small battles; focus on winning the market.

In this example, what I learned to do was apologize to the customer, accept responsibility even though it wasn't my fault, and provide them with either a store credit, ship the items back to our warehouse, waive the restocking fee, or issue a full credit. About nine times out of ten, the customer is so grateful, they calm down, and understanding that you are doing them a huge favor, re-order from you in the not-so-distant future. Hostile customers often morph into loyal evangelists when treated supremely well, who end up promoting you to many more customers. Lemons into lemonade my friends.

You have to change your mind to think of a negative, as an opportunity to show greatness. It's harder to delight a customer when nothing has gone wrong — they have a baked-in assumption that you'll deliver on your marketing promises. But when shit hits the fan, that's the real test. Step up!

A Recipe for Small Business Failure:

A big issue SMBs (small to medium size businesses) face today, is that consumers are accustomed to the next or same day delivery time of Amazon, the 24/7 customer support, free (no questions asked) returns from big box retailers, and 25% off coupons for every holiday. This is absolutely killing small business owners, who treat *every* single sale and *every* dollar as if it were their last! They try to lock in every bit of margin, and never allow the customer to make a return, change their mind, or explain an issue that arose from the experience with the item. This is a recipe for small business failure.

The founder who flips a 180 — from helpful (before the purchase) to jerk (after the purchase) — creates a recipe for attrition, bad word of mouth, and startup self-destruction. Consistency in customer relations matters.

True, as a startup founder/small business owner, we don't have the time nor resources to acquiesce to every customer, provide full refunds, and free return shipping labels on every order. However, consumers have the ultimate choice as to where they vote with their hard-earned dollars. More and more customers are choosing big box retailers and Amazon®, not because of the low prices or convenient selections, but rather because of the trusted post-purchase experience they have come to rely on.

Zappos®, the online e-tailor of shoes and apparel founded by the late Tony Hsieh, offers both free shipping and free returns (with a delightful, turn-key return policy). They built their business model on a free end-to-end, no questions asked shipping experience.

So, how can small business owners compete against free end to end shipping and returns? My suggestion is to offer superb customer service, be quick to admit failure, but establish some firm rules around what you will and won't tolerate so that it's clear to customers in the beginning. Macy's® offers a 60-day trial period on their mattresses. If they offered say a 30-day period, customers might only try the mattress for a week and then set up a return. Macy's actually encourages you to keep the mattress for two months. Most customers by that time, fall in love with the mattress, or at least move on, and Macy's is able to minimize customer returns.

Simplify the rules for orders and returns to avoid complaints. The more rules you make, the more friction you build. Ask yourself, would *you* order from your company?

So, You're Not The Market Leader?

When you launch your product, it may be first to market for a while, but typically what occurs, is that it will become one of many choices in a sea, vying for customer's attention. Instead of trying to appear to be the biggest, take the counterintuitive position to position your business as something *different*. If the leader has thousands of employees, offices, and complex products, how can you be the opposite and own it? In being smaller, you might prove that you can be nimbler and offer more customized features. In being smaller, you might build custom features for a client that are unique to them.

Whereas the big player might never do that for even their largest clients.

The goal is not to act like the biggest — the goal is to position your company as different, to build a loyal fanbase that favors customization, speed, service, or a feature over size.

Selling Large Companies:

Typically, large companies *feel* safer working with other large companies. It could be easier to justify partnering with a new supplier who also is a public company or has offices around the world. Your job, should you want to sell larger companies, is to position your startup as a specialized tool that fits a unique problem that plagues that particular enterprise.

After selling hundreds, if not thousands of small businesses, and closing dozens of larger accounts, I'd argue that selling smaller companies might appear easier to close, but in reality, can require the same or more effort for a lower ROI on your time. The big difference is in the payoff. If it takes you a year to close a large company, earning your firm a $1 million annual contract, and it takes you three months to close a small business yielding you a $10,000 annual contract, the difference is $990,000. However, that small company in reality will only deliver $833 in new revenue per month in return (per year) should you get them to a "Yes", whereas the large company will give you $83,333 in revenue per month in return – a 9,900% difference. You would have to close one hundred small companies to yield the same revenue per month as one large one.

The Money-Back Guarantee:

A friend of mine has a local, family-owned Italian restaurant. It mainly serves pizza and pasta and gets a lot of families in there. On the wall and on each menu, the owner has a photo of his face, and he states in bold, "Welcome to my restaurant, while you are here, you are family. If for any reason, you are unhappy with your meal, let me or my staff know, and I will personally pay for your entire meal." I'm sure he gets very few disappointed customers and rarely has to make good on his offer. Satisfaction guarantees do work, by instilling trust that if there's a wrong, they'll make it right. If you can offer one, do so — you'll build deeper trust with your customers.

In your business, you have to find out what the main objections are going to be with customers, and fashion your pre and post-purchase experience around that. By preparing for the unhappy camper, you more holistically understand the true issues of your users and turn haters into evangelists.

Design to Share:

Look at how you hear about a new concert, product, app, event, news article, restaurant, etc. It usually derives from our social spheres of influence — friends, co-workers, mentors and family members. Electronic sharing is not just a nice thing to add to a website (social media), or politely mention in customers, "Hey, like our page on Facebook!" Founders need to design their entire business to *want* to be shared by customers.

For example, take a local restaurant — from the menu, to the interior décor, to the dessert even — they must leverage their own customers' social circles and influential reach to market their business for them. But how do we make someone so enthralled, so impressed, so inspired, that they *want* to share?

The K-Factor (Viral Co-Efficient) & Network Effects:

In Silicon Valley, VCs often talk about network effects and refer to a calculation called the viral co-efficiency, or K-Factor, when looking at the exponential growth potential of a new venture[12]. It says that every member of a network is considered a node, and each nth node that is added onto a network has x number of nodes that they can potentially reach. As more users join a network and share/invite others in, they add more nodes to the network, thus creating an exponential growth-rate that compounds in its magnitude as each successive, nth user is on-boarded. Tech jargon and math aside, while this may sound like it only applies for software/web businesses, the social media pages of traditional brands, Brick-And-Mortar retailers, and even coffee shops can benefit from its power. There's a free calculator online that you can use that will show you the viral co-efficiency of your product or service[13].

The Power of Sharing — Network Effects:

# of Customers Your Business Has Today: **100**
# of Invites Each Customer Sends to their Network: **10**
% of Sent Invites that Convert to New Customers/Users: **33%**
Your Viral Co-Efficiency: **3.30**

Compounding Growth Rate:

Customers after 1st loop:	430
Customers after 2nd loop:	1,519
Customers after 3rd loop:	5,112
Customers after 4th loop:	16,971
Customers after 5th loop:	56,106
Customers after 6th loop:	185,252
Customers after 7th loop:	611,436
Customers after 8th loop:	2,017,844
Customers after 9th loop:	3,424,252
Customers after 10th loop:	4,830,660

You can see by getting your small customer base today to share your business for you can yield an incredibly fast-growing customer base. If you simply rely on just serving one customer at a time, and never implore them to grow your business for you, you're greatly missing out on the power of network effects. I highly recommend you encourage customers to either invite people into your platform for you or incentivize them to share a special offer with their family, friends, or co-workers. Both will either yield a network effect that drives faster revenues and delights current and future customers to use your service. Next, let's look at a non-software-based business to paint the full picture.

But first, coffee™:

A perfect example is a coffee shop in LA called Alfred's®. This stylish, modern, cafe is not your regular barista bar. They've cleverly crafted the slogan "But first, coffee", which by nature, is designed to share across social media. From the printed cups[14] (figure 9.1), to the signage and in-store design[15] (figure 9.2), to the social media pages and t-shirts they sell — everything urges one to share. "But first, coffee" speaks to the share everything generation that loves to post their every waking experiences across social media, and in particular, share brands that speak to their sense of me-first-ism.

Figure 9.1

"Ready for my go-see modeling meeting in LA, but first, coffee" (Insert tagged picture of coffee mug with hashtags — #coffeefirst #LA #Alfreds #Love). If customers just took a picture of a boring coffee cup, would that excite them to *want* to share? Contrast that with this post, which is bound to be tagged with a map of the store's West Hollywood location so others know where they are, and where they just picked up this epically poured, non-corporate cup of life altering coffee. It will be liked and shared by hundreds of her friends, and will often have multiple comments on the post, thus driving more engagement all for free for good 'ol Alfred's. Alfred's didn't have to spend a dime to get this virality. Alfred's designed for the shareable moment, and they did just that.

Figure 9.2

The Power of Referrals:

Rakuten® (formerly Ebates®), an online affiliate marketing company that offers a shared commission with its users who click on coupon links prior to shopping online, receive a quarterly check with earned commissions from their accrued purchases. Rakuten offers a $50 referral check just for sharing the page with friends. When your first three friends sign up, you get a fifty-dollar bonus in *your* next commission check. This in reality, only costs them fifty dollars, but they pick up three new customers — and avoided the customer acquisition cost that may well be north of one-hundred dollars. Those new shoppers will spend thousands of dollars and net them hundreds in affiliate fees over years to come. For virtually little capital up-front (fifty-dollars), Rakuten wins three new customers (K-Factor), and potentially more when those three decide to also invite their networks in to save. Talk about designing your business to go viral!

Online Contests Drive Traffic:

Online contests are a cost-effective way to get a ton of exposure, site traffic, and build your business quickly. There are many online tools that can assist with contests like Rafflecopter®, that for free, you can set up for your own giveaways. The key to these giveaways is that they require entrants to complete a number of tasks for your brand in order to increase their likelihood of winning the grand prize, like liking your Facebook page, re-posting, re-pinning, re-tweeting, sharing your page, entering their e-mail address and more. As you build social media traffic and engagement, your algorithmic relevancy (popularity) rank across platforms rises, which spurs new followers, who convert to new customers, and builds viral, word-of-mouth campaigns that yields future market adoption.

Often, you can solicit companies and get decent prize packages donated if you partner with another business and explain to them that they will be getting exposure when you promote their brand in your giveaway. You might also want to take advantage of credit card reward points — so that you can use your American Express® points to buy a gift card on Amazon® or a prize and use that free item that cost your business nothing, as the main prize for the giveaway. Be sure to collect e-mails with an opt-in form and add those followers to your future e-newsletter for future offers and promotions.

We must leverage the power of our customers' social circles to exponentially grow our brand — this is the most powerful way to amplify our startup's reach.

Measuring User Experience (U/X) with G.P.S. Rank:

When most business owners or managers look at a customer's journey, they start with the moment a customer enters their store, or when they buy a product outright. For online stores, owners think the customer journey begins with a click to the Homepage and ends with a checkout.

The journey *actually* starts a lot earlier than that, and also doesn't end when you hand them a receipt, or they check out online. The customer journey has different phases that pass through various emotional, physical, and digital experiences or touchpoints, as we call them in design thinking. In design thinking, there is a concept called journey mapping, that when done properly, helps business owners, management, and customer service employees identify problems and opportunities within the customer experience.

It is a mistake for an entrepreneur to solely focus on the product, as that is actually only one touchpoint of the experience.

Social media is an important opportunity, that when executed properly, can be the starting point for the emotional ligament between the company and a new customer, and can also be the follow-up or post-purchase relationship, that helps bring them back for a repeat order.

Yelp® is a great example of a pre-purchase touchpoint, that helps engage and educate the consumer on small business. For restaurants, in the highly competitive dining market, Yelp is a lifeline to stay relevant, build trust, and drive new foot traffic. The Yelp experience happens both pre-purchase (during the search phase when a tourist is researching what the top steak restaurants in Boston are), and also happens post-purchase, (when the customer had a stellar dining experience and now wants to give a 5-star review).

For SaaS (software-as-a-service) companies, online review sites are also a vital element to the discovery, research, and ultimately, the sales experience. Having excellent photos of the product, online videos, user testimonials, examples of the tools, and completed outcomes is critical to convincing new customers that their solution is worth their time and money. For hotels, online review sites like TripAdvisor® are also a very important element to drive traffic and build excitement for the customer's up-coming trip.

It's not good enough to simply build the world's best product, you have to also convey that in your imagery, messaging, reviews, and community online so that you both win digitally *and* physically. Consumers live in both worlds — an omni-channel experience designed well, positions you to win. Many companies focus too much on just the physical product or service and fail to realize the importance that all physical products and services have a digital counterpart that must be managed and fostered tastefully, and with substantive appeal.

During journey mapping, you want to mock-up a walk-through of a potential customer. For most businesses, they have different types of customers, or user archetypes, that represent specific groups. They can be broken down by demographics, psychographics, geographies, modalities, or even preferences. These should be split up into specific cohorts, so that they have a specific identity in your management team's mind, instead of just, "Here's the customer."

The reason for journey mapping, is that every customer's journey is different. By choreographing and mapping this, you unlock valuable new insights, strengths, weaknesses, and opportunities to beat your competition.

Case in point, a stay-at-home mom let's say, may have more time to review your company online on a desktop computer, while a busy working professional, Joe, may only be able to quickly check your company on his mobile app before he walks in the door of your establishment. There is a difference in the amount of research each can do *prior* to making a buying decision, and thus, various types of influences will push them to on-board. For example, social proof in the way of five-hundred Facebook likes or a dozen 4 out of 5-star reviews might persuade the busy professional to walk into your restaurant, but the stay-at-home mom, may wish to read individual reviews (the good, the bad, and the indifferent), peruse up-close photos of the food, and read about the background of the restaurant and also see the kid's menu. She may also get interested in your ambiance by way of a 3-D virtual walkthrough that's posted online or a video clip on Instagram stories from a social media Influencer with 250,000 followers.

G stands for Customer <u>Goals</u>:

Before you build out a solution in the form of a digital or physical product or a service, you must know what problem you are truly solving. But, before you even know what problem you are solving, you need to know your customer's goals. Are they seeking an epicurean once-in-a-lifetime experience that they can boast about to their friends for years, or are they seeking a quick fix bite on the go because they only have fifteen minutes to eat before duty calls back at the office? Are your new running shoes going to provide greater stability for a post knee surgery patient, or are you just offering another one-hundred-and-fifty-dollar orthopedic shoe? You have to think about what <u>goals</u> they are looking to accomplish, before you can identify how they can accomplish it.

Step 1: What is your particular cohort's goals? What are they seeking to gain today (pleasure) or avoid tomorrow (pain)?

The more specific you can be, the better. For example, "Save more money" is not as clear as "Save one-hundred dollars a month over the competitor's subscription service."

Step 2: How are they currently accomplishing this goal(s)?

Be very specific. If you don't know this, you need to go out and watch how users get it done today. Cast a wide net to capture all ways.

Step 3: How do they find out about, create, or get the solution?

Again, researching, interviewing, listening and observing *unbiasedly* uncovers this. Even if a market doesn't exist today, many alternatives typically exist.

Step 4: How does your solution compare to the above solution?

Be *brutally* honest with yourself. Don't sugarcoat your product or service and sell yourself back on it. If your solution is ten percent better, then state it. The goal should be at least fifty percent better. At ten percent, you are just another option, but the switching cost is too high — too easy to ignore. At twenty-five percent, you are one of a few that are candidates for a buying decision — in the running essentially. At fifty percent better, you are top of mind in a category, but still a choice among a few — an oligopolistic situation. At ninety percent better, you are both top of mind, the clear winner, and also in viral country, where they will promote your solution to others for free. This is what you should aim to go.

P stands for Customer <u>Problems</u>:

So, we've touched on the user's goals, and what they are seeking to accomplish. Here comes the problem(s) in their way to accomplishing their goal(s). By identifying the user's current series of problems that arise when they are in the pre-experience, experience (in), and post experience, you will gain clarity of their entire journey.

Phases might include:

1.   Researching all available solutions in-person and online (**Pre**).
2.   Finding available solutions near or accessible to them (**Pre**).

3.   Finding solutions in their budget (**Pre**).
4.   Finding solutions that solve their pain or create pleasure (**In**).
5.   Seeing alerts from a service post-purchase to buy again (**Post**).

Sometimes problems have nothing to do with available solutions in the marketplace (your competition) but have more to do with *access* to get them. This can be geographic isolation (distance), price point (high entry or on-going use cost), resources gap (the solutions are there but require a technologist or an expert to put them into use for them), the other available solutions require too many steps to reach the intended outcome, or the other solutions are not presented in a simple, easy to understand way.

Thinking about problems, let's look a bit outside of your competition and the other available solutions in your chosen industry, at other problems that you may have never even thought about.

For instance, let's say you run the local men's clothing retail shop. Around you are other retail chain stores that also service men's clothing needs, and so there you are, competing against the big dogs, fighting them on in-store planograms, marketing, professional interior décor, and slashing prices left and right just to be considered.

However, the *real* problem that customers face is not choosing one retailer over the other or deciding how much to pay at your store versus theirs, it is a matter of something that comes *before* the experience — parking. Parking? Yes, Parking! Near your store, there's no parking garage, because you chose the cheaper rent on the side street, and although you're saving a few bucks a month on rent, you're losing customers left and right because your parking situation is abhorrent. When people can't park, or park in a safe, well-lit area, or in an area that provides free or very convenient parking, they opt out of your store, and head over to the local mall where thousands of free spaces exist. This is an absolute killer to your sales, and one that you should have thought about if you had journey mapped before you signed your leasehold agreement. In retail, the adage goes, "location, location, location" (and don't forget the parking).

If you are an online e-tailor of outdoor pool supplies like cleaning solutions, cleaning equipment, towels and chairs for the pool, you would think that those are the keywords that you should solely focus your SEO (search engine optimization) around online. However, the problem you are really facing is that to break out against other online competitors, you must think in terms of your intended *user's* goals and problems, and not solely the keywords used by the industry.

John is planning a welcome home party for his wife who just spent three months on a work trip in freezing cold Minnesota in March. She is flying home this weekend and today's Wednesday. So, John needs to clean up the pool fast (in two days) and decorate for the pool party he is planning as he already invited a bunch of her friends and family members to join. John isn't going to just be searching "chlorine for pools", he is going to be searching Google for "fun pool party ideas" and "welcome home pool party décor" among other phrases. If you solely show up in SERP (search engine results pages) for "chlorine", you may have lost John.

Instead, think about John in terms of his goals and his problems instead, not just the keywords of the component parts that make up the solution. He has never done a pool party before, so he has no clue as to how to prepare everything and get it cleaned-up, decorated and staged for a big event. Here's your opportunity. Show John that you know what he's up against, and how your solutions will help solve his pain and create the outcome he wants — to impress his wife. Remember, he doesn't just need a clean pool. He needs a smile and kiss from his wife. That's the *user's* goal. The clean pool is just a means to an end. By showing John how to both clean up the pool *and* decorate for a fun party, you solve both issues.

S stands for Customer <u>Solutions</u>:

What really is a solution? As we learned above, it actually is not just the thing that solves a problem. It has a by-product too. However, if you solely think of a solution as a way of solving a specific problem that may also help you save a little time, money or effort, you will still struggle to differentiate your business from others in your space. For example, if you sell tequila, you've got mega competition. From Jose Cuervo®, to Cazadores®, to Patron®, the list goes on and on from anejo to blanco. I see too many beverage companies try to sell features of their brewing process, their backstory about their history as a craft distillery, etc. The problem with all of that, is that it's all about them, and not about how that translates into value for the customer.

Certainly, while some customers may find that interesting, that might not be the underlying reason they buy tequila over soda. Let's just say, for them, tequila gets the party started, and a great party means a heck of a time with friends, and most importantly, a night to remember forever. Well, with tequila, the photos might remember better. When you're there pitching your wood oak aging process from pure agave plants, and your seventy-five-year-old history from your great grand daddy's ranch in Puerto Rico, as cool as that is, it is what *you* care about, and why *your* story is compelling to *you* and *your* staff. What a twenty-four-year-old shopper might care more about in his tequila outcome is to get the party started as I've said, so where does your backstory and his weekend party plans connect? They don't. Create the connection for him. Make *your* story match *his* story.

Every customer cares a little about a lot, and a lot about a little. You need to find out what the majority of your users care most about to make them buy your products and use your services. Selling into the majority moves the sales needle the fastest.

If you focus on the small group that only care about your distillery process, you will only serve that small segment. If you focus on being the solution that get's the party started, you serve a larger majority. Now, this is just a generalized example, but you get the point.

Your story, your product, and their goals must be in alignment.

So now you know G.P.S. - <u>G</u>oals, <u>P</u>roblems, and <u>S</u>olutions, and can visualize exactly where everything is on your customer's journey map, and with this, you can dive deeper than your competition in your own customer journey mapping, to identify problem areas, sticking points, and uncover magical opportunities that will set you lightyears ahead of everyone else in your space. A simple way to remember G.P.S., is to think about where your customer was at *before* they discovered your solution, where they are at *while using* your solution, and where your solution helps them get to where they want to go (*post* purchase).

G.P.S. is so important, that if you give me only thirty minutes to evaluate a business, using the G.P.S. approach, I can quickly identify a company's inbound customer acquisition model, their user engagement experience, and the results of their intended solutions and marketing efforts on creating lasting outcomes for their customers. Plus, I have a toolset to compare them to other incumbent competitors rather quickly — thus, summarizing their competitiveness.

Implementing G.P.S. Rank for your Startup:

You can implement G.P.S. at home by taking any business and journey mapping them in your mind. Write this down:

1) How did you find out about them? (Social Media - which one? Word of Mouth - Who? Online Ad? What platform? Google Ads®? Bing®? Facebook Ad? Other?)

2) What did you experience *before* you arrived at the company's offering? (Research phase - SEO results? Social Media Websites? Blogs? Forums? Yelp? OpenTable? Trade Magazine?)

3) When you approached the company's offering, what *friction* points did you experience *before* you even had a chance to use their services? Was parking an issue? Did their website take a long time to load? Was their website not mobile friendly or secure?

4) During the *actual* use of the company's products or services, did you experience an "A ha!" moment that made you realize their value proposition was coming to life for you? Or did they fail to deliver? Were there other friction points with using their actual service? (customer support, tech issues, overly complex, high signup requirements, high prices, too technical, not elegant enough for your needs, felt insecure or cheap, etc.)

5) *After* the use of the company's products or services, what was the exit experience like? Was getting out from their building a nightmare? Was getting back onto the highway a problem from

their parking lot? Did someone follow-up with you after your order? Did you get a survey? Did you get a coupon for referring someone else to use them? Did your problem re-surface after you left their facility or website? How likely would you be to revisit or refer a friend?

A Customer Experience Example of Touchpoints:

Touchpoint 0: Contemplation Phase (pre, pre-experience)

- *Were you top of mind when the customer was deciding on how to solve their pain or seek their pleasurable experience? Yes or No?*
- *Were you not even on the radar screen? Yes or No?*
- *Why or why not? If not, how are the other sources able to be "top of mind" before you?*

____

Touchpoint 1: *Discovery Phase (pre-experience)*

- *How did the customer find you? What was your rank online in S.E.R.Ps? What website did they inbound from?* _______________
- *Was it easy to find? Yes or No?*
- *Did you even show up? If not, how are the other sources more discoverable today over you?* ___________________________
- *What else can you think of here?*

____

Touchpoint 2: Research & Analysis Phase (pre-experience)

- *Were the reviews or referrals from locals positive? Yes or No?*
- *Did the photos look very enticing? Yes or No?*
- *Was there an online coupon for a free appetizer or 50% off wine that encouraged client flow? Yes or No?*
- *Was their social proof available of prior good experiences from other patrons? Yes or No?*
- *What else can you think of?* _________________________

Touchpoint 3: The Arrival (experience phase 1)

- *Was there ample parking in front of your Restaurant? Yes or No?*
- *Was the outdoor signage easy to read? Yes or No?*
- *Was there a line outside proving built up demand for the establishment? Yes or No?*

- *Was the restaurant enticing with colorful décor, a menu posted outside, a Zagat® star or Yelp® recommendation sticker in the window?* <u>*Yes or No?*</u>
- *What else can you think of?* _______________________________

Touchpoint 4: Engagement (experience phase II)

- *Was there a long line or were you seated quickly?* <u>*Yes or No?*</u>
- *Did the waiver come over to greet the guests with a smile and offer wine recommendations and a complimentary something, say a bread tray?* <u>*Yes or No?*</u>
- *Did the food arrive quickly and delight the customers with its presentation?* <u>*Yes or No?*</u>
- *Did the waiter offer to take pictures of the guests for their online sharable moment?* <u>*Yes or No?*</u>
- *Did he bring out a complimentary dessert or after dinner port (wine)?* <u>*Yes or No?*</u>
- *Was the check quickly presented or did you have to wait for 30 minutes for it?* <u>*Yes or No?*</u>
- *What else can you think of?* _______________________________

Touchpoint 5: Post-Engagement

- *Did the waiter thank everyone and hold the door on the way out of the restaurant? Was the parking lot well-lit and safe?* <u>*Yes or No?*</u>
- *Was it easy to get back to your hotel from there?* <u>*Yes or No?*</u>
- *Did the restaurant send you a follow-up e-mail thank you for your visit and request for feedback and an online review?* <u>*Yes or No?*</u>
- *In 3 months did you get a coupon to come back as a guest and receive a free glass of wine and appetizer?* <u>*Yes or No?*</u>
- *What else can you think of?* _______________________________

While these are just examples for a simple restaurant matrix, they help outline the progression of a customer throughout their engagement with restaurants. By contrasting the other local competitor and a national restaurant chain to your restaurant, you can quickly map out how you stack up against them at multiple touchpoints throughout the customer journey, during the G. P. S. phases.

G.P.S. Rank - How to Measure the Customer Journey:

So how do you compare the sum total of your overall customer experience to the competition? With the G.P.S. Rank (see figure 9.3), we can see the specific areas and sum totals to gauge the effectiveness of their experience. This uncovers the forest for the trees and helps us find ways to improve the incremental touchpoints that make all the difference for customers over the long-term.

Areas Needing Improvement: The specific areas where your competitor's touchpoints are highly rated (8-10), and you are lower (1-7), your company can stand to improve and meet (or exceed) the bar set by your competition.

Areas of Achievement: The touchpoints where you are performing higher (8-10), and your competitors are lower (1-7), you are winning in those areas, but still must maintain your rank at that particular touchpoint to outpace them over time.

Ranking Metric: By averaging all of the touchpoints and comparing them to all of your competitors, you can see holistically, where you rank in a quantitative manner that is actually driven by rather qualitative (subjective) experiences.

In figure 9.3, we can see how the chain restaurant has done an effective job at being discoverable online in the pre-experience stage with SEO (search engine optimization), so they draw the majority of their patrons in to dine due to this fact. Whereas, our restaurant might have some online visibility, and possibly a bit more than our local competition. In the research and analysis phase, our online videos, menu and customer testimonials on Yelp™ are helping to persuade leads to come visit us over the local competition. On arrival, due to our limited capacity and service staff, often times patrons have to wait longer than expected as compared to the chain restaurant, so we may need to improve this segment Lef the experience to deter people from walking away or waiting too long. During the dining experience is where we really shine, however, as we can see, most of the restaurants all do a successful job, so while we think of a restaurant's food as what differentiates it from the competition, it may be harder for us to break out from the pack here as the local competitor and the chain restaurant all win here.

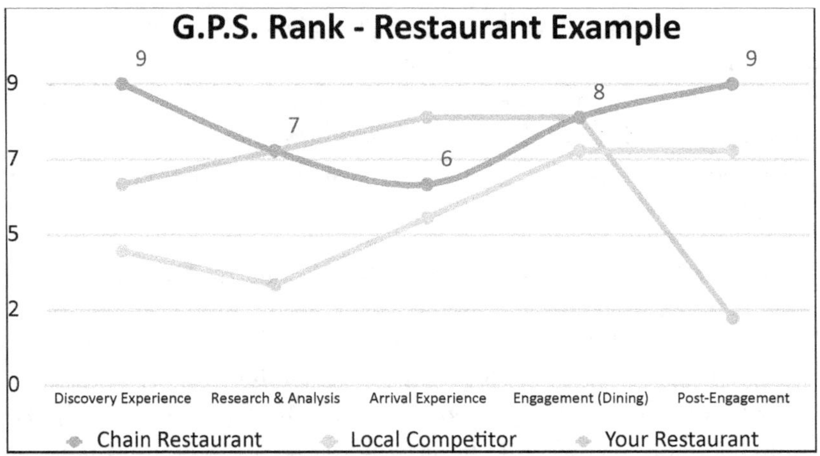

	Chain Restaurant	Local Competitor	Your Restaurant
Discovery Experience	9	4	6
Research & Analysis	7	3	7
Arrival Experience	6	5	8
Engagement (Dining)	8	7	8
Post-Engagement	9	7	2
Average:	**7.8**	**5.2**	**6.2**

Figure 9.3

Lastly, the post-engagement experience is where we really see the big miss for our restaurant. The chain restaurant provides all patrons with a 15% off coupon to come back on their next visit, and they also send a follow-up "thank you" email to everyone who visits. The local competitor, unbeknownst to us until we tried their experience, has been giving a "be our guest" referral voucher to each diner who visits, that rewards their friends and family with a "free appetizer" should they come in. G.P.S. Rank helped us to see that our post-experience segment could use much refinement to bring our service up at least to the level of our competition, if not exceed theirs.

Find areas where your competition ignores or fails the customer and use that to delight them instead.

G.P.S. Rank is a powerful tool to use as you launch or grow a business. Customers may not be able to explicitly explain to you what they didn't like about your product or service or what they really didn't love about the competition, but this breaks a multi-touch point experience down into bite size chunks that your team can focus in on and improve. By splicing these moments into manageable user experience segments, you can raise the bar for your company, and in the process, delight more customers and bury your competitors because you will more clearly see the *entire* experience from your customer's eyes, and not just from up in your corporate tower, or behind a P&L Statement.

Dealing with People (How to Get Collective Buy-In):

Heuristic - any approach to problem solving, learning, or discovery that employs a practical method, not guaranteed to be optimal, perfect, logical, or rational, but instead sufficient for reaching an immediate goal. Where finding an optimal solution is impossible or impractical, heuristic methods can be used to speed up the process of finding a satisfactory solution.[16]

Being around startups, boards, investors, entrepreneurs, small business owners, suppliers, customers, agents, lawyers, bankers, and more for over a decade, you learn people — the types, their motivations, and their patterns— however, most of this, you will discover on your own, over time, as my examples should be used as a heuristic — an approach, not a hard rule.

Most of the world's problems come from people — destruction, anger, wrath, envy, greed, revenge, indifference, pollution, etc. Conversely, most of the world's beautiful creations, joyous pleasures, humanitarian aid, helpful mentorship and bountiful opportunities come from people too. So, how we deal with and persuade people makes up nearly most of business — and for such a high percentage, I think it is only fitting that we spend some time exploring at it.

When you build a product — you need people. When you raise capital for your business — you need people. When you sell your product to someone — you need people. People are around us, within our organizational walls, and externally, inside of their own camps, defending their own castles, needs, and focusing on their own outcomes.

I believe that being great with people, sets you at a differentiated level that is really hard to compete against. You might have a better product than I do, but if the same customer just flat out likes me better, often times they'll buy from me. This isn't fair, but it's true. Ever pitch a buyer with a hands down better product, and wonder why she still stays with the same supplier year in and year out? Well, go to the annual tradeshow and you'll see them boozing and schmoozing while laughing together at the bar over things totally unrelated to business.

Unfortunately, humans let their personal opinions and biases blind them to better products, better people, and better results for themselves and their organizations.

Same goes with hiring the "best" people — a reiterated phrase that virtually every business book and leadership guru implores you to do. What the hell is "best" anyway? How do we identify "best"? And if we can, how do we get them to work with us and buy into our dream? Furthermore, "best" today, may be utterly ineffective tomorrow — so let's replace "best" with "most effective at solving/building X" today.

Developing social skills with people takes time. I've found a few ways to practice, so that when you really need to connect with important people, you can. This, by no means, means that I turn on the charm or try to BS someone on who I am, or how I think. Rather, this is a social skill — being able to connect *authentically* within sixty seconds with virtually anyone, about anything.

The best entrepreneurs I know, can connect with anyone, at any time, over anything. They know enough about most topics to jump in a conversation, add their two cents, and get the other person to engage deeper, building camaraderie.

Most people, when they first meet you, are on the defensive. This is normal — we are human after all — and the way the human brain is designed is to determine a safety score so to speak, when scanning another human to either signal a fight, flight or bond reaction. Humans are greeters — we routinely walk by others at an airport and nod to acknowledge the other person, we make sure on a flight that we provide the other person with ample personal space, we say, "Excuse me" and "Thank you" (most people do at least) — there is a flow to being human — greeting, engaging, requesting, receiving, giving and departing. An ebb and a flow.

So where am I going with this you ask? Here's where. Your startup is a direct reflection on you, the people you hire, how you collectively think, your standards, your rules of engagement, and you as the founder are its chief socializer.

In today's hyper competitive global business world — it's not enough to have a more compelling price, a more differentiated product feature set, or a better user experience — you have to be able to get people to like you first, before they will be open to buying your product, or investing in your startup.

Humor is one of the easiest ways to connect with strangers. It disarms the defensive, it breaks down invisible social barriers that divide us, and it opens people up for a few moments to hearing more. Self-deprecating humor can be a great way to show you've come to grips with yourself and your failures, and that shows humility — a trait I believe many great leaders possess. Neutral humor about topics can often be a helpful way to bond two strangers in just a few minutes. People love to laugh — that's a fact. Heck, people pay for stand-up comedy just to forget about their day and chuckle for an hour.

They say laughter is the best medicine. I say laughter gives the best sales presentations. Make people laugh, and you'll effortlessly swoon new customers over.

Think about the buyer who has scheduled your meeting for the 4:30 pm slot on Friday, towards the last thirty minutes of her long week. She's obviously not giving you priority on a Monday bright and early, but she is interested just enough to give you some space before she jets out of there to grab a happy hour and get, well, happy over a cocktail and have a few laughs. Do you see where I am going with this? If you open the meeting by saying something like, "Thanks for the meeting, I'm about ready for that happy hour, aren't you?" (with a smile on your face), she will probably laugh and agree with you, and all of a sudden you just took the exact thought that she was thinking, claimed ownership of it, brought it out into the light and showed her that you know how *she* thinks, because you both think alike! Now you're a team, you're thinking alike, and she's a bit more open to hearing more from you. You bought yourself five more minutes.

Another way to get buyers to open up, is to immediately admit a negative off the bat. Here is an example:

"Listen Donna, I'm not gonna waste thirty minutes of your precious time giving you some spiel on how our widget is gonna be the best thing since sliced bread - I love bread, and it's not better (she laughs). But hear me out, the one thing I can show you is that it saves your company one-hundred thousand bucks a month in cost over your current supplier - She's *sold* folks (I exclaim!) Just kidding, but can I show you what I'm talking about? It'll only take three minutes of your time." "Sure, let's hear it." she replies.

Regardless if she buys today, you've left a favorable impression which allows you to follow-up later on (rejection free) and see if she's open for doing business.

People have titles, and often times, they inherit the prototypical mannerisms, outlooks, and personality types of their titles for no good reason other than that's what's expected of them from others.

For example, think about a buyer at a large retail chain. What's the image that comes to mind? Did you think of a fun, wild and carefree girl that loves Pilates class and listens to J-Lo® all while dancing the night away on weekends at the local nightclub? Well, she may indeed love and do those things, but when she's at her office, the wild and carefree girl gets packed away, and the "buyer" persona has to come out — analytical, cost conscious, risk averse, etc. However, that person is still inside, and she's waiting for 5pm to close up shop, text her friends, and grab the Frosé! So, who do we want to pitch? The buyer that's been trained to say "No", because that's the default response mechanism for most pitches, or the fun, open person that wants to say "Yes!", and give us a shot? We can't just pitch like everyone else —we have to unlock the human inside, not face the title – Buyer, Investor, or Customer.

Business logic only gets you so far in life. Social skills get you a lot further, faster, and builds deeper relationships that endure.

Again, at the end of the day, we need all kinds of people, from all kinds of backgrounds, and we are both reliant on them and they are reliant on us. My father always reminded me, "Reagan, we're all buyers and sellers of goods and services — buyer beware, seller beware." There are days where people will be totally open and receptive to your pitches, and there are days where they will be closed and slam the door in your face. My sister used to remind me, "If you knew what everyone is going though, you would forgive everyone for everything." Be mindful that people have lives *outside* of work that matter more than their work. They have aspirations that are uniquely theirs, and that most, by nature are risk averse for fear of making a mistake and being blamed by their boss, or worse, fired. As an entrepreneur, it is your job to have empathy when needed, reduce prospective fear of failure in their minds, and develop deep relationships that are a win-win for both parties.

As my father used to tell me, "Sometimes putting yourself in someone else's shoes for the moment is really hard, but if you can do it, you can better understand where they're coming from." He was and is a hell of a salesman and entrepreneur.

CHAPTER 10:
MARKETS

Understanding the Consumer Psyche:

Today's consumers are more connected than ever before in history. They are linked in, face-timed out, liking, up-voting, reviewing, critiquing, favoriting, sharing, pinning, posting and more every hour. E-mails are fired off a mile a minute, and every moment is now captured, shared and liked within seconds from being experienced. Yet, many consumers feel completely overwhelmed, even disconnected, while some pay money to have others show them how to *not* check their phone for an hour! How we leverage (or don't leverage) technology is just one piece of the puzzle to unlocking success in your startup. Remember, tech is a tool, not an outcome. Before we get caught up in what the hottest new industry and buzzwords are, we have to get back to basics — psychology.

No matter what business you start, what industry you serve, or what product or service you attempt to sell, you've got to win the mind of your customer *first* before you have a chance to win their loyalty in sales thereafter. Tech aside for a moment, the inner workings of the right hemisphere of our brains control our emotions and drive impulsive, consumptive behavior. Our analytical, rational, number crunching left-brain hemispheres help to validate and approve/disprove the emotionally driven right. So how do we build brands that favorably trigger the correct psychological sequences that drives the behaviors that we want? If we can better understand how the mind processes information and ultimately makes decisions, we can more acutely engineer our branding to close the path to purchase loop in an expedited manner.

Different consumers seek different information to understand the available choices in a market and make an informed buying decision. While every industry and market have different players, aspirations, challenges and solutions, the bedrock of all markets is the way that the brain is structured to digest information and buy.

Maslow's Hierarchy[17] (figure 10.1) is a psychological representation that depicts a triangle pyramid of five successive levels to organize the essential elements that humans focus on in life. As humans meet the needs of level 1, they intuitively (and often subconsciously) move up to level 2 and so on, until eventually seeking to attain the experiences that level 5 offers. The theory goes, if we can't take care of the basics like food, water, shelter and sleep, how can we focus on other things like building our relationships with others, developing our own self-esteem, or even fueling our artistic creativity? As entrepreneurs we must understand this model in relation to our own business, and where on a psychological level we hope to push our customers up into with our marketing efforts.

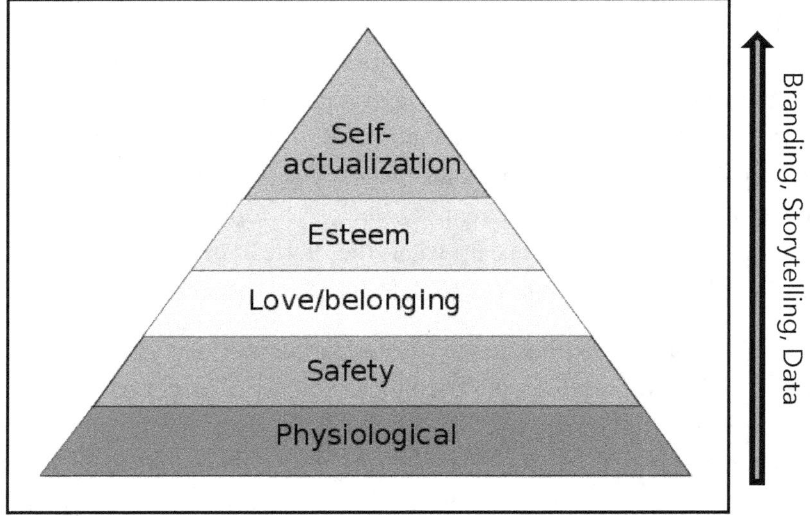

Figure 10.1

For example, it may be hard to get a shopper to consider and buy your farm's organic kale, when they are living on food stamps, paycheck to paycheck, and hoping that they can pay rent next month. For someone who is making $100,000 a year, they've achieved levels 1 and 2, and are working towards levels 3, 4 and 5. They would be a better candidate to consider switching from the competitor's lettuce to your organic kale. Your branding is what will move them over.

Level 1: Physiological: Food, water, shelter, reproduction, sleep, homeostasis, excretion.

Level 2: Safety: Security of body, employment, resources, family, health, property.

Level 3: Love/Belonging: Friendship, family, sexual intimacy.

Level 4: Esteem: Self-esteem, confidence, achievement, respect of others, respect by others.

Level 5: Self-Actualization: Morality, creativity, spontaneity, problem solving, lack of prejudice, acceptance of facts.

Thanks to Maslow's Hierarchy of Needs we've got a framework for understanding humanity and their sequentially motivating elements. While Maslow opened our eyes to the goals behind the actions, marketers took the model one step further to position their brands at the right level to win hearts and minds. Branding, to many marketers, appears more of an art, than a science. However, if psychology is rooted in science, and we as humans yearn to continually evolve, grow and progress, one could argue that there are two areas where any brand can be mapped on Maslow's Hierarchy of Needs.

One, the actual layer where the product would be categorized by a retailer (e.g. Men's Apparel), and the other, where the marketer *should* position it (e.g. Esteem/Achievement)

Notice how there are two layers, and you, as the entrepreneur, have the power to set your own positioning. This is one of the most important jobs that a CEO has to figure out — where to set the brand so your market both understands what is for sale, and also desires where it will *take* them. This is akin to crafting the branding Ying and Yang. For this to work, there has to be a piece footed in reality associated with the marketing to make it believable within relation to the category, but the imagery, wording, metaphors, references, should appear more. Brands connect best with customers when they appeal to customers in a real, meaningful manner. You must think about the level of need a customer is trying to meet today and position your product/service in a way that appeals to that aspiration for fulfillment tomorrow (physically, emotionally, aspirationally, spiritually).

For example, Nike's slogan, Just Do It®, appeals to Maslow's Level 5. Their branding tells consumers, you put in all of the hard work and practice, and you can achieve greatness too like [Tiger Woods, Serena Williams, etc.]. It is an *aspirational* brand — its users are motivated by the challenge to be better, look better, achieve physical greatness, and display athletic prowess to capture titles. What are they physically selling? Sneakers, shorts, socks, t-shirts. Did you buy greatness at the register? No. But you bought into the *motivation* to unlock your own greatness. Nike helps you *realize* your potential — even if it is buried deep within the burrows of your soul.

Think about your new brand and ask yourself the following:

What does it *physically/digitally* sell today? ___________________

What could it *emotionally* sell tomorrow? ___________________

If you recently opened up a coffee shop, are you just another coffee shop? Or, are you the fresh start to a new day? Are you the cup that muses the next John Steinbeck to write a classic? Are you the meeting place that connects two lost souls for the first time? Are you the choice through which people show others that they support local, organically sourced beans over corporate coffee sellouts? If this sounds like a bunch of sugar puff thinking, think again. Rolex doesn't just sell luxury watches, and their branding perfectly encapsulates it all — "It doesn't just tell time. It tells history.™"

Great branding builds a narrative; a new experience that *moves* people beyond the product in their hands.

Become *more* than just what you sell. Elevate your brand from the category it technically fits inside of a grocery aisle or retail store, upward to unlock your customer's deeper, hidden goals. When done properly, a bond is forged for a lifetime.

The Ice Cream Cone, The Vitamin, and the Pain Killer:

As we've discussed, a business's goal is to deliver value to a specific audience by way of a product, service or experience. For said value creation, members of this specific audience remunerate the vendor with continual usage of and/or payment for the product or service. Where many startups fail, is to clearly identify to the market, prospective investors, and partners, their true archetypical role that they play in the creation of the value they hope to pass along.

**Nearly every business shares the *same* identity crisis. Most businesses fail to understand what they truly sell —
an Ice Cream Cone, a Vitamin, or a Pain Killer.**

While evaluating startups pitches, VCs in Silicon Valley routinely ask founders "Are you creating a pain killer or a vitamin?" A pain killer is a *must* have product, while a vitamin is a preventative cure, which is a lot harder-to-sell. In addition to which, I believe, there's one more category to add — the Ice Cream Cone.

The Ice Cream Cone is not technically solving a direct pain, nor is it preventing something in the future from happening, rather it is providing one of life's memorable moments today. Think about attending a Disney® theme park with your family — the kids are happily running around, playing on the rides, laughing and dancing while the parents are relieved that their children are satisfied, and that they have a day to take a break from their cubicle coffins. Or think of a movie. Going to the movies with a date may solve the pain from staying single and sitting alone in your studio apartment on a Friday night, but it is really an Ice Cream Cone experience — delivering romance, attention, adoration and a sense of wonderment. Part of the human condition is to simply experience something in the present moment that provides *immediate* gratification. Sure, we're locked in a constant battle between offsetting future pain, eliminating past painful situations, and buying and using things that prevent us from experiencing something painful and costly. God, it's totally exhausting to be human.

Most startups fail to understand if they are selling an Ice Cream Cone (ephemeral satisfaction today), a Vitamin (pain prevention/ potential satisfaction tomorrow), or a Pain Killer Product (pain relief today/tomorrow).

Your business, marketing, sales pitches, and conversations —must *clearly* define if the solution(s) that you provide aims to increase someone's pleasure or decrease their pain. Failure to clearly define if your brand is an ice cream cone, vitamin, or a pain killer leads to customer indifference, and ultimately, early startup apathy.

Humans are obsessively thinking about increasing life's pleasure and decreasing life's pain.

Take one minute and think about everything you have done in the last five minutes. Did you adjust your seat so it was more comfortable? Did you take another sip of coffee while reading this as it quenched your thirst and gave you a spike of energy to flip the page? What else have you done to reduce pain or create pleasure? No action is too significant or too insignificant to write down. The goal is to see that you too, share this fundamental truth with all of humanity.

The dichotomy of pain v.s. pleasure defines the human condition. Startups are the shuttles transferring passengers expeditiously between the two worlds, for a fee.

These two categories are some of the macro categories that define most of humanity's day-to-day thinking. A customer is calling you because she can't find the instructions for using the product properly on your website (saving her time, thus relieving pain). An employee is scheduling a meeting with you to discuss her compensation package (can be either increasing wealth to obtain more pleasure or decreasing pain that her current salary provides). When a supplier offers you a lower price (they are attempting to curry your business to increase their revenue, or their pleasure). Over the course of the next hour, walk around and look at what people do — they are locked in a battle with themselves and the world to increase their personal pleasure or decrease their personal pain — fidgeting between Heaven and Hell, smartphone in hand.

Emerging Markets Driven by Human Emotion:

With Maslow's Hierarchy in our tool-belt, let's look at some macro/micro trends that savvy marketers, entrepreneurs, and their venture investors are currently tackling, and their implied psychological tier that they appeal to within the consumer's mind. Your next startup idea might just come from one of these hot, burgeoning growth areas.

As you read below, don't fall for the trap of looking just at the *what* each category does, rather, think about the underlying human *emotion* and *desired* outcome. Industries, services, and products come and go. Underlying needs evolve over time. Deep rooted human emotions *never* change. Are the companies who operate within these fast-moving markets selling ice cream cones, vitamins or pain killers? Will these industries and trends continue for decades or fade away?

Social Media Virality:

Discovering something new for the first time used to happen by word-of-mouth at a dinner party over a few beers when your family member would show you their new gadget, on a road trip when your pal would pop in that flashy new CD, or in the newest monthly trade journal when it hit store shelves. Today's products, services and experiences are discovered in a totally different way. From ping notifications on your smartphone, to hashtags (#NewProduct) and tagging (@InsertNewStartup), to podcasts, YouTube® videos, celebrity endorsements — today's consumers are force-fed ads day and night. The difference between yester-year and today's ads, is — wait for it — they don't look like ads! Today's ads — wrapped in the disguise of technology, web, and social media — feel more like organic content, custom tailored just for you. Think that new pea-based protein shake just naturally arrived on the doorstep of that toned looking girl's Instagram page because, oh, she just loves it so much to do she *had* to share it with you? Think again — it's sponsored content — she was paid to do it. Sorry to burst your bubble pal.

Marketing has shifted from direct advertising to storytelling by way of organic content that *moves* us to buy. Becoming a great storyteller is one of your startup's most valuable secrets.

Here's a tectonic move: Banner ad click-through rates have fallen precipitously over the years, and to counter that, newsfeed providers like Facebook (Instagram), YouTube, Twitter, and others have found clever ways to hide ads within the feed so they appear part of your chosen feed. Marketers are encouraged to develop user personas and craft interesting, compelling stories that attract eyeballs, clicks, and conversions. And the stories not only speak emotionally to us, they make us want to share them with others. Whether they make us laugh, cry, or get irate — video vignettes featuring a product, a video user testimonials, or when an interstitial ad loads (the ones that play before you play a movie, song or watch a video) — there is a viral component designed into all of them. Watch, Share, Buy Me.

The Growth of Online Communities:

The Web has blossomed over the years from AOL® chatrooms, to Google Hangouts®, to Facebook groups, to Linkedin groups, to VIP subscription-based clubs centered around specific topics. Next will be Virtual Reality full immersive experiences akin to teleportation. Want to learn about Real Estate investing and chat with like-minded investors? There are groups for that. Want to learn about Day Trading Stocks? There are groups for that. Want to learn about traveling the world on the cheap? There are groups for that. If you can think it, there are others that are into it — and there are groups there to either charge you for exclusive access to it, or will provide it for free (so long as you see sponsored ads in the group online or in their e-newsletter).

With today's web building tools like WordPress®, Joomla®, Wix®, and more, you can create a unique focused website tailored around any community or topic you can think of. You can install plugins (pre-engineered code) for free or less than $50 per asset, that will set up a recurring subscription that you can charge customers on a monthly or annual basis to gain access. You can even build exclusive content, have guest writers from Fiverr® collaborate with you to drive traffic to new topics/articles, and provide special reports, tools and features for your members for a small fee.

Limited Flash Deals and Coupons:

The days of GroupOn®, LivingSocial®, GILT Group® and more may have come and peaked but deals and coupons are still big business. Companies like Rakuten® allows you to sign up for free, enter in your basic info, and then so long as you are willing to click an affiliate link that tracks your purchases online before you buy something, they will pay you a percentage of the affiliate fee that they earn as a reward. It's not uncommon for people to earn hundreds of dollars a year just through Rakuten. Prefer to just get a discount up front? Companies like CouponCabin® and RetailMeNot® have you covered. Just search for your favorite Retailer on their site/mobile app, click the affiliate link, and voilà, the coupon is automagically activated for you at the destination URL. Bottom line — people love saving money — and deals are not going away anytime soon.

Organic Food/Lifestyle:

Think that 2020 Chardonnay from the Russian River Valley might have some trace minerals that don't vibe with your new organic lifestyle? No problem. We've got organic wine, that's sustainably farmed and harvested in eco-friendly packaging that minimizes packaging materials and carbon footprints, delivered right to your door by online mobile web apps Drizly®, WineDirect®, Minibar® Delivery, and Saucey®.

Epicurean Lifestyle:

From Foodie blogs to TopChef® competitions, to downright overindulgent decadence — the epicurean lifestyle brings access to all things gluttonous right to our smartphone, dinner plate, and belly.

#FoodieNation — seriously. We've got HD quality, professionally shot, artistic pictures of food, wine, desserts, and epic scenery flooding into our Instagram® feeds, tempting us to go big or go home (and if you go home, we deliver too, so don't worry). Think GrubHub®, Postmates®, and DoorDash® for fast, convenient restaurant quality meals delivered right to your door for a small convenience fee. Think Amazon Fresh® (need groceries but don't have an hour to spend going to the mall to buy Wholefoods®?) — no problem, Amazon will drop it off in a 2-hour window for a small fee on a minimum order. Need a little meal inspiration? We've got popular shows like Man vs Food® on the Food Network, TopChef®, Chopped®, Hell's Kitchen®, MasterChef® and MasterChef Junior, IronChef®, CuttThroat Kitchen®, Barefoot Contessa®, America's Test Kitchen®, 30 Minute Meals®, Chef's Table®, Throwdown with Bobby Flay®, Worst Cooks in America®, Rachael Ray®, Giada at Home®, and UglyDelicious®. You can't go to the gym without watching a food show! Are you stuffed yet?

Extreme & Remote Fitness:

Harder, faster, slower & downright dirty have become the new, *new* fitness regimes of the world. From small community run competitions like marathons and swim meets, we've grown beyond local and gone global with fitness. We've thought outside of the box and curated one-of-a-kind fitness challenges, experiences and programs that blend Navy Seal style training, with Gold's Gym® power lifting, and Buddhist Monk mindfulness.

Fitness Competitions - Think ToughMudder®, IronMan®, CrossFit Games® - workouts are getting harder, more diverse, and more outlandish. Forget the good 'ol fashion push-up, sit-up, squat and 30 minutes of jogging — now we've got burpies, double unders, air squats, knees to elbows, pistols, walking lunges, band-assisted pull ups, rope climbs, sumo deadlifts, thrusters, handstand push-ups, muscle ups, box jumps, snatches, clean & jerks, ring dips, wallballs, and more. That's not all — we now call our workouts by specific names too - WOD (workout of the day), CrossFit Total (3 attempts to find your max squat, standing press and deadlift), Hero WODs (named supportively after fallen military servicemen, police and firefighters who have died in the line of duty — these difficult workouts give us an extra challenge and patriotic reminder of their sacrifices so we should push harder to honor them), Metcon (metabolic conditioning), Frans, Murphs, Isabel, Filthy Fifty and more. Whew, I'm exhausted.

Fitness Endurance - Think SoulCycle®, CycleBar®, Peloton®, Bikram Hot Yoga, Pilates Reformer, Kickboxing, etc. Be sure to buy your Lululemon® designer yoga mat and foam roller because you're gonna need those too. Did I forget to mention at present a SoulCycle® 1-hour spin class starts around $40 a pop (including $5 shoes), and you've got to book ahead of time on the mobile app to reserve your exact bike in the classroom. The physical and digital worlds are melding together, from GPS enabled watches/ smartphones that track our every step, stair and heartbeat, to GPS running mobile app mapper like MapmyRun®, to sleep tracking apps like Whoop®, FitBit®, Emfit QS®, S+ by RedMed, Beddit 3 Smart Sleep Monitor, Jawbone UP3 and more — our health data has become our new prescription that guides our motivation, sets our goals, and predicts our demise. Couple this with the COVID-19 pandemic era, we've seen a tremendous spike in at-home fitness apps, exercise equipment, and fitness enthusiast communities emerge. Fitness is adapting to the 'new' normal quickly.

Mindfulness - Think online mediation apps - HeadSpace®, InsightTimer®, SimpleHabit®, 10% Happier®, Calm®, The Mindfulness App®, Smiling Mind, Meditation Timer Pro, Omvana, Simply Being, Breethe, Stop, Breathe & Think, Buddhify, MINDBODY and more. Namaste is here to stay. Many have predicted that uncorrected cellphone usage, social media addictiveness and longer work hours have caused us to essentially fry our peaceful equilibriums. But no one would have guessed that the exact mobile device that causes us our pain, would actually become the antidote that brings us peace too, for a monthly fee of course. #TheMindfulMobile

The On-Demand Goods Economy - Clothing, Furniture, Crafts:

While this covers multiple sectors, the core concepts are built around i. Ease of browsing unique, custom pieces that fit our bodies, homes or lifestyles, ii. On-demand access via the web to massive selection at a fraction of the traditional cost, and iii. Rapid delivery of goods right to your door.

Think brands like UnTuckIt® (shorter men's shirts), ProperCloth® (custom tailored clothing for a slice of the normal tailor price), Rent-the-Runway® (rentable designer wedding dresses at a fraction of the traditional cost), WayFair® (discounted designer home-goods with unique style), HomeGoods® (retail chain with trendy, sophisticated home-goods at a bargain), ETSY® (one-of-a-kind, handmade, artisan crafted goods), Minted® (crowd up-voted embroidered prints & home-goods).

Global Causes (Social Impact):

The world has many problems, and they assuredly need your physical assistance, social likes, and frankly, donations. Want to round up the change for a cause when you buy a soda? Just press here on the P.O.S. credit card machine at your favorite Supermarket, Gas Station or Retailer. Want to donate in a little bit bigger way and get public praise for it from your network? GoFundMe®, Kickstarter®, IndieGoGo® and the like help startups, projects and ideas get the funding and support they need at inception.

Green Movement (environmentally focused products sustainably sourced, carbon neutral service providers & companies that donate or giveback to earthly causes):

It seems like most companies today are either partially, or fully committed to protecting the planet. They've come to learn that going green has benefits: higher sales, lower costs, and strong brand identity.

Think companies like — UPS® (Carbon neutral program charges shippers a small fee to offset their carbon footprint for package delivery), Paperless Billing (essentially who needs that paper statement mailed to you anyway — just check it on your laptop or smartphone guys), GreenWaste® (seems like recycling has become the norm — did you know they sell your freely donated items and make a ton of money off of it?), Patagonia® (durable clothing designed to last a lifetime — if your clothing falls apart, they'll fix it. If your clothing is unrepairable, they'll reuse the material to make a new item without any waste), Starbucks® (recycled, post material coffee cups, lids, and coffee sleeves), Preserve® (from toothbrushes to storage containers to recycled razors), their slogan "Nothing Wasted. Everything Gained®" ensures you've gone green even in the smallest of places. Method® (household cleaners, laundry products, and personal care products that are both naturally derived and biodegradable — helps you stay green around the house too). And before you go to bed at night and turn out the lights, you'll be happy to know that Edison's invention no longer uses filament — rather, it is a high-tech LED designed bulb that sucks significantly less electricity and lasts, oh, twenty years! And we can't forget our LEED® Certified buildings that use less power, are greener in design, and give property managers something to market. Aren't greener buildings supposed to cost you less, so why is rent so high? (says everyone in San Francisco).

Cloud Computing:

A very broad category indeed, but the main concept offers worldwide storage of data on distributed servers 'in the cloud', thus lowering local storage and transaction costs, increased connectivity and greater convenience, and possibly security. The category also includes Analytics, Operations, Security, Customer Support, Marketing, Collaboration Tools, Finance and Other.

Think companies like — AWS® (Amazon web server hosting), Stripe® (CC payment processing), DropBox® (file storage/ transfer), DocuSign® (multiparty e-signatures), Slack® (global business messaging platform), Canva® (free graphic design platform), etc.

Crypto & Alternative Currencies:

From online wallets to store currency, to trading brokerages to transact trades, to research platforms to perform analysis, to coin-based marketplaces to exchange coins & more, alternative currencies are all the current rave:

Think companies like — Binance®, bitMEX®, KuCoin®, Changelly®, Coinbase®, Bitfinex®, KeepKey®, Treznor®, MyEtherWallet®, Jaxx®, Electrum®, CoinDesk®, BitcoinWisdom®, BitcoinTalk®, LedgerWallet®, Gdax®, and more crypto platforms, wallets, and exchanges.

Music/Audio Streaming/Podcasts:

Free or cheap monthly subscription-based music streaming delivered right to your mobile phone, computer, car or IOT device (Alexa®/ Google Home®) has arrived in full. No longer do we trek on down to Sam Goody®, Tower Records® or Walmart® to buy a full $20 CD or even download a $0.99 single on iTunes®; music consumption has exploded, while artists and record labels continue to struggle to replace the good 'ol record label days of substantial sales and royalties.

Think companies like — Spotify®, Pandora®, Amazon Music®, Apple Music®, iHeart Radio®, Google Play®, Audible®, etc.

Drones:

Unique footage, never before accessible for cheap — only when pigs fly right? Wrong! — from GoPro® Karma®, to DJI® Phantom, Mavic Pro® and Spark Drones®, we've got you covered from the sky. Even Apple® Stores got in on the retail market of distributing drones that work in conjunction with your iPhone®. The drone market has so many players, from consumer toy and professional grade brands like DJI®, Uvify®, Hubson Drones®, Parrot Drones®, Yuneec Drones®, Autel Robotics Drones®, GDU Drones®, to high end photographic drone companies like FreeFly®, to even personal flying machines (the future has arrived sir), like Intel Drones Volocopter®. We've got mini drones that use your smartphone as a flying camera to large military plane size drones called UAVs that carry weapons equipped with infrared thermal cameras and night vision that keep our world safe domestically and abroad called the Predator® and Reaper®. We've even got alternative fireworks drones that use LEDs to replace traditional (flammable) fireworks, border patrol drones, safety surveillance drones that fly high above construction sites, power plants, oil refineries and offshore rigs — how else could you see if that coal burning power plant smokestack CO_2 scrubber needs to be replaced?

Online Subscription Box Businesses:

Discovery Boxes & Convenience Boxes are either highly customized or selectively curated by staffers with monthly deliveries of product right to your door.

Think companies like — Birchbox®, StitchFix®, Blue Apron®, Dollar Shave Club®, Hello Fresh®, Ipsy®, BarkBox®, Dia®, Bespoke Post®, Gwynnie Bee®, Le Tote®, Grove®, Loot Crate®, FabFitFun®, HomeChef®, NatureBox®, etc.

Cannabis Distribution:

With the legalization of recreational Marijuana in states like Alaska, California, Colorado, Maine, Massachusetts, Nevada, Oregon,

Vermont, Washington, and Washington DC, and other states have legalized medicinal Marijuana like New Jersey, Michigan, Kentucky, New York, and even Georgia at time of writing — the list continues to grow as the taxation upside has finally convinced law makers that there's green in green. The industry is up for grabs — from farmers, to retail distributors, to online medicinal e-marketplaces, to ancillary supplies — it seems like everyone is looking at the cannabis industry as the next green movement, literally.

Even publicly traded Constellation® Brands has made a massive investment in the Cannabis industry — to the tune of $3.8 billion in Canadian Canopy Growth Corp.® as of August, 2018 according to this Denver Post article[18] — put that in your pipe and smoke it.

According to a The Motley Fool® article[19], "the cannabis industry could grow by an impressive 25% to 35% per year through 2021 — or beyond. This sales growth, aided by the expectation that Canada will legalize recreational pot soon (at time of writing), is a big reason why pot stock investors have piled into this industry recently. But it's not just sales growth that has investors excited. It's the shift in consumer opinion toward cannabis. Within the US, no fewer than five national polls since April 2017 have demonstrated overwhelming support for legalization (often 59% to 64% support, depending on the survey). With the public so strongly behind the idea of legalization, investors expect sales growth throughout North America to continue climbing."

So what industry verticals are ripe for the picking? Farming companies like Canopy Growth Corp. (NYSE: CGC) currently operates grow facilities that spread 665,000 sq. ft. and is in the process of developing greenhouses on 3.7 million sq. ft. of land in British Columbia, according to the same Motley Fool article.

Medical marijuana farmers & distributors — at $3.47 billion and growing, Aurora Cannabis® NASDAQ:ACBFF is giving Canopy® a run for its money for the medical marijuana and therapeutic space. Other players include Aphria® (NASDAQ:APHQF), MedReleaf® (NASDAQ:MEDFF) and more.

Retail Distribution has taken Colorado by storm since their announcement of legalization. Chains like Native Roots® have expanded rapidly to twenty stores, LivWell® to fourteen stores, Green Dragon® to eleven stores, and Lightshade to eight locations at time of writing, according to this article in westword[20].

Ancillary Goods — from paraphernalia to consume, bake, smoke, inhale, and evangelize, the list goes on. The marijuana subculture is no longer a thing of 70s Wild Childs and concert going teenagers. It's now gone mainstream, and there's big capital at play in this new growth market.

The Selfie Movement:

#MCM - Man Crush Monday, #WCW - Woman Crush Wednesday, #TBT - Throwback Thursday, Photo Editing Apps and Selfie Sticks. The world of Instagram®, Facebook®, Snap®, WeChat®, WhatsApp® and more is here to stay. Every moment has become a sharable moment. See a great looking champagne bottle? Got to snap it, share it, and build likes. See a great view? Got to snap it, share it, and build likes. See a funny bumper sticker? Got to snap it, share it, build likes. Everything requires a photo, and every photo requires a hashtag (#) for SEO. Designing apps, products, even situations (e.g: photographical elements in your store, restaurant, hotel, etc.) that help facilitate selfies is key to riding the selfie wave.

Online Dating Apps:

When's the last time you got a real answer from someone when you asked where they met their boyfriend or girlfriend? According to a statista.com[21] report, fully 19% of all US Internet users are currently using a dating website or app as of April 2017. 30% of all US Internet users aged 18-29 were currently using dating sites or apps, and a further 31% had done so previously. Think about that for a second. That's one out of every five people you meet on the street, and one out of every three Millennial/GenZsters — even Cupid would be impressed.

Why such explosive growth? Is it the sheer ease of use, the overabundance of choice down to the extreme granularity, or just the basic addictiveness of a smartphone — we buy, do and research everything else on there, why not our dates and mates, right? We used to have Match® and eHarmony®, and it used to be an oddity to say you "met online" — images of classified page stalkers flash though our heads. However, now we've gone wide and deep with online dating — we've got Tinder® for quick matches connected by geolocation, we've got The League® developed by a Stanford business school graduate for the elite singles with pedigree, we've got ChristianMingle® for, well, Christian minded folks, we've got FarmersOnly® for our Wrangler® wearing friends in the Midwest, and the list goes on and on - Bumble® (only the girl can initiate a conversation if she *wants* to. Enter, Aphrodite), It's Just Lunch® (for, well, lunch dates — rather see you in the daylight sir, thanks), Coffee Meets Bagel® (which I used to think was for bagel lovers, but apparently it's not — too bad, bagels rock), How About We® (no clue what this even means), Hinge® (because if my friends don't trust you, why would I?), OKCupid® (after a long interrogation style questionnaire, they deliver suitable matches), and more. What's the future of dating? Maybe genetic match-making — why haven't we seen 23andMe® or Ancestry® jump in on the action? Maybe our biological genes hold the truth for predictive dating analysis that yields our soulmates? I predict this will come next. Whatever it is, dating is big business, and online dating, no matter how you slice and dice it — by age, geography, shared interest, degrees of separation, timed dating, contests, new rules of engagement, or even genetic symbiosis — online dating is here to stay. If you can reimagine the rules, you might just find your share in this crowded space.

The Surveillance Economy:

Protecting our homes, offices, and valuables has never been so easy. From Ring® (doorbell camera/audio theft prevention system) to Arlo® (portable, Wi-Fi enabled, high quality video security systems for households and offices), to Nest® Hello (a 24/7 video recording system with AI-powered motion deception and facial recognition), the eye in the sky has arrived, and it's cheaper, more powerful, and ever connected. However, you'd think that theft would be a thing of the past, but oddly is hasn't been eradicated fully. San Francisco, for example, still boasts one of the fastest growing auto theft markets with nearly 30,000 break-ins in 2017 according to recently published police reports, as the crime was recently downgraded from a felony to a misdemeanor[22].

The Access Economy: (Goods, Experiences, and Luxuries):

Ah, dreams of sipping Champagne while relaxing in a hot tub on a 250 ft. mega yacht in the balmy sea just off the coast of the Amalfi Coast in Italy have become accessible for the moderately rich (no longer reserved for only the ridiculously wealthy billionaire elite). It seems that our generations have *shifted from the ownership model to the access economy,* and that simple, yet powerful shift has unlocked new business models, companies and experiences.

Do you really want to own the Ferrari® Modena or do you just want cruise up and down Ventura Blvd. watching everyone stop and stare at you as you whizz buy? The *experience* is the desired result. Ownership just gets in the way. Rental companies that allow you to gain a peek of the lifestyle of your dream give you the ultimate power without a lifetime of work, capital, and sweat and risk to buy it. Want to get front row tickets and backstage passes to a nearly sold-out rock concert or famous golf tournament like the US Open? Companies like MasterCard® have special VIP programs that select card holders gain exclusive access to just by being an owner and modest spender. Want to sleep like a king but don't own a palatial bed? No problem — products like Tempurpedic®, Sleep Number®, and mattress firms like Casper® offer high end slumber at a fraction of the historical price — and they'll deliver and install for free too. Want to win a dream round of golf on an epic Irish course with famed Major Champion Rory McIlroy? Mobile based, on-demand golf booking service company GolfNow® routinely offers once-in-a-lifetime contest opportunities to book now and win a trip of your dreams. Do you follow famous Instagram® pages that document Millionaire experiences like $30,000 watches, sports cars, yachts, mansions and enviable model wives? Why not jump in a private jet? You don't need to do what Mark Cuban did (he apparently bought his private jet for nearly $40m online), you can simply join a fractional ownership club like NetJets®, WheelsUp®, or others that give you access when you want, how you want it, without the unfathomable invoice that leads to ownership (that also includes maintenance, insurance, jet fuel, and salaries). Getting access to the millionaire and billionaire experiences has arrived — and it costs pennies on the dollar.

Artificial Intelligence (AI):

According to a Forbes® article[23], artificial intelligence was developed by John McCarthy, who first coined the term artificial intelligence in 1956 when he invited a group of researchers from a variety of disciplines including language simulation, neuron nets, complexity theory and more to a summer workshop called the Dartmouth Summer Research Project on Artificial Intelligence to discuss what would ultimately become the field of A.I. At that time, the researchers came together to clarify and develop the concepts around "thinking machines" which up to this point had been quite divergent. McCarthy is said to have picked the name artificial intelligence for its neutrality; to avoid highlighting one of the tracks being pursued at the time for the field of "thinking machines" that included cybernetics, automata theory, and complex information processing.

Merriam-Webster defines artificial intelligence as[24]:

1.   A branch of computer science dealing with the simulation of intelligent behavior in computers.

2.   The capability of a machine to imitate intelligent human behavior.

So, what's a world where A.I. runs everything look like? God only knows. But what we do know is virtually every major company globally is investing like mad and hiring technologists, A.I. engineers, and consultants to figure it out for them. It seems like the future's competitive differentiation and thus advantage, will be for companies to leverage A.I. to compete for them. We're not just talking elimination of the low level, routine operations that take up a majority of service jobs, we're talking the whole stack. Despite what leadership tells us — that the future will feature a hybrid of both autonomous and human-based work balanced to optimize the customer experience — once executives get a taste for A.I., we know they will go full throttle to A.I.-ify their companies. Recall outsourcing? We outsourced it all — from service support call centers, to engineering, to tech support agents, to even product management — it was cheaper, they worked while we slept, and they competed for our business. It also meant the ability to cut labor as we needed, so that we could rebalance our bottom lines when Wall Street demanded it. Outsourcing was the last tectonic shift. The future is A.I. Artificial Intelligence will become the sales force we always wanted — continuously hunting for the ideal client to pitch, convert, and close. A.I. will become the customer service desk we always asked for, but never got. Instead, companies got cantankerous, un-loyal workers who complained about their jobs and would quit for a 10% pay increase from the competitor across the street. Computers don't get disgruntled, they don't tire out after eight hours, they don't petition for raises, and they don't leave us for someone better. They are loyal, they work until they break, they never complain or accuse management of less than standard treatment — they are downright an executive's dream. But they are an employee's competitive nightmare.

Facial recognition software coupled with A.I. will replace store greeters at your local retail chain and recognize every shopper, every time. Drones equipped with facial recognition software, machine learning, and a real-time connection to a database with billions of data points with predictive analysis will prevent crime before it has a chance to fester. Websites will dynamically adjust themselves and offer consumers personalized, real-time updated product selections that appear curated just for them — making a buyer or shop owner's product selection seem out of touch and obsolete. Cars will be continuously updated via software and in-sync with each other in real-time to prevent traffic jams, accidents, and car chases. Are we getting closer to Utopia or George Orwell's <u>1984</u>? Not sure. In the process, jobs will be lost, humans will be outworked, outpaced, outperformed, and severely marginalized. This will be the greatest industrial revolution *since* the Industrial Revolution. Any company equipped with A.I. that stands to offer another business lower HR costs, increased margins, enhanced customer retention, and greater global reach, will be of great value moving forward. Eventually, A.I. empowered companies might be competing against A.I. empowered companies, instead of humans competing against humans. The competitive moat armed by a company's one unique competitive advantage, that famed investor Warren Buffet always alludes to, might just be replaced by continuous learning, A.I. powered hovercrafts equipped with night-vision, thermal sensing cameras and a digital arsenal of weaponized offers that are statistically calculated to win — because when the house always learns, it always wins, every time.

Blockchain Technology (Platforms, SaaS, and Dapps):

For years, companies created corporate silos that separated customers from the value that they created and put a cash register between the two entities. That was the name of the game — we make something that you want, pay us, and we will let you have it (or have access to it) so long as you keep paying. While this historically has been the standard operating procedure for nearly all for profit businesses, it comes with its flaws, as evidenced in recent year debacles. Namely, what happens when I sign up for your service, give you my personally identifiable and confidential information, and your site or servers get corrupted or worse, hacked? How about when I sign up with your service, become reliant on it for my business or life, and you decide all of a sudden to jack up the price by a ridiculous percentage, and I have no choice but to accept. Lastly, what happens when someone that you hire, as your service provider, decides to commit an act of corruption and steal money from customer accounts just like mine without you nor I even noticing? How can we prevent many of these situations from occurring?

In the wake of the 2008 Global Financial Recession and the Real Estate market collapse, a new form of technology called Blockchain was developed, as the underlying foundation of cryptocurrency. While cryptocurrency provides a digital alternative to Fiat money printed by central banks, they might be more secure, traceable, and not subject to the manipulation of big banks and institutions (so they say as of today, but undoubtedly might not be in the future as more capital pours in). Blockchain is a new technology with many applications outside of just currency. Without getting too deep, as you can research blockchain elsewhere (by experts), blockchain is decentralized code, submitted to the chain ledger in the form of coded blocks. When a user wants to say, make a purchase on eBay®, currently, they have to log onto eBay, find the item, buy the item, and then the buyer and seller take the required steps to accept the order, ship the goods, and make the payment *through* eBay. That is a centralized transaction, whereas Blockchain is decentralized. Your computer essentially makes a secure transaction directly with another computer, writes the mini agreement (sometimes called a smart contract) into the ledger (a widely agreed upon online recording system), and the transaction is confirmed. The key here, is that it shifts the transaction to the ledger, and does not route it via a company's server silos. The transaction is validated and stored on the public blockchain ledger for all to see (it is encrypted, but still there), so no internal manipulation can occur by a company or employee.

In so doing, companies that deploy blockchain can shift the power *away* from major incumbent players, create an end-to-end secure transaction, and thus, charge much lower fees. There are less middlemen — often, there are no middlemen — so, fees are reduced, security is increased, visibility of the transaction is made public (no private backdoor deals), and no manipulation or changing of the terms of the transaction (or smart contract). A new contract would have to be written and agreed by all parties for it to be made effective. The downside? The company no longer operates in a data silo, storing information and restricting access for a high fee. The upside — to be determined over time. Every week more and more startups emerge that are dreaming up new ways to shift existing transactions like car rentals (where it has a ton of friction points — shopping, waiting in line, dealing with the customer service clerk, booking, renting, returning, etc.), to the blockchain. Imagine pressing a button on an app, the phone is authorized to open up the car, it shows you where the car is, you open the door, and drive away. When your rental is done, just lock the car, the app updates to a new smart contract for someone else, and you don't get access to the car anymore. No friction points dealing with browsing for cars, booking and returning, just get it, click, and go.

NLP (Natural Language Processing):

If only my computer could talk to me…wait…it can! With the invention of SIRI®, Amazon's Alexa®, and Google Home®, NLP or natural language processing systems have come to be our friend, personal shopper, newscaster, and assistant. NLP covers a broad range of verticals — speech recognition, to spelling, to full comprehension and understanding — NLP is a massive and growing space. Of course, companies like Google®, Apple® and Amazon® have a first-mover advantage, but other startups are emerging for specific use cases, new products, and OEM partnerships that use NLP in exciting forms. The ultimate goal of NLP won't just be a one-and-done request — "Hey Siri, what's the weather outside?" — rather, it will be a conversation in the not-so-distant future whereby NLP systems will begin conversations, use bio sensors to detect our moods, behavioral patterns, and will use predictive analytics and big data to forecast solutions to problems before they begin, diagnose us and our desires, and show recommendations tailored to our individualistic lives.

Machine Learning (ML):

Coders used to build code in simple terms — if x, then do y statements. You could rely on these statements to take a user generated request, field the appropriate data from a stored database, crunch the numbers, and dump out a y statement result. What's 2 + 2? (*if* two adds to two *then* that equals four). Today, we're building computers that do way, way more. ML, or machine learning, takes computational functions to a new level. The difference between a standard engineered system was that it had a fixed series of code, that could only produce the results that its engineers allowed it to output. That's history. Take Amazon.com for example — ever log in to see a product's price and today it's one figure, and the next day, it's another? It's not a buyer changing the figure when she wants to — it's the machine learning about supply and demand and learning how to forecast the willingness of its customers to pay. Imagine television that learns what you like to watch, and instead of you having to spend twenty minutes flipping channels, it's delivered curated, customized content right to you — enter, Netflix®. These systems are continually learning what their users click, watch, browse, touch, buy, and share. Algorithms are designed to progress in their design, output, granularity, and accuracy of results over time. The more data comes in, the more finely tuned they get. That's why big companies like Google®, Facebook®, Apple®, Amazon®, Microsoft® and others have such competitive advantages — they have tremendous data, cheap computational power, and powerful algorithms that get better and better by the minute. Traditional companies, without machine learning as their backbone, don't stand a chance in competing against systems that continually learn, react, and improves thousands of times a day.

CHAPTER 11:
PHASES & PATTERNS

"Based on my business plan, once we launch, we should be cash flow positive in eighteen months, as our subscriber base should scale out at a rate of 50 new users per day," I boasted proudly across the table at my quarterly shareholder meeting, pointing to an X/Y chart on the board with a diagonal line that started at zero and soared up and right towards $28 million in year five. As Chief Executive Officer of WorldMusicLink (WML), I had the fiduciary responsibility to update my shareholders on our projected growth. By projected, I mean my best guess without appearing blindly näive or timidly conservative — after all, projections, when you're a public company, have years of historical data points to be projected off of, but in a new startup, you're starting with nothing and trying to convince yourself (and others) that you'll be something someday.

What I failed to realize in my projections, was that growth doesn't start at zero and travel up and right in a straight line; hell, it doesn't even stay in positive territory for long post-launch. If we're really being honest with the facts as outlined in Chapter One, most startups don't even get into positive territory at all! The truth is, there are inflection points along the way that accelerate or decelerate your startup into a new tier. The challenge is in articulating to investors and to your team, just what those will look like, and more importantly, *when* they might occur.

Financial pro formas are a projection into the future. They don't actually tell the story of how you got to the bottom line; they only show your dream of achieving a bottom line.

So why do so many founders rely on their five-year projections if they don't actually tell the important pieces of the tale? There are two reasons that come to mind. One, because historically the venture capital and investing community would compare different startups by evaluating their projected sales, gross margins, cash flows and net incomes, all to guide an investment thesis and decision. And two, because we all love a success story. As newbie founders, it's intoxicating to adjust a few numbers on a spreadsheet to see how fast we'll become a millionaire in just a few years. We paint a mirage in front of our screens and calculate how our 30% equity stake at a future sale price of $100 million, will net us $30 million in cold, hard cash. Problem is, we've created a document that sets us up for heartache — if we don't hit those numbers in that timeframe, we've lost, and if we don't have a large enough figure in year five, then an institutional investor might pass on our round — it's death by projection.

Stop Thinking Proforma. Just Start Performing.

The most important narrative of your startup is actually not the tale of a pro forma but is rather a list of milestone events that accelerate you from point A, to point B, to point Z. True, milestone events don't sound as cool as boasting about a $50 million-dollar run-rate in year five does, but these moments define significant inflection points that trigger a radical shift in the trajectory of your business.

Inflection Point: An inflection point is an event that results in a significant change in the progress of a company, industry, sector, economy or geopolitical situation and can be considered a *turning point* after which a dramatic change, with either positive or negative results, is expected to result. Companies, industries, sectors and economies are dynamic and constantly evolving. Inflection points are more significant than the small day-to-day progress typically made, and the effects of the change are often well known and widespread.[25]

Want to really attract an investor? Prove it with an inflection point, *not* a pro forma statement.

Investors are always looking for companies that have just had, or are about to have, an inflection point. It is the calling card of *significant* momentum, of scalability, and of a return on their investment. What's more mouth-watering for a VC, you tell me, "Here on the board is our 5-year projected (bullshit) revenues from zero to $100 million with 80% gross margin in year-5, priming us for a $1 billion Unicorn IPO" — says every entrepreneur in Silicon Valley — or B, "Last month we partnered with fifteen new universities including

Stanford and Cal, and saw a 220% increase in our recurring monthly revenue. This month we've closed an additional dozen university partners and locked in $500,000 in new sales. Next month we plan to scale to the Northeast and are already in discussions with eight more colleges to sign on." Well, if you want to believe the hype, invest in company A. If you want to invest in a startup demonstrating traction and in the middle of an inflection point break-out, invest in startup B.

However, inflection points can also go the other way, meaning, south. For my first startup, WML, we had projected that one of our inflection points would be when we inked a partnership with Musician's Friend® (the subsidiary of the largest music equipment retailer at the time, Guitar Center®). Musician's Friend® boasted over ten million subscribers to their mail order catalog, and a partnership with them, we thought, would surely result in an immediate jump in free and paid subscribers for us. So sure enough, we baked that partnership right into our projections and waited for the money to pour in…and waited…and waited. While I was able to strike a partnership with the Director of Business Development of Musician's Friend, right around the same time, unbeknownst to us, he was about to leave the company. They put up ads across their website for WML, and only a trickle of traffic from Harmony Central™ came in, their subsidiary musician community website. Once our contact at Musician's Friend left, our deal was toast, as no one was there to pick up the balance of the partnership details we agreed upon despite my countless e-mails and phone calls. There went our projections, and our anticipated upward inflection point with it.

What happens if we can't bank on inflection points materializing? Well, it turns out that most startups perform similarly across four pattens over time. Try to spot what kinds of inflection points may contribute to the shape of the growth curve of each type below and for your own company.

1. **The Hockey Stick Startup:** This startup dips into negative financial territory for a period of months or years, and then hits an inflection point, and begins an exponential rise towards growth, scale, and/or financial solvency.

Wikipedia[26] describes a J-Curve as, "a curve (that) initially falls, then steeply rises above the starting point." For all intents and purposes, think of this J-Curve as a giant NIKE® symbol, where on a standard X-Y linear graph, the starting point (line) starts above the x-axis, and quickly dips below for a period of time, and then rises back to the x-axis at a later point, and accelerates up and out to the right into quadrant I, also known as the profitability quadrant.

Retail operations like clothing stores that require a significant amount of up-front investment in clothes ($100,000 of new inventory), a $5,000 monthly building lease, a $3,500 computer system for inventory management, etc., follow this model. Or consider a new restaurant that requires a $200,000 investment in new kitchen equipment, $25,000 of food and supplies, and $10,000 of advertising before the doors even open. Each company will require a period of time to return back the invested capital by way of new sales, hence the shape of the J-Curve.

2. **The S-Curve Startup**: This startup grows slowly initially, but (usually) stays in positive financial territory for a period of time, then hits an inflection point, grows exponentially, and then hits another (negative) inflection point, levels off and then declines back to a constant rate or back to zero.

Encyclopedia.com defines an S-Curve, or sigmoid growth curve, as "A pattern of growth in which, in a new environment, the population density of an (organism) increases slowly initially, in a positive acceleration phase; then increases rapidly approaching an exponential growth rate as in the J-shaped curve but then declines in a negative acceleration phase until at zero growth rate the population stabilizes."[27]

Consider a new software gaming company that requires a relatively small up-front investment of say $100,000 to build a new game (app), and then as they reach a sizable number of paying subscribers with viral marketing on social media platforms, see an exponential spike in their revenues. Then, after 24-36 months, the hip factor begins to cool off, people stop paying for their app, and sales level off. Startups like this are banking on an initial up-front investment that yields a rapid, exponential growth curve to provide them optionality to sell the company off during the rapid growth period or IPO, before things cool off.

3.   **The Heartbeat Startup**: This startup either sharply dips into negative financial territory out of the gate, or quickly gains traction, then has a very abrupt series of high highs and low lows that zig zag throughout the company's lifecycle. These startups often raise capital, burn through it all, raise more, burn through it all, raise more, burn through it all. Like a heart rate monitor — up, down, up, down.

Think seasonal businesses like pop-up shops that require fast implementation to take advantage of the summer season like a boat rental company. They require timing to get the required inventory of boats ($500,000) in May just before the summer season hits, then they see a sudden spike of revenue between June through September, and then a steep decline in sales when the season is over. Alternatively, a new technology company may raise a large round of investor capital (which makes the company act like they are artificially operating at say a $5 million run-rate per quarter), to then see a steep decline in user growth in eighteen months when their capital begins to dry up, triggering another round of financing to pump the sales back up; hence the up-and-down pattern of cash.

4. **The Flat-Line Startup:** This startup launches and just never materializes into anything. Some call them the Zombie startup, where they experience a small hint of progress — an inked partnership, some new sales contracts, a product launch — and then just never break out into significant revenue territory or have any sustained traction that warrants additional bets on growth or funding rounds. They typically stay on life-support for a period of time, until they run out of funding or the founders call it quits. Think of a heart monitor, without a beat.

Most startups that don't raise any outside capital, but are self-funded by the founders, can find themselves in flat-line mode until a break-out inflection point. They show a little bit of progress, make a few sales early on, and then sustain just enough paying customers to keep the dream alive, but never really move the needle to trigger a sizable updraft. The only way to reach a new inflection point is either by a miraculous partnership, a major product tweak, a 180-degree pivot, an infusion of VC or external financing, or an out of the blue event that rains in new luck — think of being featured in TechCrunch®, a famous celebrity posting your product to their ten million followers driving an absurd amount of new traffic to your site, or some other display of the startup Gods.

When we launch a new company, it is near impossible to anticipate what kind of growth or stagnation we will experience. Most entrepreneurs are bright eyed and bushy tailed, confident that their projections will jump off the page and into their checking accounts. However, even if we can't tell you what kind of startup growth you may experience, I find it helpful to illustrate the aforementioned scenarios so you can better prepare for any pattern and spot it early on.

Inflections and Patterns:

To simplify this, let's think back to our lemonade stand example. You start this pop-up lemonade stand business because it is the middle of summer and it is roasting outside. Demand is building for a thirst-quenching beverage and no other vendors (supply) is in sight. You've scouted the street corners and you've got an instant monopoly waiting for you. So, you put some money into it by buying some lemons, a stand, some signs, paper cups, water (to mix with lemon juice), sugar, etc. to produce your best tasting lemonade. At this point, your startup went from zero (neutral financial position) to negative, as you prepared to open. Once open, you get some customers to stop by on their way to and from town, and they start buying your lemonade. You begin to make some money (profits), and then your hockey curve begins to rise and rise until it breaks through the total of all of your historical fixed costs and continues rising. For simplicity sake, I am not including variable costs (these are the actual on-going costs to produce and sell each 'nth' cup of lemonade).

The model is simple, yet many people forget how long it may take to go from neutral, through negative results, to break out into profitability. To help you best prepare for any launch and growth, you should become familiar with the above models, so that you can identify the general peaks and troughs where your business will journey through. Diving deeper, from product design, through development, deployment, refinement, growth, and eventually plateau/stagnation/demise/re-invention, it will become paramount that at each stage, you identify the constantly changing needs: people, product, promotion, capital requirements, publicity, partnerships, and psychology needed to get to the next inflection point.

When I think back on all of the startups that I have been a part of, while in the trenches, it was ridiculously hard to know where we were at, as I could never put a title on exactly every phase. One day we would be in ideation mode, and the next day in business development mode, and the next day in product design mode, and the next day in hiring mode. A giant mess from A to Z and back to A.

But I do know now that there were definitely phases of growth, and similar patterns, and that if I could have better understood what each chapter was going to more or less be structured around, I would have been able to plan for our needs better. Clearer planning can help you overcome the obstacles that seem to crop up at just about every stage. One day it will be that you are totally out of cash, and that you should have not paid that invoice just because it arrived in the mail. Sometimes delaying that payment by a few days before your deposit will clear or before the next credit card cycle begins will save you, literally. Knowing when you really need to make that hire, versus knowing when, if you spent a few days reading about a subject yourself, could save you the trouble of paying someone to do the basic entry level stuff, and reserve that hire for the more advanced product design/build. These are just some examples of timing and knowing what's coming up next in the life cycle of your startup.

Finding Product-Market Fit:

One of the underlying elements that drives each phase and progress of a startup is Product-Market Fit (PMF). According to a great article written by Tren Griffin posted on Andreessen Horowitz's blog a16z.com, "The product/market fit (PMF) concept was developed and named by Andy Rachleff (who is currently the CEO and co-founder of Wealthfront and is a co-founder of Benchmark Capital). The core of Rachleff's idea for PMF was based on his analysis of the investing style of the pioneering venture capitalist and Sequoia founder Don Valentine[28]." As Andy Rachleff explained:

First to market seldom matters. Rather, first to product/market fit is almost always the long-term winner." "Time after time, the winner is the first company to deliver the food the dogs want to eat." "Once a company has achieved product market fit, it is extremely difficult to dislodge it, even with a better or less expensive product.

PMF may not specifically be a quantitative metric, but it is commonly used among investors to qualitatively determine and rank where a company is at in their startup's engagement with a market, often referred to as "traction". By understanding PMF, investors are better able to gauge when to write checks, when to hold out a bit longer, and when to pass.

Griffin quotes famed Venture Capitalist, Marc Andreessen, co-founder and general partner at Andreessen Horowitz (A16Z), "product/market fit means being in a good market with a product that can satisfy that market."

In my opinion, your goal should not only be to get to product-market-fit as fast as possible — so that your business has the highest chances of survival — but also understand *what propelled you* there.

Again, there is no mathematical formula that says if A event + B event + C event occurs, then that equals a PMF percentage of D. However, as a founder, there is a growing sense of the amount of connection that your startup is experiencing when you have a fast-growing customer base, the marketing channels that you are using are yielding the best return of any you have tested, investors are agreeing with you on your traction and willing to write checks, and customers are raving about your product to others. Sometimes it takes twelve to twenty-four months to get to product market fit, and other times you just never get there.

To illustrate PMF, and how it evolves over time in correlation to both the activities that are needed and the cash on hand required to perform those activities, see the figure on the following page — a fictitious example of a startup dating app I created called Love Birds.

Love Birds helps U.S. collegiate students connect with each other in a fun, playful way by gamifying the courting process to win a date that uses your intelligence, not just your looks (as other apps do). Users download the free app, answer mini questions about each other, and as they answer more and more correctly, they unlock access and win a date! The app is downloadable for free on the app stores and will be launched as a freemium model — free to download and use, with up-sells costing $1 per unlocked question (to bypass them) if the user either answers incorrectly or wants to skip to the next question to win that date.

In figure 11.1 (Product-Market-Fit Analysis)[29], even though there is no firm calculation that drives the percentage of PMF, the chart is to be used as a heuristic that helps you see the correlation between PMF, cash on hand (vis a vis fundraising or sales), and the milestones that demonstrate inflection/traction. As you can see, PMF remains at zero percent during the initial four months of product design, research and development. Once launched, between months five and twelve, the estimated PMF percentage rises to just over twenty percent, meaning they have demonstrated a potential market and have a small, but growing number of paying subscribers. Between months fifteen and eighteen, a venture financing round is received, and that event marks a significant step in proving to investors the demonstrated traction. In months nineteen through twenty-four, as subscriber revenue increases, another round of financing is secured, and the percentage of PMF rises from sixty to ninety percent, thus signaling PMF might be achieved.

If you are part of a startup that has yet to find PMF, you'll know it. Some of the calling signs when you have not reached PMF are:

- Challenging time defining who your target customer is.
- Challenging time understanding where to spend your marketing dollars for the most effective return on investment (ROI/ROAS).
- Low ROAS (return on ad spend) on your marketing campaigns.
- Low checkout conversion rate on your e-commerce store (less than 1%), above average would be 2%, good would be 3%, great would be 4%, and superb would be 5% or higher (in most markets).
- High attrition rate of early adopters or infrequent repeat purchases.

- Low customer referral rate (Net Promoter Score®, NPS, that I highlighted earlier, can define this). If your metric is under 50 you should deem your PMF as low, if 50-70 it would be ranked as good, and 70+ as outstanding. NPS measures the willingness of a customer to refer your service to another person, by ranking 1-10 on a scale. 1-7 are detractors, 7-8 are passives, and 9-10 are promoters. Your goal is to get 9s or 10s, suggesting higher PMF.
- High customer returns, negative online reviews, frequent customer phone calls, too many sales objections or pre-purchase questions.

What are the Phases of a Startup's Growth?

1. Problem Identification/User Empathy:

In this phase, you are using the Insightrepreneur method to listen, ask, and understand to gain insights into friction points, underserved customer cohorts, and market dynamics to isolate the top problems that a given group of people are experiencing. You are not jumping to solve them or monetizing them — you are just emotionally and objectively evaluating, documenting, and understanding how they interconnect.

2. Solution Ideation:

In this phase, you are building off of your findings of the problem identification and user empathy phases and ideating on potential solutions to various problems. Again, you are not getting caught up in the monetization phase or business model, just mapping a solution to a problem and ranking them in the order of most critically important to solve vs the nice to solve ones.

3. Initial Market Research/Product-Market-Fit (PMF):

Here, you are conducting one-on-one interviews and gaining feedback on a prototype version (wireframes, paper mockups, presentations, etc.) that highlight current pain-points and proposed solutions. You are seeking product-market-fit so that your proposed solution fits well with the specific user type(s). If not, then you refine and adjust until it starts to hypothetically solve user pain.

4. Solution Refinement for Prototype/Alpha:

In this phase, you are refining the initial prototype version or alpha version. You may have launched a private or even a public alpha version. Yes, there are bugs and yes, it likely sucks, but you are not trying to win a medal. You are proving a thesis of observation with a draft of a solution. Do your utmost to quickly refine the product here as you collect feedback.

5. Resource Collection to Develop Prototype/Private Alpha/Skills Building/Team Building (Recruitment):

In this phase, you are planning out all of the key resources that you need to execute in the first six-to-twelve months of your startup and launch version 1.0. You are talking with the most important people first — engineers, product designers, a technical co-founder or an operational partner depending on your needs. If you can recruit just one or two people here, it is often better than four or five because sometimes too many people early on can ruin the startup soup. Teams of three are typically the best — A businessperson, technical co-founder, marketing/sales/business development or specialist like a scientist, chef, PhD, etc., depending on your market and needs.

6. Incorporation/Legal Setup:

In this phase you are having uncomfortable conversations with your co-founders or initial hires, by splitting stock and determining the legal structure. Get a proficient lawyer who specializes in business law or even better, startups. There is a lot to cover in this phase: Incorporation, Meeting Minutes, Corporate Charter, Voting Rights, Stock Issuances, Capitalization Tables, Legal Structures (C-Corp, S-Corp, LLC, LLP, B-Corp, Non-Profit, etc.). Have equity conversations openly, honestly, and early on with co-founders and early employees. Set up an ESOP (employee share option pool) so that early employees have options that they can buy into at a low strike price per share. Plan for future financing rounds with your attorney so that you have a sufficient amount of common (or preferred) stock, and that you are incorporating in a startup friendly state - DE, NV or CA are the common ones.

7. Prototype/Alpha Testing for User Feedback/PMF Targeting:

In this phase, you have launched the prototype, or alpha version to the public, and are working out the kinks, removing bugs, and are attempting to on-board as many users or early adopters as possible. The goal is not monetization (yet). The goal is either first to market position, attaining product-market-model fit, and/or disrupting a market with a radical solution. You will be experimenting a ton here — different marketing copy, price points, product feature sets, advertising channels, A/B testing, recipes (if cooking) & packaging.

8. Product/Service Refinement:

In this phase, you are building off of the earlier release, and are adding incremental releases that solve earlier bugs that pissed customers off. You might be developing some internal tools, systems, or processes to solve bugs, reach out to companies to win new sales, or figuring out if you need to pivot and change your model, price point, product, feature set, market or distribution channel. Pivoting is ok, and I encourage you to pivot early and iterate as often as you need to.

9. Resource Collection to Develop the Beta/v1.0/Open Business to Public/Team Building (Recruitment):

In this phase, you are getting increasingly better at solving a customer pain point, delivering value, and are building early customer evangelists that spread the word about your product. You're launching a Beta or version 1.0 of your product and have a good grasp on the target customer, market, solution, and cycle of the machine that you have built. You are now thinking ahead and looking to hire that great operations manager, that killer sales lead, or that Rockstar engineer — to help you scale. To do so, you may need venture capital, so you start preparing your financial docs, investor deck, and map out who could be the right Angel or VC firm(s) to partner with. You begin networking your tail off and start lining up meetings with associates and partner investors if you can, to whet their appetites for a VC round.

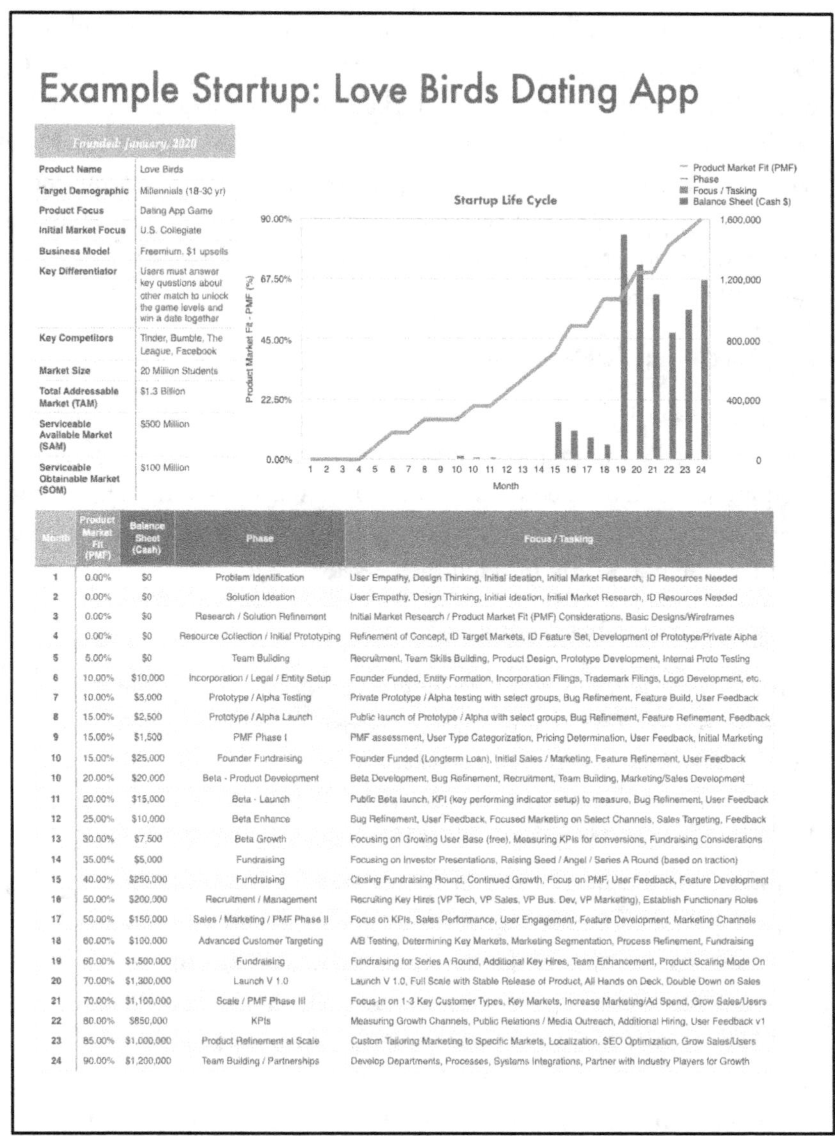

Product Name	Love Birds
Target Demographic	Millennials (18-30 yr)
Product Focus	Dating App Game
Initial Market Focus	U.S. Collegiate
Business Model	Freemium, $1 upsells
Key Differentiator	Users must answer key questions about other match to unlock the game levels and win a date together
Key Competitors	Tinder, Bumble, The League, Facebook
Market Size	20 Million Students
Total Addressable Market (TAM)	$1.3 Billion
Serviceable Available Market (SAM)	$500 Million
Serviceable Obtainable Market (SOM)	$100 Million

Month	Product Market Fit (PMF)	Balance Sheet (Cash)	Phase	Focus / Tasking
1	0.00%	$0	Problem Identification	User Empathy, Design Thinking, Initial Ideation, Initial Market Research, ID Resources Needed
2	0.00%	$0	Solution Ideation	User Empathy, Design Thinking, Initial Ideation, Initial Market Research, ID Resources Needed
3	0.00%	$0	Research / Solution Refinement	Initial Market Research / Product Market Fit (PMF) Considerations, Basic Designs/Wireframes
4	0.00%	$0	Resource Collection / Initial Prototyping	Refinement of Concept, ID Target Markets, ID Feature Set, Development of Prototype/Private Alpha
5	5.00%	$0	Team Building	Recruitment, Team Skills Building, Product Design, Prototype Development, Internal Proto Testing
6	10.00%	$10,000	Incorporation / Legal / Entity Setup	Founder Funded, Entity Formation, Incorporation Filings, Trademark Filings, Logo Development, etc.
7	10.00%	$5,000	Prototype / Alpha Testing	Private Prototype / Alpha testing with select groups, Bug Refinement, Feature Build, User Feedback
8	15.00%	$2,500	Prototype / Alpha Launch	Public launch of Prototype / Alpha with select groups, Bug Refinement, Feature Refinement, Feedback
9	15.00%	$1,500	PMF Phase I	PMF assessment, User Type Categorization, Pricing Determination, User Feedback, Initial Marketing
10	15.00%	$25,000	Founder Fundraising	Founder Funded (Longterm Loan), Initial Sales / Marketing, Feature Refinement, User Feedback
10	20.00%	$20,000	Beta - Product Development	Beta Development, Bug Refinement, Recruitment, Team Building, Marketing/Sales Development
11	20.00%	$15,000	Beta - Launch	Public Beta launch, KPI (key performing indicator setup) to measure, Bug Refinement, User Feedback
12	25.00%	$10,000	Beta Enhance	Bug Refinement, User Feedback, Focused Marketing on Select Channels, Sales Targeting, Feedback
13	30.00%	$7,500	Beta Growth	Focusing on Growing User Base (free), Measuring KPIs for conversions, Fundraising Considerations
14	35.00%	$5,000	Fundraising	Focusing on Investor Presentations, Raising Seed / Angel / Series A Round (based on traction)
15	40.00%	$250,000	Fundraising	Closing Fundraising Round, Continued Growth, Focus on PMF, User Feedback, Feature Development
16	50.00%	$200,000	Recruitment / Management	Recruiting Key Hires (VP Tech, VP Sales, VP Bus. Dev, VP Marketing), Establish Functionary Roles
17	50.00%	$150,000	Sales / Marketing / PMF Phase II	Focus on KPIs, Sales Performance, User Engagement, Feature Development, Marketing Channels
18	60.00%	$100,000	Advanced Customer Targeting	A/B Testing, Determining Key Markets, Marketing Segmentation, Process Refinement, Fundraising
19	60.00%	$1,500,000	Fundraising	Fundraising for Series A Round, Additional Key Hires, Team Enhancement, Product Scaling Mode On
20	70.00%	$1,300,000	Launch V 1.0	Launch V 1.0, Full Scale with Stable Release of Product, All Hands on Deck, Double Down on Sales
21	70.00%	$1,100,000	Scale / PMF Phase III	Focus in on 1-3 Key Customer Types, Key Markets, Increase Marketing/Ad Spend, Grow Sales/Users
22	80.00%	$850,000	KPIs	Measuring Growth Channels, Public Relations / Media Outreach, Additional Hiring, User Feedback v1
23	85.00%	$1,000,000	Product Refinement at Scale	Custom Tailoring Marketing to Specific Markets, Localization, SEO Optimization, Grow Sales/Users
24	90.00%	$1,200,000	Team Building / Partnerships	Develop Departments, Processes, Systems Integrations, Partner with Industry Players for Growth

Figure 11.1

10. Fundraising (Seed Round):

In this phase, you are hunting for capital. You've got a somewhat stable version of your digital product or have a physical product in a dozen or so retail stores, or have your experience being enjoyed by hundreds if not a few thousand users — all depending on your business type. You're busy planning to raise funding and have worked with your lawyer to determine the right structure for the round — debt, equity, or convertible debt or S.A.F.E (that converts into equity at a later date). You have your cap table ready and have looked at a few scenarios for what your team's equity might look like based on various valuations and financing amounts. You may be raising an early Angel round or a Seed round depending on the PMF and traction you have, and growth prospects. With new capital under your belt, you're able to ink a few more new hires, and better match the product, marketing, business model and customers together — hence PMF increases.

11. Development/Refinement:

In this phase, you have raised a round of financing and are continuing to experiment with your marketing and are refining the product or service based on user feedback, analytics, and A/B testing. You begin to ignore the things that are not working and focus in on the things that are truly moving the needle.

12. Pre-Launch Marketing/Sales:

In this phase, you are again drilling down deeper into your customer journey, removing friction points, increasing your conversion rates, and optimizing your marketing messaging.

13. PR Announcement for Launch:

In this phase, you are seeking publicity and editorial write-ups to publicize your company, product or service. The more attention you get now, can either make or break you — depending on how prepared you are for it. Make sure your website can handle all of that traffic if you get picked up by a national news outlet. Make sure you can order sufficient inventory amounts if all of a sudden, a big customer wants to order a few pallets or a full container of product. Make sure you can hire that special new team member if she reads your article and expresses interest — if you wait for too long, she will get picked up by a competitor or another firm.

14. Launch of Beta/v1.0/Open:

In this phase, you have launched your product fully to the public, and have nothing to hide. You are focused on delivering value, increasing your customer base, finding early partners to help scale your user numbers or give you added value or publicity. You've come a long way to get to this point and should be proud to have taken an idea to market. Now, the salesmanship begins.

15. Marketing/Sales/User-Feedback/Product Refinement/PMF Narrowing in around 1-3 Key Groups:

In this phase, you are continually refining the product, differentiating against competitors who may be cropping up in the market, attending trade shows, and soliciting feedback from users on what features or products to launch next. You have eliminated the "service every customer at all cost" mindset and are really focusing in on the one to three that matter most, who have the most satisfaction with your brand, and who provide the greatest amount of revenue or future growth potential.

16. Measuring Data/Sales/PMF/A/B Testing:

In this phase, you are using data to drive your actions. You are no longer operating solely on hunches and user conversations, but are really leveraging technology to track, test, and adjust your product to best fit of the market. You are using analytics to adjust the marketing copy, price points, packaging, feature sets, and ultimately shape of your company. This helps you differentiate and optimize for future growth.

17. Refinement of Product/Service to Enhance Marketing/Sales Process/Operations/Development Cycles for Effectiveness/Team Building:

In this phase, you have a good grip on where your business is at today, and so you begin to focus on team building and developing processes within your organization that help you accomplish more, at a faster pace. You hire an operator or VP of development who helps structure the company, process, and deliver more traction at a faster clip. You are no longer a startup seeking to get to market, you are a company seeking to increase your market share.

18. Fundraising (Angel/Series-A) planning (as needed):

In this phase, depending on your balance sheet, cash flow, and overall scaling goals of your startup, you may need to raise an institutional round of financing. Again, you go back to your projections, investor presentations, and networking your tail off to get you your Series A round. It may take several months to close a round of funding, but you're on your way to becoming a fast-growing startup.

19. Team Building (Recruitment):

With a fresh round of funding under your belt, and a greater percentage of PMF, you start hiring people to fill the various management roles that you will need to run each division — (CTO, VP of Sales, VP of Business Dev, VP of Marketing, etc.). The goal is to remove yourself as the CEO of everything, and have these people take the reins to hire, manage, fire, and report back to you.

20. Scaling Considerations (defining key channels for marketing/ identifying key growth markets/defending competitive barriers):

In this phase, you shift from a survival mentality — whereby you solely focus on the launch and survivability of your startup — to that of a developmental mentality. Your goals and priorities, while still focused along the lines of delivering increasing value for your users, morphs into one of long-range scale. You start to ask your team — what's blocking us from amplifying our results by 10X or 100X? How can we double our business every quarter? What resources — people, platforms, products, partnerships, publicity — do we need to scale the model out regionally, nationally, and ultimately globally?

21. Partnership considerations:

In this phase, you have identified the key elements to scale, and are approaching them with fervor. Your role, as Founder and CEO, is to step back from the day-to-day operations when possible, so that you can bridge new relationships with vendors that can add better products, resources, and support for your company. You are also seeking distribution partners where your service is a value-add to their offering, so that you can leverage their breadth and scale by standing on the shoulders of giants. You may be needing to raise another round of financing soon, so inking key relationships and partnerships now, can set your squad up with an inflection point that will help you close a Series A or bank loan as needed.

22. Fundraising (Series A/Bank Loan) planning:

In this phase, you are increasing the PMF and thereby, the valuation of your company. You may have some revenue coming in, or at the least, have compounding month-over-month user growth — either of which might land you a deal with a private financier or institutional investor.

23. New Product Feature Build/Product Refinement:

In this phase, after you have raised additional capital, you go back to the drawing board to continue the build-out of new features, new offerings, add locations, and other expansionary developments that further increase your market share and organizational reach. You may be launching ancillary products or entering new markets, but the goal here is to use the added capital and PMF that you have built in the initial channel to hit the ground running in follow-on launches.

24. Additional PR/Social Media Community Building/Customer Engagement Events:

In this phase, you are leveraging the power of public relations, newspapers, social media, contests, and other coverage and/or brand activation events to build traction with your enterprise or consumer segments. Your goal is to establish yourself as the clear-cut leader in a space — that space can be local, regional, national or international.

25. Team Building (mini teams/departments/developing operational workflows, systems, protocols, and improvements):

In this phase, your management team begins setting up formal structures, workflows that guide the innovation process — design, development, testing, feedback, iteration, budget approval, launch, marketing collateral, refinement, etc. You are continually striving to decrease operational costs, increase operational output, and minimize product downtime, bugs, customer returns, refunds, and more.

26. Scaling - Doubling down on marketing in channels that work best, A/B optimization, elimination of features as needed for growth, CapEx investments for growth, additional PR:

The goal in this phase, is to say to yourself, "Look, we've got a proven model, we've got the team, we've got some funding under our belts and a runway, now we're going to drill down on the unit economics and really strive to ween ourselves off of investor capital and skate towards profitability." For every company, every market, and every product/service, scaling means something a little different. You might be looking to scale the proven model within a specific industry vertical — say the retail space. Or you may be looking to expand into a regional market, say distributing your new coffee drink to the Pacific Northwest by way of a regional grocery chain or distributor. Scaling can even mean hiring an extra fifty people to help in various segments of your business — you might need an extra fifteen back-end engineers, ten front-end designers, five inside sales reps for the West Coast market, and two C-level executives.

27. Continual feedback from customers to improve the product, divisional growth, off site or remote offices/workers, localized marketing budgets, SEO to drive growth, data analytics to monitor KPIs (key performing indicators):

Our job, as a founder, is never over. Our job just morphs from one challenge to a different looking one, as we gain traction, PMF, and financial capital or sales. One thing should always remain a constant — seeking unbiased feedback from users and integrating it to improve your offerings. Even at this stage, with all of your success, if you start ignoring customers, you'll quickly be out of a job. At this phase, we are drilling even deeper than before to uncover patterns among all users, to help us drive innovation at a product level, that we can deploy to select users or site wide to all. We are breaking up specific markets into user cohorts and putting feet on the ground in various markets to help on-board them, convert more paying customers, and scale out even further. We are monitoring our KPIs, so that we understand what campaigns and product features truly move the needle for us, and we start to focus in on specific growth areas that set us up for the future.

28. Replacement of key people with more experienced veterans to scale faster and more effectively:

It's not a secret that skillsets are like tools, and tools are good for getting jobs done for specific purposes, at different times. Sometimes when you build a house, you use a hammer. Other times you need a screwdriver. And other times you need a professional electrician. The takeaway is this — the people you hired twenty-four months ago, may have expired in the skills department. They were awesome at building the first version or two of the software, but now, running a department of fifteen people requires managerial skills, financial planning, and a willingness to hire and fire people, which might not get so well with your buddy Chad who was the Rockstar coder on the alpha and beta sites. You may need to up-skill Chad, or move him to a different squad, or, sadly fire him. Sorry Chad, you still get your stock options.

29. Scaling Continues:

For some companies, growing from startup to fully fledged business is the furthest they'll go. For others, the journey never really ends. For companies that raise venture capital, the journey usually involves regional, national and international expansion, coupled with increasingly larger and larger rounds of financings from Series B, C, D, E and possibly an IPO or acquisition. While I won't get into the specifics of those, because if you are in that territory, you will have counselors, investors, and advisors all guiding you on what to do next, I will tell you that the scaling journey should always continue. You don't always need to grow bigger, expand more retail sites, or spread yourself across four continents, but you do need to scale your offering, stay modernized with your marketing and distribution channels, and stay close to the customer to remain top of mind and continue to win. Notice that an acquisition/IPO are not a part of this list? Don't get distracted by thinking about a liquidity event until you get later down the road.

Your job is to ideate, develop, launch, scale, hire, and grow — all to create as much PMF and user value as possible in as short amount of time as possible.

The more you prepare for each successive phase of the startup journey, and understand the correlation between PMF, cash on hand, and successive growth phases, the faster you will be able to focus on the things that actually move the needle.

CHAPTER 12:
UNIT ECONOMICS

What does it *really* cost to acquire a new customer, and how long do they stay with us as a *paying* customer? Marketing to acquire new customers is expensive, and customer retention is the key driver for growth for most companies. As a general rule, for many businesses across various industry verticals, repeat customer purchases drives growth rates, gross margins, and offsets the initial investments in sales, marketing, administration and operations. Why? Because if you just win one sale, then you just win one sale. The cost of acquiring that one sale is usually a lot higher than you actually think. We call that cost, the CAC, or Customer Acquisition Cost. When that customer converts from a one-time sale to a repeat sale, then we call that period the CLV, or Customer Lifetime Value, or as we reference herein, LTV, or Lifetime Value of a Customer.

When I think of early-stage startup marketing, one of my favorite business professors and advisors, Bob Caspe, comes to mind. As a successful tech entrepreneur turned business consultant, Bob has been in the startup trenches more times than most founders can dream of. I asked Bob when a founder should start thinking about marketing and the cost to acquire their first set of customers, he astutely replied:

> My observation is that for most, the problem is in the cost of customer acquisition. Think of selling your product as a process of "buying" a customer's behavior. You need to spend some money in marketing and sales to provoke a transaction with a customer. And, how much you pay to acquire each customer can determine the difference between your survival or bleeding to death.

> In fact, my experience is that the hardest part of starting a new business is finding and convincing customers to buy. Yet, virtually all entrepreneurs leave the process of sales and marketing to the end of their development cycle, preferring

first to finish their product. At first glance, this seems logical. After all, you can't sell from an empty wagon. It makes sense that you need a product to show before you can go out there and sell. Well, nothing could be further from the truth!

My advice to start-ups is that it's never too early to engage with real customers to test whether the value that you propose to deliver is adequate to pry the money from your customer's clenched fists. It's not until you ask for the money that you will truly test their resolve to not share it with you. And, having the product is irrelevant. In fact, it's a distraction. Because it's not about the product, it's about the value that is delivered. The customer doesn't really care "how you do it," they really simply want to know "what's in it for them?" or if you can do it, what will it cost? In the best of all worlds, a purchase decision by a customer can be conditional upon your delivery of value when you finish the product. This is how Kickstarter works."[30]

CAC: The total cost to acquire a customer.

LTV: The total value (revenue/profit) received by the customer.

CAC and LTV are one of your most important metrics, or KPIs (key performing indicators), that you will need to be aware of in both the assumption phase (business planning/projections), as well as in the actual launch and scaling phases. The formula — the ratio of LTV to CAC — determines the amount of profit that each marginal (nth) new customer provides to your company, hence, how much growth potential you have without additional marketing costs.

When CAC is higher than you anticipated, then you will spend more money acquiring each new customer which puts a strain on your margins and operating cash flow to keep forging ahead. When the CAC is lower than you planned, that's great, however, it is really only ideal in the right proportion to the LTV for that customer segment.

Revenue vs. Gross Profit LTV/CAC:

If we are calculating just the accumulated total of revenue that a customer, over its life, delivers for a business, that metric is only half of the battle, as it does not take into consideration the true cost of servicing the customer, also known as, Gross Margin.

So, while you *can* use Revenue to calculate LTV in your ratio, it might be more accurate to also look at Gross Profit-based LTV. Many investors believe a scalable ratio for LTV:CAC is 3:1. For every one dollar you spend, the business yields 3 dollars in return. If your ratio is less than this, then you are likely acquiring customers for far too high of a price (and may be running losses), and if you are operating at a ratio of say 5:1, you might be growing *too* slowly, as you are leaving customers on the table that you could be acquiring if you spent more on marketing to scale faster.

Again, this is a heuristic, and each business, market and business model requires refinement to find the proper ratio. Often times companies that can clearly articulate their LTV:CAC, can prove to investors that they understand how the business cycle works and how capital is efficiently spent and returned. Enough with words, let's show you some numbers so you get the picture.

Example Coffee Company: Bob's Java

For a simplified version of this, let's say at Bob's Java, owner Bob decides to put a coupon ad in the local newspaper. That ad costs Bob $1,000 and will run for one week. That ad then yields (over a testable period that he is tracking, say one month), one-hundred new customers in week one who walk in and present the coupon, with more to follow. Each of those customers buys, on average, $10 worth of a coffee and a bakery item. For simplicity, let's just track this one campaign who uses that one coupon and ignore any other customers that might buy.

<u>Sale 1: Week 1</u>   <u>Unit Economics:</u>

- Ad Cost: $1,000
- # New Customers Acquired: 100
- Revenue: $10 x 100 orders = $1,000
- CAC: $1,000/100 customers = $10.00
- LTV: $1000/100 customers = $10.00
- LTV/CAC: $1000/$1000 =   1
- **LTV/CAC Ratio:**   **1:1**

Let's assume half of the customers return from the same ad coupon because they're locals and had a positive experience at Bob's.

<u>Sale 2: Week 2</u>   <u>Unit Economics:</u>

- 50% Repeat Customers: 50
- Recurring Revenue: $10 x 50 orders = $500
- CAC: $1,000/150 orders = $6.66
- LTV: $1000/100 + $500/50 = $20.00
- LTV/CAC: $1500/$1000 =   1.5
- **LTV/CAC Ratio:**   **1.5:1**

<u>Sale 3: Week 3</u>   <u>Unit Economics:</u>

- 40% Repeat Customers: 40
- Recurring Revenue: $10 x 40 orders = $400
- CAC: $1,000/190 orders = $5.26
- LTV: $1000/100 + $500/50 + $400/40 = $30.00
- LTV/CAC: $1900/$1000 =   1.9
- **LTV/CAC Ratio:**   **1.9:1**

<u>Sale 4: Week 4</u>   <u>Unit Economics:</u>

- 30% Repeat Customers: 30
- Recurring Revenue: $10 x 30 orders = $300
- CAC: $1,000/220 orders = $4.54
- LTV: $1000/100 + $500/50 + $400/40 + $300/30 = $40.00
- LTV/CAC: $2200/$1000 =   2.2
- **LTV/CAC Ratio:**   **2.2:1**

- **<u>Totals:</u>**   **<u>Unit Economics:</u>**
- Ad Cost: $1,000
- Total Revenue: $2,200
- Total Gross Profit (50% margin): $1,100
- **Revenue-Based LTV/CAC Ratio:**   **2.2 = 2:1**

- **Gross Margin-Based LTV/CAC Ratio:**   1.1 = 1:1

In figure 12.1 by the second sale, the LTV is higher than the CAC. As you continue into the future by sale three and four, the LTV drives higher than the CAC. Obviously, there is churn (customers deciding to stop buying), so that is factored in here, as 100% of customers on day one dwindled down to 30% by week four. As you project out further, that figure may fall more, or might level off at 30% retention, therefore if it does stay at that, then you know that after four sales, you have won that customer over and that they should continue to provide your business with a positive return. Nothing lasts forever, but as you can see in figure 12.1, an initial $1,000 advertising investment goes to a positive ratio via repeated transactions despite a churn rate of 70%.

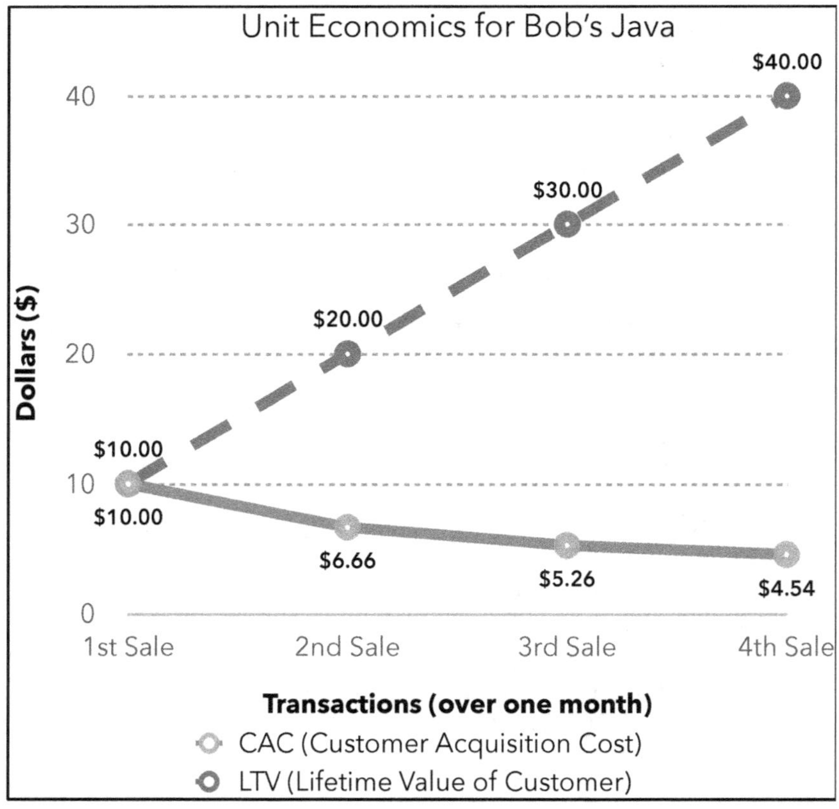

Figure 12.1

In our oversimplified example, LTV grows larger over time with repeat transactions from one ad campaign. In reality, you will continue to invest in marketing and usually (hopefully) over time, your targeting gets more effective and cheaper as you become more efficient where you spend your ad dollars — possibly you negotiate lower ad costs for a longer-term commitment — thus, CAC *should* reduce over time. LTV *should* also naturally increase over time as you get better talking with customers and creating goods and services that add value for them week in and week out. For some businesses, they simply don't have a lot of the same, repeat customers (e.g: funeral home might only sell your family one service, an airport bookstore might only sell a traveler a book once, a hotel might only have you stay there once, etc.) For most SaaS businesses, e-commerce businesses, and retailers, they do have a sizable percentage of repeat customers.

In an advanced (more accurate) version, add in all of the other operational, sales, and administrative expenses that you must spend to acquire a customer, and that sum can give you a more holistic picture of the true *aggregated* CAC. You might also add in other new sales that come in from referrals or play with the numbers to increase or decrease the total amount each customer spends on their second, third, fourth or nth sale, as they may decide to buy a few extra items each time as they come to know and like your food offerings in the coffee shop. For simplicity sake, I want you to see that there is CAC, LTV, and a relationship between the two that you must monitor closely.

LTV:CAC Ratio:

1:1   Considered a "poor" business model (loses money as it scales)

3:1   Considered a "good" business model by most.

4:1   Considered a "strong" business model by most.

5:1   Considered a "very strong" business model by most. Might also signal the business could invest more in marketing to acquire customers to scale faster (are they leaving opportunities on the table?).

**The goal is to have your fully loaded CAC (all costs included)
decrease over time, and have LTV *increase*, so that there is a
widening gap between the two. The gap represents your growth
potential and ability to profit from customers.**

What does LTV/CAC look like in the eyes of leading Venture
Capitalist? As Ryan McDonald, Vice President and Principal, at
Norwest Venture Partners (a leading venture and growth equity
investment firm managing more than $9.5 billion in capital)
explains:

> Quality of revenue is one of the most important traction-based
> metrics to me. Growth, market, proprietary advantages or IP,
> team and other factors are all incredibly important and also
> very obvious. Everyone is looking at these. But often times,
> investors value revenue and revenue growth at face value
> without taking into account the deeper properties of that
> revenue. How difficult was it to *sell* this revenue? Even if it
> was low cost, making the LTV/CAC metrics look good, did it
> take three years to win the contract? Is there something
> inherently off with the margins? Maybe gross margins look
> good, but there is a lot of embedded SG&A [selling, general &
> administrative] cost or CapEx [capital expenditure] associated
> with serving this customer. Maybe the revenue is great, and
> margins are solid, but there is no real stickiness to the revenue.
> Are customers, either B2B or B2C, going to pull away from
> your offering once they have extracted full benefit from it?
> Will you be undercut on cost when a competitor offers an
> inferior, but much cheaper offering? Just because it is
> recurring, or SaaS, does not necessarily make it valuable
> revenue!"

To highlight LTV and CAC examples, let's look at some
software companies who have shifted away from a perpetual license
of selling software once, such as Adobe® and Microsoft®, to a
recurring monthly subscription. Why? Because the lifetime value of
a monthly subscription far exceeds the former fully paid license. By
selling in smaller increments on a monthly basis, they end up
keeping the customer for a longer runway. Sure, companies claim
you always get the latest version of their software with a recurring

subscription which is true, and you do pay less in total dollars each month, but more over the course of one year hence, they net a higher LTV from you.

Tien Tzuo, Founder and CEO of ZUORA® (NYSE: ZUO), outlines in his prescient book Subscribed[31], what the future of the Subscription Economy® (his trademark) will look like. He postulates that more and more companies are shifting away from a capital expenditure (CapEx) (up-front big cash outlay) for tangible or intangible investments like new software, hardware or machinery — to an on-going, pay-as-you-go model, that becomes an operational expense (OpEx). This is a 180-degree shift from the past, as an on-going subscription model is a win-win for both the service provider and client, as it eliminates the need for long sales cycles with RFPs (request for proposals) that take months to close, big budgetary approvals, and upfront capital investments with long payback periods. Instead, subscriptions provide a better balance between service provider and client, centered around usage, on an on-going basis over years, not around a one-off sale based on capturing gross margins.

Tzuo highlights numerous industries outside of Silicon Valley and beyond SaaS that are realizing huge gains and longer customer lifetime values because of this radical business model approach. Moreover, this shift from a one-time sale to an on-going relationship helps the customer's balance sheet retain more cash, eliminates a large, one-time up-front investment in technology that may need to be replaced in a few years when those systems become obsolete, eliminates the on-going client-side maintenance, upgrades, system integrations, and expensive and time-consuming, on-site training.

For a coffee shop, could it be better to get a customer on a monthly recurring subscription such as an all you can drink coffee card for $50 per month ($600 per year) that guarantees consistent revenue and pre-payment up-front at the start of every month? Conversely today, the coffee shop opens and prays for walk-in traffic, starting each month with a zero cash balance and no guarantee that any new or repeat customers may walk in to order.

Shifting your model from a one and done strategy, to a lifetime relationship model built around your core customer(s), puts your business in a different ballpark — one where LTV becomes your secret long-term advantage, and removes the need to compete day in and day out simply on gross margin to win one sale.

CHAPTER 13:
CAPITAL

There comes a point, when you've successfully formulated your team, developed and deployed a product that is getting market adoption, and when revenue starts coming in. If you're not at this point, then you need to go back to check on the basics: team, product, market, business model, marketing, and pricing. So here you are, revenue is coming in as top line sales, and you've got your expenses managed, so you're creating sustainable growth. Remember, Sales minus COGS (cost of goods sold) equals Gross Profit. Profit fuels future growth, providing your expenses are in line to yield a positive net income.

There's a formula that was popularized by Venture Capitalist, Brad Feld[32], which he calls the "Rule of 40". While this works well for SaaS (software-as-a-service) companies in particular, it may apply to your startup. The Rule of 40 says that a metric for determining the scalability of a startup is having any combination of the following three scenarios. By using a blend of revenue growth and EBITDA (Earnings Before Interest, Taxes, Depreciation, Amortization), investors can gauge if a business is ready for a break-out inflection.

Scenario 1: 40% Sales Growth* + 0% EBITDA = 40% growth

If you have this scenario, then it may be acceptable to have zero EBITDA, because it is assumed that the company is growing so fast with new customers that it is plowing the income back into the business and its marketing activities.

Scenario 2: 20% Sales Growth + 20% EBITDA = 40% growth

If you have this scenario, you're balancing new sales growth with healthy gross margins, and managing your fixed costs well as you scale, thus, a positive EBITDA.

<u>Scenario 3</u>: 50% Sales Growth Rate + (-10%) EBITDA = 40% growth

If you have this scenario, you are growing even faster than 40%, but you could be losing money on your margins by offering discounts to attract more customers, or, something else like rapidly hiring or investing in marketing and sales aggressively to become the market leader. Thus, you could have a net loss in EBITDA, but still could mean that you are fundable as you are growing so fast that eventually you can find a way to manage the cost side of the business and correct net income out.

Sales Growth: Year over Year or Month over Month

EBITDA: Earnings Before Interest, Taxes, Depreciation, Amortization

I think the Rule of 40 is a great quantitative goal, that for some companies is a compelling metric to monitor growth and be able to convey in a smart, packaged answer to investors. However, while these above figures are helpful references when you are making money, they can lead you to develop a myopic view of what success should look like for your business.

For investors, whether they admit this or not, they are always longing to invest in the clear-cut winner take all in a category.

That means the most return on their investment in the short and long term, so in essence, they could be willing to invest in a startup that is growing so fast despite having a net operating loss or even a carry-forward net operating loss (meaning continual, consecutive losses that aggregate). The rationale being, is that any market worth investing in, will need to be growing quickly and getting big — at least $1 billion or larger usually. When they invest $50-$100 million in a company across a Seed round, Series A, B, C, D, they are betting on a 5x-10x return on that investment, meaning, they need an exit of $250-$500 million dollars. If the total market size is only $1 billion dollars, an exit worth the valuation of 50% of the market is not realistic.

Finding markets that are worth multiple billions are more attractive for most venture investors. The returns required in an exit (liquidity event for their Limited Partners) forces the math on this.

For Angel investors, a $1 billion market might work well for them, and investing in a company that can ultimately achieve 15%-30% of that market will yield a sizable return for them.

During my days in both WML and LaDolceDeal, I focused on a blend of things that I thought would yield traction. Some did, and some just didn't move the needle. So, let's define traction a bit further.

So, What's Real Traction?

As Angelo Santinelli, a leading business consultant (Dakin Management) and former Venture Capitalist (NorthBridge Venture Partners) advised me, "Traction is not vanity metrics, like [the] number of subscribers or active users. Traction to an investor means one thing and one thing only — significant and consistent sales growth."

To you as an entrepreneur, traction could look like:
- **Making a few key hires**
  - Hiring a well-known CTO, Co-Founder, Engineer, VP Sales, etc.
- **Building a workable prototype**
  - If it is a product that will actually be launched, used and tested, then it's solid.
- **Launching version X**
  - Deploying a Beta, MVP or version 1.0 or 2.0 on schedule.
- **Getting a sizable number of early adopters**
  - Signing up 100-100k users depending on if you are B2B or B2C.
- **Getting paying customers**
  - Repeat customers are the best, because you can prove retention, hence CLV - customer lifetime value.
- **Getting big publicity**
  - Getting featured in a major publication, on TV, in a journal, at an industry leading event, or speaking on a reputable panel.
- **Inking a key partnership**
  - Signing a partnership/license agreement with a well-known client.
- **LOI - Inking a Letter of Intent**
  - Getting written commitment from a Customer, VC, or Supplier.
- **Raising a round of capital**
  - Closing a round of financing/crowdfunding shows interest.
- **Grand Openings**
  - Opening an office space, restaurant, retail store, platform, etc.
- **Getting a Key Board Member/Advisor**
  - Attracting a respected A-Lister to your Board

- **Being Cash Flow Positive**
  - Cash flow positive and paying yourself shows sustainability.
- **Growing by the Rule of 40**
- Any of the three outlined earlier proves traction to most VCs.

What's Not Real Traction?

Don't fool yourself with these common traps. I should know, I've done most of them!

- **Perfecting the Business Plan**
  - Ideas are cheap, validated assumptions are valuable, proven results based on executed assumptions are priceless. Business plans are un-tested guesses. You must validate them!
- **Pitching to Those Who Love You**
  - Pitching your idea to close friends, family and colleagues — "But everyone says they like it!" - Unimportant, they're not buying.
- **Designing/Redesigning the Logo/Mission Statement**
  - Okay Picasso, this isn't an art contest, now start selling!
- **Chasing Potential XYZers**
  - Potential people in a startup are worse than none — potentials suck your time, fill you with false hope, and derail your momentum. Employees, Investors, Customers, Suppliers are either fully on board, or they're not. Run from the maybes because they'll kill you and your startup slowly.
- **The Never Ending Wire Frames**
  - This is a slippery slope. You spend nine months instead of one building the world's most beautiful wire frames of your new app, site, product, etc. People don't buy wireframes, they buy products. Investors don't invest in wire frames, they invest in products with massive potential or proven results, and employees don't work for you just because you have a beautiful sketch.
- **Chasing Vanity Metrics**
  - It's easy to get delusional when your site goes from zero to 1,000 visitors in a day. They may be competitors checking you out, Russian bots called phantom metrics juking your Analytics, or potentials (see above). Unless those clicks convert, forget them.
- **Winning Business Plan Competitions**
  - Here's a debatable one. Competitions judge presentation skills, ideas, and high-level metrics. You might be able to win despite having any real traction. Teams who enter business plan competitions are looking for validation that their idea is worth pursuing. The best validation comes from paying customers who continue to buy from you. Some competitions pay you small amounts — $10k-$50k — which is helpful, but the effort required to win is usually better served plowing back into your

startup to enhance the product, attract and retain customers, and scale.

- **Getting Validation from "Experts"**
  - By design, experts have deeper knowledge of a market over the average person. However, experts can often have a myopic, one-sided view of how things are in a space, what's possible and not, and where the industry's headed. If you're chasing idea validation from veterans in a space, you're either sharing your insights which is not wise, or you're looking for something else that you think they will give you — added credibility as you lack it in that space (the inexperienced often see the space's biggest opportunities), referrals to key customers, investor capital or warm intros (rarely happens), new key insights (why would they share these with you — unless they are part of your team or have equity?).
- **Chasing after Publicity**
  - This one is tricky. Sometimes press is a catalyst. Most often, it's a flash in the pan for your biz, and a mega boost to your ego for about a month. If you're chasing press, you're not chasing customers, and you usually aren't worthy of the press just yet anyway, right? If the press is chasing you, you're focused on customers, and usually worthy of the PR (however you're so busy, that you'd rather scale, than get publicity for vanity sake).
- **Credit Card/Payday Loans/Bank Financing/SBA Loans**
  - Anyone can rack up credit card debt with high interest rates to pay for stuff today, but it's hard to pay it all off if you don't get enough profit to pay it off later. Pledging your house as collateral for a loan, while totally ballsy and laudable (that you're willing to risk it all in pursuit of your vision), is usually not financially prudent. A balance sheet with little debt is an entrepreneur's/ investor's dream. You'll sleep better at night, the investor won't have to take more of your company in equity to offset the added debt, and everybody wins. Don't let easy cash from debt sources fool you into thinking that's traction. That's debt in disguise.
- **Pre-launch E-mail Signups**
  - While it is great to have a large prelaunch list, unless they convert soon, that list is pointless — they won't pay bills. Sure, you can convince investors that one thousand people just signed up because of a Reddit® or ProductHunt® post you did, but that may not convert into revenue.
- **Early Customers Out of the Gate**
  - This is another deceiving one. The day I went live with WML, we got our first sale (the customer decided to buy a three-month subscription instead of a one-month subscription), and I thought, wow, he is willing to pay more therefore he must really think there's value here. Hooray! Wrong. People test things out, and

often managers would rather try things for a few months and not one month so they don't see another bill on their statement, and also, they're so busy doing other things so they may not have time to check your site out for a few weeks. This doesn't necessarily mean they're *hooked* on your product. Look for continuous on-boarding, continuous subscriber/payment growth, repeat users — these are more indicative of traction versus the few who bought the first day you went live. There's usually a trough that follows right after, and while you may have a few thousand bucks in the bank and are on a startup high from the get-go, remember this is a marathon, not a sprint. People who often are leading in the first five minutes lose the race to others who build over time.

What's an Investor thinking if I say we have traction?

- **Founder**: "Here's our mock-up website, don't you love it?"

- **VC**: "Just because you created your first version, doesn't mean much, frankly. What do you want a medal? It's your job to create, it's my job to fund scalable ventures. We need a working prototype to persuade our team to cut a check. Validated proof of concept, growing users, and/or revenue helps. Do you have that?"

- **Founder**: "Well, our prototype isn't quite launched yet."

- **VC**: "Having a working product is a basic requirement of being a startup. How can I invest in something if it is only a napkin sketch?"

- **Founder:** "You should invest because the SF Chronicle® just featured us!"

- **VC**: "So you've just received a write-up in your local newspaper? Cool. No medal yet either. Why? Because PR comes and goes. People read something today and forget about it when the next beer arrives at the table."

- **Founder:** "We just launched our private Beta! Check it out here [insert URL]"

- **VC:** "Thanks for e-mailing me that link to your buggy Beta with no users yet. Keep me in the loop on your progress while you grind so I can see how far you can go without my capital first. While not investable today, I won't tell you "No" straight up, but might say "Keep me posted" for months to years. This keeps my investment options open if you begin to get hot so I don't shut that door completely on the next Unicorn."

- **Founder:** "We just got a blurb in TechCrunch®. When are you free for a meeting to fund our Series-A?"

- **VC:** "Did your PR stunt result in 10,000 new signups on your app? Now we're getting warmer to something applaudable here. Talk to my associate; he'll screen you for me and let me know if this is worth thirty minutes of my time or not."

- **Founder:** "We just stole this engineer from Apple. We're in scale mode now!"

- **VC:** "Okay, so you've managed to convince a software engineer from Apple to spend weekends helping you build out version 1.0 of your app for 10% equity? Congrats. Still, I am not investing in Apple, and you've got the beginnings of something compelling, but nothing solid just yet. Keep me posted on your progress."

The "Keep Me Posted" VC E-Mail Trap:

Beware of this line "Keep me posted" or "Keep me in the loop on your progress" — this is investor code for I am not interested today, and unless you start to get really hot, or I fear missing out on funding the deal, I will use this phrase instead to give me optionality and keep you feeding me updates. VCs rarely just say "No" outright. God forbid they miss out on the next Airbnb®, Uber®, Google®, Box®, Stripe®, etc. They'll never hear the last of it from their partners or LPs.

So, listen up, here's one of the biggest Catch-22's in entrepreneurship history: How the hell do you build and launch a company without funding, but how do you get funding if you don't have anything? Ah, the entrepreneurial Catch-22.

Try to avoid raising capital until you have a workable product in hand, and ideally, have at minimum $10,000 per month of recurring sales, or 10,000 users.

But how do I hire someone without any funding? The only way to get that product finished is to put on your salesman/

saleswoman hat and start convincing the technical folks you need to help you build it. That's where your compelling story becomes vital. If you are building software, know that engineers like tough problems that have meaning or a cool factor. Example, "If you join my company, we will be creating the world's first technogadgetgizmo that will disrupt the entire cloud computing business and render it archaic. Want to join the adventure?" For social or consumer facing ventures, they have to attract talent in the early days in a different way, by creating and portraying meaning. For example, "Here at Social Handbag Co. we think *differently* about fashion. We believe fashion should always have a conscience, and our bags should give back to society. That's why for every bag sold, we donate ten percent of our profits to this cause because at our core, that's what we stand for."

To build something requires people, and people require convincing. Getting investors requires a working product, traction, compounding sales, or a growing number of users, and that requires the former too.

I think you should only consider raising capital when you are in the strongest possible position to negotiate. The whole job of an entrepreneur is to *flip* the power paradigm to make investors jump to fund you. The only way to do that is with proven traction demonstrated over a short time horizon.

When you are growing and moving fast, investors sense it, and want to join the ride before the train passes them by. Typically, the strongest startups don't need to sell their companies, their traction speaks for itself. The weakest companies, or ones without much traction, often do much of the hyping and have the biggest smoke and mirrors up. I should know. I have had both types. Which type would you rather have?

As a rule of thumb for me, I think if you are a free app, you shouldn't try to raise money until you have at least 50,000 to 100,000 downloads or installs. If you are a consumer product or e-commerce business, I don't think you should try to raise money until you have $10,000-$20,000 in recurring revenue every month. When you have less than that, clearly you don't have market dominance and are still figuring out who your customer is and what channels and promotions work the best for acquiring customers. For B-2-B startups, I think having at least 25-50 B name companies subscribing to your service or at least 10 A name customers, or at least 3-5 Best in Class customers (if you say Google and Walmart® are our two biggest customers, the floor is yours, and so is my checkbook). Every business is different, so timing traction to know when you've got a hit on your hands is like trying to determine when you're ready to move out of your parent's house — you just know when it's time because it feels right.

If you are raising venture capital, the investor is the supplier [of capital], and the startup is the customer [buying capital]. Don't be fooled, it's not the other way around.

The best startups don't need funding, rather VCs have to sell or supply the capital to them. The cost of capital is paid out in equity (not cash). This is how you must think. If you think, oh, I only wish we could get funded, and beg for dollars, you are thinking as a supplier begging a customer to buy from you what they don't want. You have it backwards. Investors are the suppliers, and startups are the customers — spend your equity wisely in exchange for capital.

Lastly, not all financings cost you, the entrepreneur, the same amount of equity. With preferred stock, caveats like protective provisions, liquidation preferences, valuation caps, warrants, anti-dilution provisions, ESOP percentages, vesting schedules and more that are written out in the term sheet (contractual document signed between investors and startup), the amount of stock that you own today, and in the future, can vary greatly based on various scenarios. If you are not careful and have good counsel, you can easily sign off on a deal that leaves you with very little to nothing when your company sells for millions. When you have multiple offers, you have optionality, and can choose the right financing to fit your needs. You can compare different outcomes to create a win for you today and your future. For more helpful information on venture capital finance, please refer to the wonderful book Venture Deals[33] by Brad Feld and Jason Mendelson.

CHAPTER 14:
BOTTLENECKS

A bottleneck, as I learned in my Organizational Behavior/ Technology Operations Management course at Babson, is a blockage in a specific area of your operation that prevents output or increased growth. It can be a piece of the manufacturing process where all of the movement in your factory comes to a screeching halt, and thus, needs to be improved, modified, or removed in order to restore the output to normal levels, or, to increase the levels as defined by management.

I have observed that there are four key bottlenecks outside of those in manufacturing, that are less visible to the operator, but if left unchecked, can stymie the company's growth prospects. The four include emotional bottlenecks, intellectual bottlenecks, financial bottlenecks, and social bottlenecks.

Emotional Bottlenecks:

Emotional bottlenecks are elements inside of your heart, mind, and subconscious, that filters what comes in, what is blocked out, synthesized, and then affects how you engage with the world.

An emotional bottleneck could be something as simple as a negative feeling that you are harboring deep inside of the recesses of your soul, that once scarred you, and is now preventing you from taking decisive action today. I can think of a few situations that were emotional bottlenecks that once prevented me from taking swift action and created self-doubt in my abilities to implement some of my ideas.

Early in the development of WorldMusicLink, when I was 20, I invited a classmate of mine to join me and my family in California for Thanksgiving dinner. During that week, his family was already vacationing out West visiting his sister and decided to take me up on my offer and drove up to see us all. We went to lunch one day, and after mentioning to my friend my concept for WML, he quickly shot it down in front of our lunch table, proclaiming that it simply couldn't work, that it was no different from MySpace®, which was the category default for musicians to promote themselves to fans at the time. His sister, in my idea's defense, seemed to see my vision, as she was an aspiring actress in Hollywood, and had also faced a similar challenge of promoting herself to entertainment executives and managers who could accelerate her career, so she could see how this could be a helpful resource for those inside the industry, not just another band-to-fan platform, like MySpace. Despite my attempts to convince my friend to see my vision, he became even more self-convinced that my idea could never work, and instead of politely backing down, became steadfast to prove me wrong with examples and facts.

In my early days as an entrepreneur, I was simply too emotionally fragile to handle such feedback. I viewed the criticism as a personal attack on me, and not the concept at hand. That lunch emotionally scarred my entrepreneurial spirit for a number of months, and in the aftermath, I realized, that there is a difference between constructive criticism and an unhelpful public scoffing. So, I made it a point to not share my business ideas with those who wouldn't immediately praise them. In retrospect, removing friends and people from your life just because they may disagree with you is the wrong thing to do. Underneath it all, I'm sure my friend wanted me to succeed, but his approach to feedback could have been a bit softer.

When you're launching your first startup, it's important to hear feedback, and actually I would encourage you to find people who can really poke holes in your assumptions — but you need to ensure that these people deeply have your best interests at heart; they want you to win and want to make sure you have covered all of the bases for your idea, business model, investors, markets, etc. to be the best fit. Furthermore, you need to be *emotionally* prepared to hear criticism, and most importantly, get it from people who will actually be using your product, not just from friends or family. *Never* let feedback emotionally scar your creativity or ability to forge ahead.

On your entrepreneurial journey, you will meet lots of different people. Some will love your ideas, most won't care, and a few will cast doubt within you. You can't get wooed by the applauses, you need to learn to move past the apathetic, and most importantly, you must remove your own emotional bottlenecks from blocking out constructive criticisms of your business ideas (providing they have your best interests at heart).

Intellectual Bottlenecks:

The old adage, "What you don't know can kill you," sort of speaks to this, but I like to think of it as, "What you don't know can kill your business, quickly." When you start your first company, there will be a million different things you just really have no clue how to do, some of this is content based (the type of knowledge that can be acquired with research), some of this is experiential (the type of knowledge that you must experience first-hand to understand what to do when and how to do it), and the last type is hypothetical (the type of knowledge that you can never acquire as that situation could never have been planned for or predicted).

Learn to develop an appetite for knowledge, more specifically, technical, motivational, and managerial knowledge that will catapult you and your business to new heights.

You can get this from library books for free, the Internet, forums, blogs, magazines, and from advisors and other entrepreneurial mentors. Some of my favorite inspirational sources, while not exhaustive include Tony Robbins[34] <u>Awaken the Giant Within</u>, Deepak Chopra[35], Paul Graham[36] (Co-founder, Y-Combinator), Peter Thiel's <u>Zero to One</u>[37], Guy Kawasaki's <u>The Art of the Start</u>[38], and Robert Cialdini's <u>Influence</u>[39]. These books range in scope from personal empowerment, helping you break-through limiting beliefs to those that help you see the bigger picture in your life and startup, to detail oriented, that help you create a game plan for your venture. As an entrepreneur, we need a little bit of all of them to see our vision clearly, execute effectively, and lead others successfully to the finish line.

Some of the best advice I ever received came from entrepreneurs who have had both failures and successes — as

they shed light on what didn't work, why, and what worked well. Those stories saved me from walking into a lot of landmines.

The more you know, the cheaper things become to purchase and run, and the faster your business will accelerate, as you will be able to leapfrog the knowledge curve to a new level of the startup game in an exponential fashion, not a linear manner. Experiential knowledge, you may have from other jobs that you have worked in, or from running a different business in a different sector, and let's face it, sometimes you may just never have it. That's okay too.

In startups, inexperience can unlock unique insights.

Let inexperience be the muse from which you explore new possibilities with a fresh mindset. Hypothetical bottlenecks are those in which you could never have planned for — a situation or event — but now, it's you who must figure out a plan of action. Be open to learning.

I also encourage you to not get caught up in the "what would happen if *this* happens" planning mindset, but rather let events come as they may. My father used to tell me, "Too much planning is like a drug." You may have heard the other expression "Over-analysis leads to paralysis." Both are true. If you can increase your knowledge base in the area that you are launching into, great, do it — only you and your business will gain more horsepower to run faster. If you can find excellent mentors, advisors or partners who can guide you with their experienced viewpoints, then do so, they could save you big bucks when you need it and can help you shape your vision.

How might your inexperience today, see things differently, to become the new way of tomorrow?

Financial Bottlenecks:

Financial bottlenecks can make or break your business. Either you have the cash to pay for growth, or you don't.

Most businesses actually go out of business because of cash flow problems, not because of product, leadership, or marketing. Cash is king, but in startups, *cash is life*. The moment you lose it, you're either begging for investment and giving up equity, paying exorbitant interest rates, or filing for dissolution.

Cash, on any balance sheet, is the first line item that provides the most liquid form of solvency. The more cash on hand, the more you can fund growth, borrow from lenders or raise from investors, and the better you will be able to meet payroll and payables each month.

Let's say you launched a new coffee shop and have a record year. You started with zero in sales and grew it to $100,000 in 12 months. Great work! It's now year-end, and you're celebrating by opening up that bottle of champagne on New Year's Eve, but come January 2nd, you owe your coffee bean supplier ($5,000), have to pay the rent ($5,000), and also have to cut payroll checks ($5,000), totaling $15,000, but you only have $7,500 in the bank. There is no way you are going be able to pay your supplier, and meet payroll, *and* still have a storefront to walk into tomorrow with your current cash balance. What to do?

One way might be to run the invoice for the beans on a credit card that will extend your real payment date for another thirty-days and net you 5000 reward points worth a $50 credit, pay the $5,000 to meet payroll so you don't lose your employees, and take the balance of $2,500 and hand deliver 50% of the rent check to the landlord, explaining that the balance can either be paid by credit card today (if he'll accept it), or in a week when more cash becomes available. This is a tough situation to be in, but founders need to be creative and vigilant in who they pay when, why, and how. No one likes to be out of cash, but it is often a recurring situation for many companies small, medium, and large. This is where cash flow comes into play and will become your most critical component in the early days, and arguably every day, for the life of your business's life.

The key takeaway on cash flow is to visualize it like the oxygen of your business — it comes and goes — but a sufficient amount is always required to stay alive and healthy.

How to Manage Cash Flow:

Before launching a business, map out the most important elements of your cash flow — staff, rent, main suppliers, advertising, insurance, taxes, etc. Next, determine the average monthly cash balance that you might need based on your particular startup. Think of it this way, what's the bare minimum amount of cash on hand that you need to operate this business successfully? If you fail to prepare for cash flow, as I have done in the past with my first startup, you'll quickly get into a cycle of cash crunches that force you to delay payroll, halt advertising, layoff people, and miss important milestones on time. Add five to ten percent onto what you think your bare minimum cash requirements might be to provide a small cushion at all times.

While most news articles, magazines, and stories focus on garnering a higher growth rate, revenue and profits are actually historical records used for accounting purposes and don't tell the story of the *current* financial health of a business — cash flow does.

In the first 24-months, founders need to worry more about cash flow than sales or profitability. The timing of cash inflows, the net cashflow (inflow minus outflow), and implications of cash flow are the pillars that drive future sales and trigger an ultimate profit.

Let me show you an example of a startup with poorly timed cash flow, and one with a well-timed cash flow.

Startup A: A Poorly Timed Cash Flow Company

Founder Bob pre-buys all inventory, stocks every flavor of coffee in large quantities to take advantage of a 10% savings from the vendor, pre-pays for advertising every month in the local newspapers and buys a twelve-month package that gives him one month free, thinking it is the best rate. Then he hires a few more employees because they're minimum wage students and he thinks they're cheap labor.

By buying everything up-front, he drains most of his cash reserves, and banks on the advertising to drive sales. By having every flavor of coffee in his new shop, he thinks that that is the key differentiator against Starbucks® and other coffee bars in town, but all of that excess inventory, even at a 10% discount, drained even more cash. By hiring a few extra employees, even at minimum wage, he reasoned his retail shop was prepared for any surge in traffic to deliver outstanding customer service because he read that that is why coffee customers keep coming back (repeat sales). To the contrary, he over committed to his cash obligations to meet payroll taxes, wages, increased insurance, and other benefits, all that drained cash. This startup will soon run out of cash, as they have loaded their books with liabilities and operating expenses, and not retaining cash or revenue.

Startup B: A Well-Timed Cash Flow Company

Taking a different approach, founder Tonya decides to test the market for her coffee before she commits to ordering in bulk from her vendor. A deal on inventory is only a deal if it actually turns over and sells, netting a realized savings, not a hypothetical savings, she figures. She conducts sample taste tests by standing outside of her shop and giving out free samples that she received from her vendor just by asking for a few sample bags of beans of each style. After about 150-200 taste testers, she determines that of the twenty available roast varieties (flavors), there are four that resonate the best with her local market — Colombian, Mexican, Kona, and French Roast. The rest she decides are not worth stocking initially, until the market demand warrants it with another taste test.

Next up, instead of pre-buying a year's worth of advertising in the local newspaper for a one month free trial, she calls up the publisher, explains she has a new coffee shop, and negotiates to pay for a three month ad spot to test out three different ads with coupons on the grounds that the newspaper will also come by her shop to write up an editorial story and review with a photo for the new business and food sections, thus garnering her business added publicity with an A/B marketing test opportunity to determine what ad has the highest return. Finally, instead of hiring three extra baristas even at minimum wage, she secures agreements with the three to work on an on-demand basis if the shop has a spike in traffic. She offers to *double* the minimum wage, with the caveat that they must make themselves available within a one-hour time frame from when she calls them to come into work — they all agree as the offer is too sweet of a deal to turn down. She figures, if she has a spike in customers walk in, she'll have the cash flow to pay the extra staff for the day even at higher wages.

By avoiding all of the up-front inventory bloat on the balance sheet, Tonya streamlines the decision-making time for a customer when ordering, thus, decreasing the through-put time from arrival to payment. If she had over twenty options, as Bob choose to do, it would have caused customer indecision and could have created an operational bottleneck. By only stocking four coffee roasts, she pleases the majority of her patrons, while only rejecting a small percentage of those who don't find the other varietals in stock, but in so doing, preserves cash by sticking to a smaller menu.

By testing out three ads in the newspaper over a three-month term, she saves more cash and determines the best performing ad which sets her up to sign a long-term contract with the publisher knowing that the best ad will truly drive foot traffic. And finally, by not hiring extra labor (even though they were a bargain initially), and by offering to double their wages on an on-demand basis, she ensures her business has staff should the traffic surge over an anomaly busy weekend. Tonya has prepared her business to be cash flow solid.

There are countless examples of companies, even with hundreds of millions of dollars in annual revenue, who go bankrupt because of poor cash flow. They buy too much inventory, even though they have terms with their suppliers, and the inventory doesn't turn over fast enough. They expand too quickly and acquire more properties, draining cash, instead of improving the margins or sales of their existing locations. They over hire, thinking that more people will grow the business faster, then run out of cash and can't meet payroll. Toys-R-Us®, Sears®, Gibson® Guitars, The Great A&P Supermarket® chains ring a bell? Cash flow affects both the startup and the 100-year-old, multinational juggernaut. No one is immune to the perils of cash flow.

Whatever business you are embarking on, think about the *timing* of cashflows to prevent bottlenecks from taking you by surprise. Always keep a 5% contingency fund of cash in an account just in case you need to use it, and always have backup credit on your cards or a revolving line of credit from a bank, that you can use in a pinch if necessary. Defend yourself from the cash flow crunch!

My 5% Rainy-Day Fund:

If possible, it's prudent to save 5% of your sales and put it into a rainy-day fund — so if you have $100,000 in sales, reserve $5,000, if you have $1,000,000 in sales, reserve $50,000. While this is only 5%, it can be an immediate, interest-free lifeline when you need it.

Imagine if that big customer of yours is late in paying you by three weeks on a big order you fulfilled; this happens more often than you might realize. Despite what payment terms you have negotiated with them, customers often pay later than terms allow. If you can't meet payroll, payables, or rent due to cash flow, you're toast.

My father used to tell me, "All businesses have good pay, slow pay and no pay. Good pay we all want, slow pay we all have, and no pay puts us out of business." Have a reserve to temporarily provide working capital at zero interest. If you have to borrow working capital from a lender, it can easily cost you 10%-30% in interest *plus* take days to complete the paperwork and get approved. If you really want to get smart, invest that 5% in an interest yielding reserve like a three-month CD (Certificate of Deposit) or MMA (Money Market Account). While this does tie up the cash based on the term of the instrument, you can make interest on it while it sits idle. If you are concerned about liquidity, you can ask your bank if they can provide you with a high yield savings account or checking account that has a higher interest kicker. At least this helps offset the depreciating cost of inflation (2%-3% per year) while the money sits ideal in your rainy-day fund. At the very least, the peace of mind in knowing that you have thousands of dollars in a rainy-day fund will help you weather the little cash-flow ups and downs that you will face over and over again. If you are raising venture capital, you might also consider apportioning 5%-10% into a rainy-day contingency fund to ensure you have working capital at all times and won't have to go back to your investors for an emergency bridge loan.

Social Bottlenecks:

Social bottlenecks are in a category all of by themselves. The expression, "It's not *what* you know, but *who* you know" should ring a bell. In the startup days, there are key people who can help catapult your business to new levels, but unfortunately, they're outside of your immediate network. There are key customers who you haven't sold yet, who, if you did, could open many more doors for you and prove to the world that your product was a winner. There are suppliers who you don't know yet, that can lower your costs, improve your margins, give you better payment terms, and deliver at a faster rate than your current ones. There are VCs and Angel investors who you haven't been introduced to, but if they could only hear your pitch, might just invest and open the doors for more investors to join them. There are incredible editors at leading publications that should you get a warm introduction to them, would love to write an editorial review on your startup. Struggling to find that perfect software engineer to help you build version 1.0 of your idea? There are folks just outside of your network who know that person who is looking to join the next big thing.

These are all social bottlenecks. They go back to your ability, or more frankly, your *inability*, to break into better, more quality social circles — customers, suppliers, investors, media, and employees — at every level that can accelerate your venture's growth.

Make it a point to become a super connecter, force yourself to be more extroverted, and seek ways to not only grow your network, but most importantly, enhance the quality and depth of the relationships within it.

Enhancing the Quality of Your Social Network:

In the days of WorldMusicLink, when we started out, I only knew a few folks in the music industry. My network consisted of my former guitar teacher, Steve, and a part-time musician friend, Gabe, who was also a graphic designer. This wasn't a good start for a business networking portal that claimed to be the hub of the music industry that was going to help you connect with everyone and anyone, right? I realized that my own issue of finding the right folks in the music business, had to become my company's leading attribute.

So, what did I embark on doing? I leveraged social media (Facebook, MySpace, Linkedin, blogs, forums) to find thousands of new connections. I would ask people to invite their friends into the website and in return, would give them free access to a premium account. In terms of advisors, I was running a music company with no music leaders on our board. This was not a good start. I listened to the advice of my business mentor and friend Glenn Kaplus, Adjunct Professor at Babson College, to find music industry pros to place on an advisory panel. I followed suit and on-boarded Dr. Rob Klevan (former Director of Education at the world-famous Monterey Jazz Festival). After Rob joined, I moved onto the second, Bob Jamieson, famed Record Industry titan, Babson alum, and former Chairman and CEO of RCA Records® BMG North America. With Bob aboard, he introduced me to Tamara Conniff. Tamara had just left her post as the Executive Editor of *Billboard Magazine,* and was tapped by famed Music Industry icon Irving Azoff, Chairman of Live Nation®, to run Frontline Management, the artist management division. With Tamara on board, we had fleshed out the music side of our industry panel, all while ensuring that we placed other key advisors with complimentary skill sets, different networks, and from different, yet supportive backgrounds — legal, software, and venture capital.

The credibility that each advisor provided to our business's idea was impressive, but more importantly in my opinion, was their personal advice. Each helped introduce us to better quality (more connected, more experienced, more reputable) people at different stages of our growth. I couldn't have done this by myself, in that record time, and to that degree of success without them. A warm introduction to someone new is about the best introduction that you could ask for. For us, it was pivotal to getting us the seal of approval from the music industry, getting the media to take us seriously, and getting customers to trust us with their careers from day one. I owe a lot of our early traction to our Board of Advisors.

You ever wonder why venture-backed companies seem to become so successful so quickly? Let me tell you, it's not just the capital they raise. Sure, the money helps them buy credibility, office spaces, furniture, make key hires, etc., but the *quality* of the VC's networks is really the hidden gem of the deal. You are getting insider access to the decision makers at other companies who will be the first retail chain to give you that three-hundred store test of your new widget, that introduction to the bank President that will set up a $500,000 revolving line of credit to finance your cash flow, those warm introductions to new partners to help increase your site's visibility, etc.

Access to the *right* people, is the invisible check.

So how can the average business, that may not be interested in going the VC route, or may just in fact, not be a VC fundable business, mimic the effect that a VC-backed startup receives? Start by growing your local network. Join the business chamber of commerce, leverage your alumni directory, get out into the community and have real conversations with real people, and ask for help. I mean it, really ask them for help to spread the word about your new business. Ask successful restauranteurs, other founders, and local leaders for their advice on what to do next. Buy people coffee — it only costs two bucks, and you can gain so much knowledge and access to new networks in the process. People by nature want to help other people, and most want to see others succeed, not fail. But if you don't get out there and do your own cheerleading, you never get connected.

The strength of your business relies on the power of the network of your customers, suppliers, investors, and advisors. A strong network can overcome any obstacle, grow out of any phase, and reach success faster.

CHAPTER 15: WORLD MUSIC LINK

"It was the best of times, it was the worst of times, it was the age of wisdom, it was the age of foolishness, it was the epoch of belief, it was the epoch of incredulity, it was the season of Light, it was the season of Darkness, it was the spring of hope, it was the winter of despair…"

— Charles Dickens, <u>A Tale of Two Cities</u>

Passion:

My Father used to tell me, "Do what you love in life, and the money will follow." There's some truth in that. For me however, I discovered a passion for the entrepreneurial journey, not just the product I was selling, the industry I was serving, or the technology I was utilizing to deliver value to others. I don't believe you need to 'Find your passion and make it your business' which, is contrarian to what many business books and gurus indoctrinate. Let's unpack this notion of passion for a second, because it has metastasized rapidly in startup and corporate culture, that I think it deserves highlighting why it derails most.

What *is* passion? In one sentence, or word, if you had to define it, what would you say passion is?

To me, passion is:

____

____.

Did you write "excitement"? How about "a willingness to do something day in and day out, even without getting paid"? Did you say "passion is a specific project, like 'X' is my passion project"? We've all heard people boast about finding that. Or did you define passion as "a specific area, field, industry, or technology"?

When I look back on my life, when I was six years old, I was passionate about dinosaurs, then by nine, airplanes entered the picture, and dinosaurs became extinct to me. A year later, Legos® took center stage garnering my attention; I spent countless hours in my bedroom building forts, spaceships, and imaginary towns. By eleven, I discovered the outside world, and the art of fishing hooked me line and sinker. Another year hence and baseball by twelve, driving my first car, a used JEEP® by sixteen, cooking by seventeen, and playing golf with buddies by eighteen. It seems that every year I flew in and out of 'passion' with something radically new — a new hobby, a new game, a new sport, a new industry, a new world. So, if my interests in various industries, projects, and areas evolved over time, but my excitement to learn something new, get completely engrossed in building or doing never waned, then could it be more accurate if we re-define 'passion' as a *state of mind?*

So, am I measuring passion correctly then? Would I have been willing to do any of those activities day-in-and-day-out at that point in my life? Of course. Would I have been willing to be un-paid to build rocket ships with Legos in my bedroom, or sit for countless hours on the dock waiting for a fish to bite? You bet! I did it, therefore, I was passionate, right? I never converted any of those activities into startup companies — that was, until I discovered music.

Passion is *not* an external thing outside of us. It is state of mind within us. We must determine what triggers us into this state so we can stay there. We can be passionate about so many things.

For me in my twenties, my focus became music; writing and playing music was both my creative respite, and my instantaneous mood booster. But making a living wage as a musician was overshadowed by my fear to turn into the perpetual "Struggling Artist". So instead of going pitching thousands of demo tapes, I decided to launch a business that could help all struggling artists find success.

On February 5, 2007, I officially incorporated my first dot com startup, WorldMusicLink Corporation. My Co-founders were my mother and sister, Suzy and Christina. The experience of our initial team in the music business was little to none, and our experience prior was a far departure — product design, manufacturing, and marketing of printed balloons & accessories used by retailers and distributors.

Months before the formulation of this venture, I had been accepted to a small but well-respected business school called Babson College (Wellesley, MA). Babson had been ranked the #1 in entrepreneurship by every report in the book, so it was a no brainer for me to visit, as I had wanted to understand how I might someday own my own business like my parents. During that visit, I absolutely fell in love with the campus, the people, and their motto, "It's Possible. At Babson." To me, this was the beacon that I had been yearning for — a perfectly systematized program that would turn my messy creative ideas into focused, value-creating businesses that might just make a small dent in the world, as Steve Jobs used to refer to. I had arrived, and class was in session.

I spent my first few months attending Babson without a clue as to what kind of company I should try to launch, or if I had what it took to make an idea come to fruition, yet I was determined to try. For years prior, my mother and I had written, and performed (albeit in our living room), a series of original songs — her on keyboards, piano and vocals, and me on the guitar. One evening, after what we deemed a satiating jam session, we had the conversation that launched the idea:

"Are there any local recording studios in town who can help us record what we've got?" "How do other musicians connect with people in the music business?" These questions fell on deaf ears, as we had no idea where to look, who to talk to, or how to package ourselves so that we could garner the attention of connected individuals in the biz. We scoured online databases and websites to find a solution, but to no avail. It seemed that the missing link wasn't musical talent or ambition, rather, *access* to the right professionals who could elevate us to the next level — a social dilemma rather than a deficiency of musical talent.

This jam session was one of the last ones that we had just prior to my departure to Babson. I was nervous of traveling 3,000 miles away to live on my own for the first time, yet hopeful that the choice would help uncover some of my talents. I had been asking my family as to what kind of company could be the right one to launch at Babson — it seemed that most kids on campus, even in their twenties, were starting their very own companies right out of their dorm rooms. So, it was with this jam session, that we thought maybe, that this kernel of an idea could be a helpful solution — to match unconnected musicians like ourselves with the Industry, and vice versa. It was there and then, that a simple, yet fundamentally valuable question that we experienced doing something that we enjoyed doing — music — kickstarted my first entrepreneurial adventure.

As I've mentioned previously in the Four Magical Insights (chapter four), I experienced a deep situational or circumstantial insight that led me to discover the market need for WorldMusicLink. This type of circumstance which I call the Founder's Fumble, holds credit for many successful companies known today. If it weren't for the struggles that founders experience during the normal course of their life, work, or hobbies, many of today's greatest inventions, companies, and creations might have never materialized.

The Founder's Fumble: Questions that Spur New Ideas

- What's always blocking me from achieving my goal in this job?

- How do others accomplish this same thing? Are they right?

- What are some alternative ways this might be improved?

- Wouldn't it be cool if this [solution/experience] existed?

- What if we could… [do this] cheaper, faster, easier, more effectively, etc.?

- Can you think of another question you've asked yourself?

____?

If you have asked yourself any of the above questions, during the normal course of your life, then you might be ready to start the process of developing a new venture, whether you know it or not.

Most startups don't come with instructions [a business plan or conceptualized at Business School], rather, they happen drunkenly when you're failing to achieve a desired outcome that you think, logically, *should* exist, but doesn't. These fumbling moments are the entrepreneurial kindling where sparks are lit.

Connecting the Music Industry:

By twenty, while at Babson College, I officially launched WorldMusicLink.com (WML) a B-2-B (Business-to-Business) Social Networking Web Portal custom tailored to introducing Musicians to Music Industry Professionals and Companies. In one centralized platform, we would grant Talent exclusive access to key decision makers inside of the Music Industry, streamline the evaluation, recruitment, and booking processes for A&R (Artist & Repertoire) at Record Labels, Booking Agents, Managers, Publishers, and Venues. In so doing, the dream was to eliminate our own band's dilemma, and also, help millions of others in the same predicament.

Musicians could create a free (basic) profile in minutes, upload their music track, and set the search algorithm to start hunting for industry matches that meet their desired criteria. Play Grunge Rock in Reno and want to get booked at that hip festival in New York City for July? WML was your warm intro. Have a hot new Country act but don't know anyone at your favorite Nashville Record Label? WML might just be the link you were looking for.

To build this type of a platform, I knew I would need more than just a good idea, a business plan, and some elbow grease. The venture would require a sizable amount of funding, the right people, and a tireless amount of convincing — after all, I was only twenty years-old, and most people weren't about to hand over a $25,000 check to a kid in college to play with a startup in his free time. So, to professionalize my approach, I took the concept to my business plan writing course at Babson. From there, I pitched the idea to help musicians more effectively promote themselves and advance their careers to the class. I was able to persuade six students to help me write the original draft of the business plan for a letter grade. We were an eclectic group of twenty somethings — hailing from Indian, Pakistan, and me California — but we all shared a zeal for becoming entrepreneurs, a love of music, and a hope to make meaning once we graduated.

Validating the Idea:

The early draft of WML was centered around selling subscription packages to music colleges and music departments, who would in turn, give the subscription to their students free of charge as a career development tool for job placement. We built the financial model around this plan, and surveyed students in downtown Boston at Berklee College of Music, in New York at Julliard, sat down with night club owners, live music venue managers, and touring musicians to gauge their interest in the concept. To our satisfaction, the initial hunches that we had about the market need were correct — there was a need for musicians to better promote themselves to music industry professionals, record labels, managers and venues for bookings. Additionally, there appeared to be a need to better manage new artist submissions and streamline the booking process while finding the right matches for their markets.

There was something deeply gratifying about pitching our concept to strangers who fit the assumptive personas of our intended users, to discover that our hunches were validated. We documented our early conversations on videotape so we could later go back and review the footage, and we sent out a SurveyMonkey® poll after gathering business cards and e-mail addresses to quantify their willingness to sign up and pay. The market need was starting to materialize in front of our eyes, however the business model needed to monetize the solution just wasn't clicking with music schools. While we felt WML could be a helpful resource to sell into the career development centers, music schools preferred to rely on their paid career development officers to connect students with industry jobs. So, in essence, while I thought WML would be their savior, in essence, it was replacing the very people's jobs we hoped would buy from us!

When our business plan course was finished, we received an 'A', so we decided to submit it into the annual RocketPitch™ competition at Babson College — a prestigious event attended by the student body, investors, and potential partners. The night before the RocketPitch™, still riding high on my solid A, I was overly confident that we would win, so in my arrogant disregard for preparation, I crafted a PowerPoint® slide deck, practiced for a few hours in the library, called it quits, and hit a campus party. After one too many beers, I retired to my dorm room, and woke up to the loud beeping of my Blackberry® alarm clock. I was late! I had thirty minutes to get dressed, wolf something down, and run to the auditorium to make my presentation.

On stage, I recall looking out into the crowd of hundreds staring back at me. I began my pitch with the bravado of a true keynote speaker. But just a few slides in, with about four hundred sets of eyes on me, reality of the importance of the moment set it. The moment caught up with me and I felt like I was outside my own body watching myself talk on stage. Oh my God I thought — I forgot the market size! With only sixty seconds to finish the last slide to conclude the pitch, I said, "The market size is huge!" The murmurs began to grow louder, as people in the crowd started to question the validity of my "detailed" market analysis. All I could think about was my last statement — I was completely derailed. I concluded the pitch, and was later approached by a slender, tallish man from Silicon Valley Bank®, who offered to provide us with banking services. I was so jubilant to have *anyone* even approach me after that dumpster fire. I quickly called my father and told him the news. He asked me to ask them if they would be willing to provide a revolving line of credit for the startup. Off I went, asking the Branch Relationship Manager if he would be willing to do so. He scoffed under his breath, "No son, we don't provide un-collateralized revolving lines of credit — you would need to pledge assets like a house, or business assets to secure the line. Do you or the business have any assets?" "Not really", I replied. Not having any assets, I dismissed the rejection, and made an opening deposit of an $800 check that my mother had loaned to me for WML in my very first business checking account. The journey had started.

As the 2006 school year came to a close, I asked my business plan class teammates if they would be willing to commit to joining WML, as I was looking to run it full time. While they expressed interest in the concept, no one would commit to helping me work on the startup over the summer to move ahead. So, as we parted ways, I spend the next three months tirelessly working on the concept, refining the product design, and planning my next steps. When school started up again that next fall, I hit the ground running. The clock was ticking, and I had nine months to make my idea functional before graduation.

Alpha:

Babson was situated right next door to a new engineering school called Olin College of Engineering®, which had a policy of providing students with free tuition should they be smart enough just to get in. I somehow felt this could be an untapped gem to find my first web developer — a key piece of the puzzle that I needed to produce the alpha prototype. So, I walked over to Olin's cafeteria, sat down, and looked around the room. I recall thinking to myself that these kids were so different from the preppy, extroverted Babsonites I had come to know. I overheard whispers of math and coding — if genius had a look, this was it. After handing out my flimsy business card to a dozen or so kids, one evening I received an e-mail. Bret was a freshman at Olin and had expressed interest in possibly helping me code my first version of WML, as he had a background in software, was majoring in Computer Science, and also played piano. During the same time, an opportunity came up called the Hatchery — it was an incubator space that was awarded to a select few of entrepreneurial teams at Babson who were seeking to take their startup ideas and bring them to market. With Bret now interested in helping, I could apply.

I recall pitching the directors of the Hatchery program on WorldMusicLink. As I sat down across from the two of them inside of the entrepreneurship center on campus, a feeling of doubt cast over me. I brushed it aside, and out came my pitch. The concept to them seemed a bit fuzzy, after all, I hadn't clearly defined what exactly we were to be solving, as a social networking site is to this day, still a challenging thing to explain how exactly it solves a specific thing at face value. One director was intrigued — she mentioned a connection she had to a relative who was leading the GuitarHero® project (a very popular game at the time) in Cambridge, Massachusetts and she felt she had somewhat of a good grasp on the needs of musicians. Whether they believed in the idea for WML or more in my ability to pull it off, I'll never know — but I was *damn* sure I was going to try to convince them that I had a diamond in the rough and the Hatchery was my next train stop. They awarded me the keys to the Hatchery, and now with my own office space, computer, printer, white board, and mailing address, WML was alive. The momentum was building. I could feel it.

I met Bret outside the Hatchery one evening just before dark. I stood in front of a giant 75' replica globe which Babson had installed about 50-years prior on top of the hill as a beacon for global entrepreneurship, in front of the Hatchery. As I stood there in the cold, waiting for my next step towards destiny, I felt an electric feeling inside — an emotion that I had never experienced before. It was the amalgamation of anticipation, trepidation, and unbridled opportunity. With arms folded, eyes looking downward, and a soft tone, he emerged from the hill, "Hi, I'm Bret. I heard about your music idea, seems pretty cool." A smile grew on my face. "Hi Bret, I'm Reagan. Great to meet you too."

Over the next few months, Bret and I worked every week on WML. I paid him $100 per week, which for a freshman, was a nice little bonus for a few hours of coding work. We met up at the Hatchery on schedule, despite the weather outside, which in New England could mean a snowstorm at a moment's notice. Bret preferred to work between the hours of 10pm and 3am, often e-mailing me updates in the middle of the night to check out. I kept my BlackBerry® on throughout the night, never to miss an important buzz of his progress.

Seeing your idea slowly come to life is one of the most exhilarating experiences of my life. It's hard to put into words how much joy it gives you just to see the transformation of an idea be born into reality.

During Spring Break, I traveled to Puerto Rico for a little time off from the hectic routine of work, study, eat, sleep, work, study, eat, sleep. My phone rang, it was Bret. "I've got an idea for how we can build this faster" he said. "Ok, I'm listening," I replied. "We can use an open source program called Drupal® that has these pre-made modules and nodes that we can install and build off of. It's really cool, so streamlined, lightweight, and I think it would work much better than HTML," he said. "I'm not sure about that…I don't even know what a *node* is? But, if you think it would be easier and faster, then I'll trust you on it. Talk when I'm back next week on campus."

Bret was thrilled. He had discovered a simpler way to develop on a framework that was already pre-made for us — all he had to do was build out each mini part called a node to create a music player, a bio, and a simple messaging system. He had discovered a brand-new way to rapidly build a website on the fly — akin to a content management system like WordPress® or Shopify® that we take for granted today. It was undiscovered IT gold for us in 2006, and we just discovered it.

We traveled from messy concept to a workable prototype that laid the foundational wireframes for what would eventually become WorldMusicLink. By the end of our time together in 2007, a musician could upload her music track, title it, post it to her profile, and share it with the world. This was music to my ears. The cacophony of ideas in my head became a beautiful symphony once I saw WML live online. I could begin to see light at the end of the tunnel. We had something tangible, something real, something that we could showcase to others and the damn thing *actually* worked!

As graduation neared, I had a life-altering choice. I could submit my application for WML to join the Summer Incubator program at Highland Capital® (a prestigious VC firm in Boston), or I could apply for a corporate job at Accenture® the consulting firm or IDEO® the famous design thinking lab — two companies I had my eye on as a potential fit, should I not pursue the startup path. But something beckoned me like a Siren from the shore. I asked myself, "Why would I attend Babson, the #1 ranked entrepreneurial college in the US, and *not* try to start a business?" I calculated the downside, calculated the upside, and applied to the program. A few weeks later, just a month or so before graduation, I received a rejection letter from Highland Capital®. They had chosen another startup from the Babson Hatchery called Paragon Lake® — an online e-tailor of customizable jewelry. "Jewelry over music?" I thought to myself. The first beat of my startup had suddenly been muted.

With no job offers in hand, and no startup funding or incubator to bring us in, I turned to my family for guidance. As luck would have it, a small 600 square-foot office space had just opened up below my family's small business in California. The asking rent was $1,500 per month, and the landlord wanted a 1-year commitment for a total of $18,000. My mother Suzy and sister, Christina, believed in the concept of WML, and had seen how dedicated I had been all year long while away, so they decided to write the first equity checks that would go towards paying the office rent and getting the company going. They pooled their money to give WML a home. Westward bound we flew.

Alone in the Office:

The carpet had stains, the paint on the walls was chipping, and the space was right next to the building bathrooms which flushed every thirty minutes — but it was perfect.

With a fresh coat of paint, new blinds, and a new roll of carpet, we got the office set up in a few months. My mother, an interior designer by nature and degree, wanted WML to have "presence" when anyone walked in, and felt a custom awning hanging outside could do just the trick. The day the WorldMusicLink awning went up was one of our earliest high points. It was the dawn of reality, it was the culmination of an idea, brought to life. I quickly filled out the rest of the office with borrowed chairs, computers, lamps, and desks — all in an effort to make us appear that we were bigger than we really were.

I spent the next nine months rewriting the business plan, pivoting away from a subscription model aimed at selling to music schools, and focused instead on testing out a premium package called a PRO subscription to Musicians and Industry Professionals. I spent over one thousand hours drafting a page-by-page color wireframe guidebook to the entire web portal, so that when I did hire a web designer, they would know exactly what to build — something that I learned from my interactions with Bret. In software, there's dozens of ways to accomplish the same outcome — so without a clear path, an engineer can build the solution, but it could look different from what you had anticipated or intended. A wireframe is worth a thousand lines of code.

Beta:

I put out ads for Web Developers, but none were the right fit. I had stacks of résumés, dozens of meetings, and a handful of phone calls with staffing firms. The applicants were either too inexperienced, too foreign (meaning they did not have the proper documentation to work full time for us without an H1B Visa sponsorship), too expensive, or too far away in the Bay Area (a 100-mile, one way trip). After nine months of no solid leads, about to give up finding my Wozniak, I was referred to an engineering job board called Dice. In desperation I took out an ad on Dice for $400, which at the time was a lot to cough up. I received one applicant, one résumé, a seventy something software engineer named Tom. Tom had all of the qualifications I had been dreaming off — had worked for several startups throughout his career (most failures), had strong coding experience for both the front and back ends of a website, and had a friendly, affable demeanor coupled with a familiar Brooklyn accent — the same my father had, which put my hiring jitters at ease. Miraculously, Tom was also a local — a serendipitous find! I hired Tom after one interview, and a few weeks later offered him five percent of WML in an equity option, should he stay on for at least one year (called a cliff). He wanted to be an Independent Contractor, so he could come and go as he pleased and work remotely on his laptop. I agreed. For $35 bucks an hour, Tom was my knight in shining IT armor.

Over the next several months, Tom and I built the Beta site from scratch. We had to throw out some of the Alpha that Bret had built as it was an unfamiliar system for Tom, so he decided to code in L.A.M.P — Linux, Apache, MySQL and PHP — with the front end in Adobe® Flash® for the bells and whistles. The nine months I spent making the world's most beautiful wire frames helped guide Tom tremendously, and although he worked at a tortoise's pace, he was methodical, cautious, and happy coding all day long — all elements of a great engineer. Tom also possessed a slight rebellious "let's go for it" attitude, possibly an homage to his younger, more wild and carefree days. While on the outside he was conservative, on the inside, the code allowed him to run free, escape the shackles of age, and summon his entrepreneurial spirit to change the world, one line of code at a time.

While Tom worked off of my wireframes, I had a few pivotal roles that drove us to our next milestones. I had to prepare investor presentations, and mail out executive summaries of the business plan to prospective investors — Angels, VCs, and everyone else in between who had connections in the music industry. Tom would routinely call me over every hour or so to show me the progress he was making or point out some bug that was causing the dreaded "white screen of death" as he would call it. In the evening, I would report our day's progress to my two financiers, my mother and sister, who both now sat on our Board of Directors as shareholders.

Launch:

The months rolled by, and as we prepared to launch the new Beta, it became clear to me that we had a fork in the road. While Tom was excited to launch, there was an element of fear to release it to the world, and also an uncertainty about what would come next for him. Would the website be a hit? A flop? Would anyone even notice? Would I be able to raise investor money and hire more engineers to accelerate the dev cycle and take some of the load off of Tom? Would Tom be able to finally manage a small team of engineers?

Our launch date continued to get pushed back as bugs prevented us from hitting the publish button. We finally had to get to the point where I told Tom, "Listen, either we launch now, or we never launch. It's now or never, and I know there's bugs and it's not perfect, but we need to get this live to see if anyone even wants it." Tom agreed, and we prepared for the big day.

By then, I had built up a list of about two-hundred or so contacts that we had talked with, about two-thirds music industry pros and the balance of musicians, bands and DJs. This was our Beta launch list. I prepared the invite e-mail, ensured we were live, and PayPal® was off of sandbox mode and set to live. I pressed Send. We held our breath. The Outlook® chime rang out — ding! WML was free at last. We were free. We waited with anticipation for a response. Any response. Silence.

"Now what?", Tom asked. I hadn't planned for what comes after the launch.

Within an hour, I got an e-mail from PayPal® that we had received money. I opened the e-mail thinking it had to be spam or a mistake. It was for a 3-month subscription by Monterey Live, a local live music venue who decided to upgrade their subscription package to the PRO status! I couldn't believe my eyes. I ran over to Tom's desk with an enormous smile on my face. "Look! We did it!", I exclaimed. "We just got our very first customer!" We high-fived. Despite a fifty-year age gap between us, no one would ever know it — in that very moment, Tom and I were both 21-year-old entrepreneurs — full of life, and on top of the world.

There's something amazing about bringing an idea to life that is hard to explain. It is a duality — one of life's scariest yet most fulfilling moments. Scary, because it feels like you're on stage blindfolded waiting for someone to throw something at you. In a launch, you've reached the end of the creative build up and are unsure as to how others might perceive it and judge it (you), but pleasantly fulfilled because you have just made your small mark on the world. No matter how small a launch, a launch is a launch, and it deserves an applause.

Growing Pains:

I spent the next few months trying to secure additional funding for WML. While our subscriber base slowly grew, we worked tirelessly to weed out the existing software bugs, gain feedback from early users, and win publicity. We raised $123,000 of investor capital in an Angel seed round, including $23,000 of my own life savings, and grew it from prototype to Beta with over 3,500 subscribers on the platform from over fifty countries, including Grammy® award winning Music Producers, Grammy® nominated Artists, and a plethora of emerging new acts with enormous potential.

WML was expanding, we now had six Account Reps working the U.S. trying to sign up music companies onto the site, a small Board of Directors and eight notable Advisors. We got featured in *Entrepreneur Magazine* in a section called "Top of the Class" and had projections of $2 million in sales for year one. The stage was set for us as the next thing to shake up the Music Industry. I left college not just with a degree in my hand, but at the helm of my very own company. Was I scared to venture out onto my own instead of taking the safe route of a corporate job right out of school? Of course I was. But I was intoxicated by the dream — I just had to chase it.

While we worked at a feverish pace to promote WML across the earliest social sites — MySpace, Facebook, Linkedin — we had a growing sense that the user base was not converting into the paying subscriber base we have hoped for. I had projected that five to ten percent of the user base would convert into revenue, and based on those assumptions, that would yield five to ten paying customers for every one hundred that joined for free. The actual conversion rate turned out to be closer to one percent on both the Music Talent and Music Industry side. That meant that for every 100, we were lucky to convince 1 user to pay. Some would pay for a month or so, others might pay for a few, and the remainder would pre-pay for a year. But we desperately needed more revenue. One percent couldn't cut it.

In the height of the Web 2.0 days, an era hallmarked by the emergence of user-generated content, the VC community had adopted the position that the startups that they would fund must either demonstrate "critical mass" pre financing, or via their round, would quickly reach it. Critical mass meant that a sufficient amount of a target market was either hooked as users, or were paying subscribers, both of which justified the investment that poured into the new venture. Marketplaces with two sides — buyers and sellers — need a critical mass of users to make the ecosystem vibrant, rich in indexable search results, and financially self-sustainable. Should a market have insufficient users on either side, it creates a deficiency, and causes attrition from one or both groups. Short on buyers, the sellers leave. Short on sellers, the buyers can't find what they're looking for, and leave. Short on both, everybody leaves.

With this VC phrase burned into my mind, we continued to plow money and time into getting as many users to sign up to the site as possible. More users were better, and it didn't matter if they filled out their profiles to the degree we needed them too to be valuable to the community — it just became a race to acquire as many as possible.

After a few months of the "more is better" approach, a growing urgency to convert the community to paying subscribers became apparent. The invoices began to pile up — rent, advertising, payroll — and more kept rolling in, but revenue remained stagnant. We had grown to over 3,000 users by that point, and only one percent were actively paying. If we couldn't get more to convert quickly, we'd have to go out and raise more capital which would either dilute our equity, or, would add more debt to the balance sheet — both scenarios I wanted to avoid.

I held a Board of Directors meeting to explain the dilemma. Without venture funding we couldn't continue to support a growing user base, and we needed to show financial proof to both ourselves and our investors who would want to know what each dollar of capital investment would yield in return. It was a Catch-22 — grow and go broke acquiring new free users, don't convert and starve.

Monetize or Die:

I made the tough decision to try to monetize the community that we spent the last several months building. Tom and I walked through WML as various users — me as a fictitious Booking Agent, John from the Clocktower Agency, and he as a promising new musician, Tyler. We timed how long each step of the signup process took, and where we felt the chargeable value was in the product — uploading more than just one music track to show a full album, adding more than one photo to show our band on tour, on stage, and on album covers. We dissected the site, separated what would be basic features given for free to both sides, and what would be PRO features (paid). We restricted the messaging feature so you could now send, but if you wanted to read a response, you would have to upgrade to a PRO plan. We continued our monetization quest. If you now wanted to contact more Industry Pros, you would have to pay for the privilege. The paywall line in the code grew wider, as our urgency to monetize became our new design focus. It was no longer about building a great product; it became monetize or die trying. We were quickly losing patience in our users, as all eyes shifted to our dwindling bank account balance.

There's an interesting dynamic within a startup on the brink of financial collapse. The North Star mission that once drove you to put every customer on a pedestal fades, and a primal nature takes over — it becomes survival of the machine over the betterment of the user unfortunately. A wave of bitterness towards your once hallowed users begins to creep in, an unwavering voice in the back of your head pressing you to ignore the free users and prioritize only the ones willing to pay. You rationalize the switch — if we can't profit first, how can anyone else profit from what we've built?

No longer were our conversations centered around designing new cool features, they became monetary-driven. "Hey, can we throw up a subscribe button here too?" I'd ask Tom. "How can we make the PRO upgrade easier to see everywhere?" We had completely lost sight of the initial user, the one who may at some point convert to a paying subscriber. As with all subscription-based products or services, eventually, everyone unsubscribes. Some days it comes in waves — "We lost three PRO subscribers, dammit", I'd yell out. Other times, a week would go by, and our PayPal® would re-run the credit cards on file, and a few days later, an e-mail would come in with the subject line *Unsubscribe! Please credit me back.* "Shit!" I'd exclaim, clenching my teeth in dismay, Tom looking across the plexiglass divider at me.

I couldn't let him know where we stood financially. I knew it would make him uneasy, and I needed my engineer in positive build mode; marking off technical bugs on our bug list, thinking that all was fine and dandy. But a deathly storm was brewing, and I felt it. We needed cash, and we needed it fast.

The Hunt for Capital:

Over the next few months well into 2008, in the height of the worst global financial crisis in modern history, there I was, pitching and e-mailing my business plan to leading venture firms — Greylock Capital®, Redpoint Ventures®, Mayfield Fund®, Garage Tech Ventures®, Clydesdale Ventures®, Maples Investments® (now FloodGate Fund®), Highland Capital Partners®, Vantage Point Venture Partners®, and dozens of music companies and Angel investors — who, despite their appreciation for our early traction, were turned off by the music space after the MySpace® catastrophe.

If you're too young to remember the MySpace story, let me just tell you that it was akin to today's Facebook®, and at their height, was acquired by NewsCorp® for $580 million in 2005, which at the time was on par with today's Unicorn (billion-dollar valuation) companies in Silicon Valley. In 2006, MySpace had become the most visited website in the entire United States[40]. A year later, Facebook® overtook MySpace® and the cataclysmic decline of daily active users (DAUs) began. By 2011, the 125 million MySpace users had evaporated, the company was in ruins, and had become the shunned

social media website that people often referred to as a sad joke —
"Hey, are you on Myspace bro?" That fairy tale ended with a paltry
$35 million acquisition by famed musician Justin Timberlake, the
former N-Sync® star, for an amount less than the combined $37.8
million of VC money that was originally poured in[41] — the new
failed Black Sheep of Silicon Valley lore.

So, it was no surprise, at a time when investors were losing
their shit, and the global markets that provided most of the funds
from investors (LPs), was vanishing, that I was told "No" every
which way you can imagine. We were "Too early", we "Didn't have
significant revenues yet", "the Music Industry was no longer our
investment thesis" and most shockingly, I was told by the Artist
Manager for legends Dave Matthews Band and the Foo Fighters,
that, "[WML] seems like a cool management tool, but I don't even
know if I am gonna have a job next year!" referring to the dismal
uncertainty facing the music business.

Our goal to raise a Series-A round of $3 million began to
evaporate before my eyes. Instead, we changed our offer to a $1
million-dollar convertible note (debt that would convert to equity at
an agreed upon discounted rate one year from the date of issuance).
But, even with our growth and lofty goals, I couldn't convince
investors to open their checkbooks, and was forced to shut the doors
on WML. It turned out that the small amount of paying subscribers
we managed to salvage, just weren't enough to keep us afloat to
weather the 2008 financial crisis which ended up lasting nearly three
years.

The End of a Dream:

Unlike back then in 2008 in Silicon Valley, today, most entrepreneurs
aren't running around like I was with a five-page Executive
Summary, fifty-page business plan, and a fifteen-minute
PowerPoint® deck. Today, they're simply seeking proof of concept
with just a stripped-down version of a prototype aimed to prove out
an early hypothesis. Over time, their strategy is for customer
feedback to drive what features stay, what features go, and where
value-creating rubber hits the road — a concept called the MVP
(Minimum Viable Product), made famous by author, speaker and
entrepreneur, Eric Reis in his best-selling book, <u>The Lean Startup</u>[42].

However, for us, we just did everything the hard way as I had been taught, and what I read was the right way by business books. While I think in retrospect, we learned more about the overall startup process the long way, a process which had historically been *the* way for decades prior — ideate, write a ridiculously long business plan, form an early team, raise seed money, build a buggy product, launch, pray, and hope customers buy, today's — test first refine later — model is not only easier and cheaper, but also more effective at eliciting critical feedback. By getting up-close and personal with early users, coupled with today's incredibly insightful analytical tools, it drives faster adoption by showing founders what features customers value to solve their woes. It shifts the conversation away from what they *tell* you they want, to being able to *see* exactly what they use and what they don't with analytics.

During our WML startup days, we did accomplish a ton. We opened our first bank account, met with lawyers to incorporate the business, created an employee share option plan (ESOP) to attract potential talent, and met with more lawyers to file for a trademark registration for our logo. I pitched our startup to Angel investors and Venture Capital firms throughout Silicon Valley and heard more "Noes" than I can remember. I even adopted a corporate mascot (3-month-old, Black Lab/Border Collie puppy) to keep me company during the long, lonely days in my office, and named her Melody after the nature of our business.

We worked *very* hard during those five years. I took no salary, hired my first two employees, fired a third (*literally* twenty-four hours later after I caught him Googling how to write the very code I just hired him the day prior for...talk about awkward), and opened our first office space. I established a Board of Directors, raised a Seed round, assembled an outstanding Board of Advisors with notable executives from tech, music, business, and law, and co-designed the web portal from scratch.

After all of that work — the ups, the downs, the employees, the office, the banks, the lawyers, the Alphas, the Betas, and the customers — closing WML down was one of the hardest decisions of my life. It felt like the ultimate waste of my early career — a dream unrealized.

There's a saying in Business School — Cash is King. Well, it turns out, Cash is Life. When you burn it all, game over.

According to a 2018 SBA report[43], one out of every four businesses (25%) close because of insufficient sales/cash flow. We too, had joined the statistic.

I spent the following few years after we shut WML down thinking about all of the amazing things I had learned, what we did right, what I did wrong, and how it might have turned out differently, if only [fill in the blank]. At first, I blamed our early web developers for coding too slowly and taking too much time to remove bugs. I blamed the isolated location of our office outside the hiring hub of Silicon Valley talent. I even blamed our own users for being too cheap to cough up a ten-dollar subscription that was the one thing they kept telling us they only dreamed of having! I blamed everything, except myself.

Every entrepreneur with a failure under his/her belt has at least a dozen excuses as to why the dream never materialized.

Getting Honest with Yourself:

The only person that was truly responsible for the failure was me. Bitching about a lack of resources was my number one excuse. Not being *resourceful* enough was the root cause of my internal failure that came just prior to our corporate failure. The truth is, I'll never know exactly what would have happened if we just "could've [fill in the blank]", as the global financial crisis was not a part of our business plan, and although I did mention that in the *potential* threats section of our business plan called "Unforeseen market forces may negatively affect the outcome of this venture", who knew that that clause would ever be summoned to fruition?

Key Lessons Learned from My First Startup:

As I look back on WML, the lessons that I learned begin to emerge as clear as day. But, when I was in the thick of it, hot in startup mode, it was near impossible to see what was going on around us, or inside of our hectic walls. Hindsight is twenty-twenty, so let me share my key takeaways, so you can recognize them early on to avoid them.

Free users today don't equal paying customers tomorrow.

It's easy to project on paper that 'x' percent your free users are going to convert to a paid plan. How could five percent not want that beautiful subscription? After all, many software as a service (SaaS) companies like Linkedin®, DropBox®, MailChimp®, and more rely on the small percentage who pay to support the majority of free who don't, right? Yes, but they also have raised war chests of cash to float their companies until that small percentage is sizable enough to self-sustain the company's future growth.

In your projections, cut the number of conversions for free to paying customers by fifty percent of what you hope for, and you might just get closer to the actual number. If your figures all work out based on that, then you've got a more realistic base to scale from.

If your business has a freemium model — where you give away access on a trial basis or a basic plan and hope for the upgraded revenue to drive your platform — you're putting a ton of faith that that will eventually come to pass. It does work for many companies, and you've got to truly nail the differentiators between the free and the upgraded versions, by drilling down on the one or two key pain points that *really* encourages people to want to upgrade and pay.

If the difference between the free and the paid plans are minor, or you give away too much in the free version and the upgraded version is not attractive enough, you simply won't persuade enough users to move over. Furthermore, as evidenced by what we did, when you're running out of cash, if you start to pressure users to upgrade and create limitations that trap them, what you end up with is a situation where they either remain as a free user, which costs you more amounts of money supporting them with un-monetized resources, or worse, you get a bunch of defectors who not only abandon, but also bring down the intrinsic value of the marketplace or platform.

In our WML example, the value of the community was realized when a musician would do a search and there were endless pages of results for Music Companies, Record Labels, Agents, Managers, Publishers, Venues, and Recording Studios that she can reach out to and communicate with. By limiting the number of search results for the free user, which is what we ended up doing in the "monetize or die" phase, we were cutting off an already starving musician from resources that could help them find success — in retrospect, a self-defeating move. Additionally, by limiting the amount of content that the same musician can upload to her profile in the form of music tracks, videos, biographical information and storage for important items such as Stage Plots, Riders, and Lyric Sheets, we were in actuality, unbeknownst to us, stunting the artist's ability to be appealing to Industry Professionals. Talk about unplugging your user's microphone.

Imagine if some of the most popular platforms of today — Facebook, Twitter, LinkedIn — began limiting your profile, the number of messages you can freely send, the amount of information and files that you can upload (pictures, videos, PDF documents, etc.) — the value of the service would decline instantaneously, the virality would disappear, and the ecosystems as a whole would underwhelm their communities. All three of those companies have had war chests of venture capital and public dollars to float them through periods to reach critical mass, but only in recent years been forced to turn on monetize or die mode, as Wall Street demanded it from them. But by then, they had already reached global scale. Whereas, we had not.

By focusing on monetization out of desperation for cash and without investor capital, we slowly killed the value of our own product. We had no idea we were digging our own grave.

Startup costs are typically 2X-3X more than your plan.

"The rent's due again. We need more money to cover next month", I exclaimed in a tone of resentful desperation to my Board of Directors. They rolled their eyes (again) as they sat down in the oversize red conference room chairs. It seemed like every check they cut to WML was deposited on Monday and vanished into thin air on Tuesday. Where did it all go? How come I was *always* asking for money? Had I been *that* financially foolish the prior month? Was I somehow spending wildly and irrationally? I stuck out my hand and began counting up the major expenses that I could think of on the fly — "Rent $1,500" I proclaimed, with an obvious tone, trying to prove my case. "Server $204" I added. "Skype $30" I continued, not a biggie, but just to show I wasn't leaving any invoice unturned. "Oh yeah, coding $4,200" I continued building my ask, "Oh come on… what's missing? Well, I've got $5,900ish, am I missing something Christina?" I asked sheepishly. Her gaze pierced right through my 22-year-old head from across the conference room table, as if to question my financial prudence the entire time. She retorted, "How should *I* know?". The landlord routinely sent invoices for rent a week and a half earlier than the first of the month. "I *just* paid rent on the first, *another* bill?!" I gasped. "Yeah, we know, we wrote you that check too" Suzy and Christina both replied, almost in timed unison. The air was awkwardly thick; a feeling I knew too well. I felt out of my own skin, completely ashamed to ask my family for more money. It wasn't fair. It's never fair. But we were all in too deep. We were so close to reaching our break-even goal, but if we didn't fuel the fire, the flame would surely extinguish.

This was a near monthly reoccurrence, a constant state of financial panic to violently push all of the invoices away from our startup as fast as humanly possible to deflect the reality that our life swayed in the balance sheet.

By paying all of the bills as quickly as I could, I could temporarily recoil my emotions, garner my focus, and put my attention back on building with Tom downstairs. I always kept the invoices on my desk face down, so Tom wouldn't feel the mounting pressure of my financial worries, and our impending deadline to thrive or die. He didn't need any more stress, but I'm sure he felt my daily anxiety.

Near the end of every month in the last year of WML, in a hurried frenzy, I'd muster up the courage to walk upstairs to my family's office, show them the invoices as justification for them to continue to fund WML for one more month. I resented that feeling, the pressure, the gut-wrenching acknowledgement that another month had passed, and we had yet to move into profitability. The startup hadn't really *started*. The revenue hadn't "turned on" as all of the VCs in Silicon Valley claim their portfolio companies can do when they please with an air of nonchalance, as if they have some magic button that they can press to activate the revenue waterfall.

"Why was the rent *always* due so soon?" I asked myself under my breath, begrudgingly walking up the stairs, barely getting the words out between the clenched vice of my teeth.

There seemed to be no end to the invoices that flew at us from every side; arrows in the dark that suddenly struck me when I least expected it. I developed a paranoia of even checking the mailbox downstairs because I knew it always represented *more* bills, hard earned money that would soon enough fly out the door before it even had time to settle into our checking account.

"Oh yeah, we had Howard (our attorney) review our cap table and write that convertible note document" I reluctantly proclaimed as if I had discovered the missing link to WorldMusicLink's expense scavenger hunt of the day. Another $1,000 arrow struck me in the back. A bill I had completely forgotten about, and far worse, I had not planned for it in my ask upstairs for more capital. "We *actually* need $7,500, you know, just in case something hits us again," I said hesitantly with a look of anguish.

There room went silent. I was covered in arrows marked "Due on receipt", my breathing stopped. Another ten seconds passed which felt like ten excruciating minutes. I had to fill the void. "Plus! Silicon Valley Bank makes us keep at least $500 in the checking account otherwise they start charging us $15 a month in low balance fees again" I added, thinking that further justification was needed to regain their confidence in my financial stewardess.

I despised those $15 a month fees our own bank charged us, the same bank that *knew* we were a startup with no money, that approached *me* as a student and wanted to partner. What a partner…I thought to myself, as they both wrote another check, splitting the sum between the two of them. My Angels had re-appeared. Out of the panicked darkness, a beacon of light began to glimmer once more. The pain of the arrows began to fade. I could breathe again.

As I walked back downstairs, both checks in my hand, a remorseful stomach in tow, all I could think about were those $15 a month fees. They weighed on my mind as if they were 150-pound boulders on my shoulders. I felt caught between two worlds — the king of my startup, and the beggar for it.

"They're slow leaks in *my* ship" I thought to myself as I walked outside and around the building to open our office door. Adding insult to injury, if you listened closely, you could hear the leaks — drip, drip, drip. I returned to my desk. Tom kept coding, knowing well not to look in my direction for a few minutes until I calmed down. He'd seen this monthly routine many times before. WML was breathing again; we could reset the clock for another thirty days.

Don't startup expenses cost what they say they will? Sorry to burst your bubble. There are hidden charges, lack of resources on lower software tiers that force you to upgrade to handle your growing needs, re-filing with lawyers and accountants when things don't go as planned, additional employee benefits that you didn't anticipate, minimum franchise taxes before you even have any sales, and things simply take more time to launch and learn from than you planned for.

Take your projections and double or triple the costs of nearly every line item. Alternatively, take your fully loaded profit and loss statement (P&L), add a line called Contingency and put 2X-3X of your expense totals in there for each month out until year two. This way, you will have provided yourself a more realistic buffer against unforeseen costs that may (and assuredly do) creep up as you grow.

The most astute investors realize that early founders underestimate the cost side of business and overestimate the revenue side. Having a contingency plan in your raise shows investors that you have a keen eye for planning when delays and the unexpected strike.

Product development takes 3X longer than you planned.

I reached into my pocket, pulled out my trusty Blackberry®, and began nervously scrolling through the calendar. We were more than behind schedule. Our private Beta launch date had come and gone; the technical bugs were now eating us alive. Completely overwhelmed by the number of glitches that the platform still had, Tom had me create a bug list — a detailed log that outlined the issue, when it first occurred, how it *should* work, and highlight in red the ones that were the most critical to the product. It was our triage list

— our own IT Emergency Room with a list of patients on stretchers bleeding out and desperately waiting to be fixed. When bugs were in progress, Tom would mark them yellow. When they were resolved, green. The 2-page list was full of reds and yellows. If they remained yellow for too many days, unsolved, I would usher Tom on to fix the next one, hoping that in the interim, he might think of some genius way to fix the one that perplexed us.

I looked across my desk at the bug list — 70% red, 20% yellow, 10% green. Death by one thousand bug bites. If we didn't fix the critical issues that prevented users from uploading their content, sending messages, and receiving notifications to revisit the site — we were toast. A few bigger questions weighed on my mind — with my self-imposed deadline, was I pushing Tom too hard? If he felt overwhelmed, could he decide to quit leaving me without a way to fix the system? I approached Tom with caution. I reassured him that it was ok if he just couldn't solve some of the bugs. "You can just move on to the low hanging fruit if that's easier for you Tom, fine by me," I explained from my desk across the office. But it wasn't fine by me. They were *all* critical — every bug was a major hiccup to the user experience — I knew it, but we weren't a full team with dozens of coders who could solve it all in weeks. We were just two doctors, one operating room, and a line of patients in the waiting room.

Fixing product bugs became our daily purpose and our mutual joy when they were finally resolved. When we would get stuck trying to tackle a bug, I'd say to Tom, "Come on, let's grab coffee." "Yeah, sounds good," he'd reply in his Brooklyn accent. We'd walk over to the nearby coffee shop, Tom would order his routine — black coffee and a tuna fish sandwich, and I'd order a coffee with cream. We'd sit together in the sunshine outside on the metal chairs that flanked our office door. As the sun bared down on Tom's bald head and my freckled skin, we'd delight in the few moments away from the operating room.

As we waited for Divine inspiration, I'd ask Tom about his true passion — flying his single-prop Cessna. He would often tell me his favorite story he liked to call the $400 Hamburger — where he would take his wife on a day trip from Monterey up to the Half Moon Bay airport, a small private landing strip where he'd order the world's best Hamburger as he'd call it, and fly back an hour later, a trip that cost $400 when you add in the cost of fuel, airport fees, and lunch he'd remark with a smile. For a few moments, we both dreamed of escaping for that delicious $400 Hamburger.

"I've got it!" Tom exclaimed, mayonnaise from the tuna sandwich still on the edge of his lips. If we add one more step to the upload flow, we can have the musician name his *own* album and then in step two, upload *and* re-order each track so that it gets mapped accordingly in chronological order, just the way the artist wants it." Another bug was miraculously solved by the coffee break.

Want to launch by March? Expect July and hope for May. This is the kind of thinking that you must develop as a startup CEO. You can't plan for March and get March. If you're not comfortable with finding bugs that set you weeks back, then don't start a web business. If you're not comfortable with waiting months for an ABC liquor license to be approved, then don't start a new restaurant. If you're not comfortable with delayed shipments of inventory, then don't start a retail business. Get used to waiting longer than you think, because that's how startups work. Hurry up and wait.

In my beautiful business plan, I had a timetable that outlined on a month-by-month basis the objectives and milestones that we would be hitting. This, I was told, was to provide guidance to prospective investors, and also align our vision in actionable milestones. While it did provide a good exercise at thinking through each stage from ideation, to prototype, to Alpha and Beta, it was actually used as more of a suggestion as opposed to a firm deadline. Why? Because things happened that we didn't expect. Tom would get sick for a week and couldn't fix bugs that prevented users from completing their profile page. The magazine article that we were banking on to go live in May to promote WML got pushed to July. So goes life, and so goes your momentum. Plan for delays. Be delighted by early arrivals.

A Co-founder's skills should not be identical to yours; they should be complimentary, yet different.

As I sat at my gray, plastic desk fumbling through a stack of résumés, each one looking identical to the next; "Lead Developer",

"Experienced Developer", "Advanced Developer", I thought to myself, "How the hell am I going to find *my* Developer?"

Every leader I'd ever read about or heard speak, always said "Hire the best people", "Every company boils down to their people — hire A+ people because A+ people will hire A people, and A people will hire A- people", they'd forewarn, as if there was some letter grade posted on the front of every résumé. I wished.

Well, what does that even look like? There must be some imaginary ranking system that measures one person against the rest and labels them an "A+" I thought, right? As I continued flipping through the one-inch stack of résumés, they seemed to blend into one; one big confusing decision to make. I needed a Technical Co-Founder, and I needed my A+ hire, but the process was overwhelming.

When I eventually interviewed Tom, the lead developer that I hired to build the Beta for WML, he not only looked different from me, but he also sounded different. Sure, we were over fifty years apart in age, me twenty-two, him in his mid-seventies, but age wasn't what made us so different. Tom had over five decades in the corporate world. He had battle-scars and wins from his former startup days. He had seen the promise land that founders yearn to conquer, and in many cases, never attain. That sage experience was invaluable to me, for avoiding failure, was my single greatest fear as a first-time founder.

Tom had developed a calm in the face of uncertainty and had learned to persevere despite the many battles. I had no such comprehension of what the battle might look like, as I had only read about it in books, listened to successful entrepreneurs boast of their triumphs, yet I knew that I needed to surround myself with a co-founder who had tasted defeat, and had forged ahead. I figured Tom would know where the landmines were. He would not run away at the first sign of a missed paycheck. Tom still had faith in dreamers like me — to change the world with our ideas. Yet, he also possessed a priceless knowledge of the arduous journey ahead of us. I hired Tom for his technical skills, but more so for his battle-tested wisdom.

If you want another you on your team, then just look into a mirror and keep dreaming. People who are just like us — they dream like us, they think like us, they work like us — and who have the same skills as us work in a new company up to a certain point. These kinds of people are attractive early on in a startup (for ideation and launch), because there's no conflict of opinion, they're on the same page with your ideas, and they work well in developing the initial product. But that's where they can stop functioning so well it turns out.

If you're like me, you hate conflict and love when people agree with you. The big issue with that is, if you are pursuing something worth pursuing, you need both someone who can see the dream, but also challenge you and push back at various stages of the game. You need someone who has overlap in skills so you can systematically execute on goals, but also someone who has complimentary skills that ripen over time and can become the Ying to your startup's Yang.

Reid Hoffman, Co-founder of LinkedIn® and Partner at Greylock Capital®, says "[Early on] Startups need Generalists[44]," — people who can wear all of the hats, as the needs crop up. [As the company scales], Specialists are needed." That's why a technically minded Co-founder and a generalist-oriented marketing/business type work well together in a founding team on a software startup. That's why a seasoned chef and an operationalist work well to launch new restaurants. That's why a creative, introverted designer works well with an extroverted, passionate operationalist. You need complimentary, not replicative skillsets.

PR before a product is ready can be deceivingly attractive.

I couldn't believe I forgot how to tie a tie. Today was the day, I needed everything to go smoothly. My hands just wouldn't tie the damn tie! I rushed to the office and began turning on all of the computers which I had put out to make us appear as if we had hired more employees. I had been selected for a feature in *Entrepreneur Magazine* for a section called "Top of the Class", and they were sending a professional photographer down from San Francisco, over 100 miles away, to take my photos for the magazine. I was on Cloud 9 — out of my mind with excitement. Thoughts of the magazine hitting newsstands across the country flashed in my mind. Images of Venture Capitalists, Angel investors, and music companies who would come flocking to WML all flooded into my thoughts. Once they would read my article, the phones would be ringing off the hook — we would escape the startup struggle, *finally*, I thought.

A knock at our office door, it was the photographer. We shook hands, and he began to set up his equipment — an oversized camera, tripod, lighting, and reflectors. He asked me to sit at my desk in front of the WorldMusicLink sign that flew proudly behind my tiny throne. I smiled, with entrepreneurial confidence and pride — "This is it," I thought to myself. "We're going to be famous."

A few months later, I e-mailed Nicole, the writer for *Entrepreneur,* and impatiently asked when the issue was coming out. She said it should be next week. I couldn't wait. I asked if I could buy some extra copies, and she e-mailed me a link. I bought 2 full cases — around 50 or so copies! My plan was to mail a copy of the magazine out to each prospective investor along with my executive summary for WML. I was expecting them to urgently reply with a million-dollar check in hand to fund our Series-A round. I figured, we had made *Entrepreneur Magazine* — you only make that when you're about to blow up big, or you've already made it. The magazines arrived at my office and I opened the box like a kid on Christmas morning. The cover was blue and orange and read "Get Rich 2.0". I flipped to my article, and there I was in living color — I was a *real* entrepreneur now.

I sent out copies of *Entrepreneur* as planned along with our investor documents, and it did open the door for meetings and help us with a halo effect for a few months. But as the issue faded into history, so did the halo that it brought us. That big break we were hoping the publicity would provide, never materialized even into a phone call. As time passed, the urge to get more publicity intensified. But there remained a gap between our financial traction, and the projections we hoped for in the articles. An urgency grew inside my gut to bridge the gap so we could live up to the hype. So instead of boasting about our financial milestones, since none were materializing as fast as we had wanted, we opted to feature user stories and talk about our platform's aim to ameliorate the music industry's problems. But as our publicity amplified, so did the competitive landscape; publicity created the exact opposite effect we were hoping for.

Want to get market approval for your new product? Why not get it featured in a national publication? Won't that make you feel like a million bucks. Sure, but it also exposes your newborn concept to the world, but quite possibly, and in WML's case, a bit prematurely.

If you're looking to get publicity, it usually means you're lacking significant *traction*. Traction can't help but get attention, and *that* wins you effortless media exposure. Publicity for vanity's sake, gets you nowhere frankly, if anything, it encourages more competition.

When you artificially bloat your early success, it both attracts copycats and sets your company up to actually hit those lofty goals — which you may or may not be able to achieve. The best PR comes when media approaches you, not when you have to nudge them to publish your Beta. When you're ready for PR, you'll know it. Don't get PR before you launch, don't get PR during your Beta until you've found product-market-model fit and loyal early customers, don't get PR to validate your entrepreneurial brilliance — if you want a pat on the back, ask your mom to read your executive summary. She'll love it because she loves everything you do.

More features don't equate to more perceived value. Users buy what solves their acute pain; more features distract from the ones that matter the most to them. Less is often more — Do no more than two or three things *exceptionally* well and be recognized for those alone. This is how you win categories.

In our office I mounted an oversized white board that would be our roadmap for all of the features that Tom and I were going to build together at WML — the profile page, music player, video player, document storage system, calendar widget, communication center with messaging, an address book with incoming, outgoing and pending contacts, a full search engine with basic and advanced search capabilities, and a settings panel to control notifications, privacy options, and other account functions. My wireframes were transcribed into white board work flows that showed how the data would be created, transferred, stored, and accessed from one module to a database and back across to another section. Scribbles on the side highlighted by stars ranked the features of most importance, and red, black, and blue colors denoted the user type — Non-Logged-In User, Logged-In User (basic free account), and Logged-In User (PRO subscriber).

If you walked into our office during our development sprints you would think we were playing a technical game of "Who's on First", whereby Tom and I would routinely act out as a user visiting the site's pages for the first time, attempting to complete the sign-up workflow, walking through the profile, adding biographical information, uploading music tracks and videos, and then viewing other people's profiles. The layers of the system's architectural complexity began to crash over us as we had not anticipated the various levels, functions, and features that each user had access to, or should be denied access to, based on their role and subscription status. To say building a social networking platform is a computational nightmare is an understatement.

Up until that moment, I, like many other people took websites like LinkedIn® and Facebook® for granted. I'd just log on, browse around, look somebody up, check out their profile, and get a lay of the land of the website, completely oblivious to the vast amounts of code, authentications, and scenarios that allowed read and write capabilities that were running 'under the hood'.

Under the WML hood, our engineering engine had burst into flames. We had never anticipated creating variants of user roles depending on if a user is logged in, logged out, if they were Music Talent or a Music Professional, if they were a *paid* Talent account or a *paid* Professional account — all different visuals were required, different feature sets, different capabilities, and different authentications/permissions. Instead of just building a simple one-size-fits-all website, we had created a multilevel, multiplayer game that demanded bug correction at every level!

As Tom and I worked tirelessly through all of the scenarios, the architecture began to take shape, bugs started to be eliminated one by one, and the user experience began to appear seamless. I'd begin, "Okay, so I'm John Smith, I'm a PRO subscriber (paid for an annual subscription) and I am trying to add this Basic (free) musician to my contact page…can he see *my* connections?" Tom would reply, "No, once you add him to your contacts, he can see them, but only once that request is accepted by the musician, not before." "Well, what happens if I want to add him to my contacts list to follow up with him at a later point, but I don't really want him to have access to all of my other contacts, can I restrict his access or is he totally in once I send this contact request and he accepts?" I'd ask. "Oh, he's fully in," Tom would reply. A moment of silence between us, Tom on one end hoping I wasn't about to throw one more layer of permissions into the workflow. "Ok, well for the Beta that's fine for starters, and we'll just have to poll the Pros to see if they're cool with that or not, because if it were up to me, I'd want to have access to the musicians, but wouldn't *really* want to give them access to my key contacts, right?" Tom paused before commenting, knowing that if he gave in too much to my side, he'd be forced to re-write the code entirely to add that function, but if he fought me, it might show a lack of appreciation for my opinion and possibly that of our users. "I agree that would be a good feature, but maybe we can push that for version 1.0 later if we find that it becomes an issue" he said, in both an appeasing yet firm tone. We agreed — on the future to-do list that feature request would go.

New Feature Bloat:

It seemed we always had bit off more than we could chew, but we were entrepreneurs — our eyes were always bigger than our stomachs. New features would force themselves into the product as we developed them — they were relentless, always auditioning for our attention to build them out. We had to develop a callous for new feature build — otherwise we'd drown in them. Features are like supplies on a ship that just set sail — surely the right ones are needed, but too many, and the entire ship slows, takes on water, and sinks.

More is better, right? This is America, home of the combo meal! No. A larger menu at that fast food chain we all know and love does *not* equal more sales, it equals more customer indecision, inventory management, explanation, and delivery discombobulation.

Simpleness is bliss. Steve Jobs, Apple's Co-founder, was a guru at minimalist design, often stripping away everything — the wires, the complex paper instructions, the frivolous bells and whistles — to get down to the most beautiful, magical moment, where value is served on a platter, not an all you can't eat Beta buffet.

We thought more bells equaled more revenue. That was a mistake. In early product design, less is more.

The 3-Minute Checkout:

Here's a rule I came up with to ensure you're delivering the right features and not feature bloat — **if your customer only has three minutes to do the task you hope for them to do because they've either got 1% battery life in their phone or their parking meter outside just expired, can they** *actually* **do it?**

Can they get from search engine to checkout on your website in three minutes? Can they order, pay and receive their cup of coffee off of your menu in under three minutes? Can they walk through your retail shop, find the item they want, checkout and go? If it takes more than three minutes to educate, convince and convert — game over. You've got to go back, eliminate steps, remove functions, strip away copy, simplify the workflow that they need to fight through to find the golden nugget, pay, and get the hell out. Lower the time to one or two minutes if you really want to test yourself and the U/X (user experience).

While for some industries or services a three-minute process is impossible, this test should highlight touch points that can be streamlined, removed, or combined to skips steps and *reduce friction*. To understand friction, visualize a static charge building up as you play customer traveling through your workflow. Each element you ask them to do builds up a charge that causes friction. Too much friction and you make it easy for customers to emotionally or transactionally give up. An often overlooked area that guarantees failure, is too much friction in on-boarding, registration, transactions, and re-ordering.

Example Friction Point One — A Long Line:

Imagine a person walking into your coffee shop and a huge line awaits them. In their mind, they are both intrigued because a line typically signals high demand, and if there were no line, it might signal no demand for a particular reason — bad food, bad service, overpriced products, unsanitary conditions, etc.

As they step into line, they are calculating in their mind the estimated time to arrival at the kiosk, and internally are plotting an X/Y matrix comparing their demand to order with the time they estimate they need to complete the order based on prior experiences with other similar establishments. While every user, industry, and service are different in these mental values, for many, there is an *expected level of friction* needed to complete a cycle. If your experience is greater than that expected level, you are substandard and considered a challenging experience. If you beat that expected level of friction, you could be considered a frictionless, easy transaction.

Example Friction Point Two — A Confusing Menu:

As the prospective customer looks up on the big menu board, they are completely overwhelmed with five-thousand options of food and beverages. The print is tiny, the names are confusing, there are no headings like "Hot Beverages", "Cold Beverages", "Sweet Treats" or "Lunch Items", but rather a big laundry list, leaving them to guess what the heck is what. Friction builds — What to order? What's it going to cost me? What does anything look like as a finished item?

Example Friction Point Three — We Only Accept Cash:

After a near ten-minute commitment to waiting in line, fumbling through a smartphone to find the "complimentary" WiFi only to realize it doesn't work, a snarky barista says "Next!" and without a smile or flicker of eye contact, says, "What do you want?" After placing an order for a cup of coffee and a blueberry muffin, the total is due and the barista says, "That'll be $7.50." The customer reaches into his wallet, pulls out an AMEX® card and hands it over. "Sorry, no AMEX". He puts the card back, in dismay, and reaches for his Visa® — everyone assuredly takes Visa he thinks to himself.

"Sorry, no credit cards." In astonishment, he realizes he only brought his two credit cards with him as he was out for a morning walk and left his wallet with cash at home. He has no means to complete the transaction and feels like an idiot for both wasting his time and now causing a public display to all of the other patrons waiting behind him. "How about Apple Pay®?" he remarks in a final attempt to pay and end the transactional nightmare. "Nope, sorry," she snarks back, "Next customer!" He has no choice but to walk away. The friction was too thick to overcome. The merchant killed her own transaction and created a defector in the process who will most likely never return.

The Three Minute Rule is highly effective when you're in a highly competitive market, your product may be undifferentiated against other choices (in the buyer's mind, obviously not yours — we always love our babies), the buyer's attention is limited or expensive to capture, and therefore the ease of your buying experience can become your startup's secret weapon.

Much of today's innovation is actually *not* focused solely on product, pricing, or market disruption, despite what it appears to be, but rather, on transactional disruption (a seamless use and checkout experience). Ultra-fast transactional design is driving how products are built, and what markets respond best to them. By working backwards, from rapid checkout to customer touchpoint number one, a startup is able to see more clearly the extraneous moving parts that cause friction and eliminate them. I've listed a few examples below.

Instead of calling a Taxi, waiting thirty minutes, and not knowing the cost ahead of time for the trip, we can thank Uber® and Lyft® for a one-tap experience to order a private car for $5 to $20 on average. Sure, a Taxi may be 20% more expensive, but that's not the sole reason why the markets migrated away from cabbies. The experience was frictionless and magical. Got just twenty blocks to walk but only fifteen minutes until your meeting? Sure, you can call an Uber or Lyft, but rush hour may eat you alive. Enter Bird® or Lime® — just step on the scooter, scan and go, starting at only $1. Yes, this is a new category of publicly available transportation, but if you had to have a rental store for the scooter that took fifteen minutes to rent one, and then have to return it and pay with a credit card, you'd never use one. Rather, the scan and go functionality of the app is so seamless, it makes riding a scooter at forty pretty cool.

Need to buy toothpaste, deodorant, and some batteries? Normally you'd get in your car, drive down to the nearest mall, hunt for a parking spot, walk inside, spend twenty minutes browsing the store, and five minutes in line to earn that nine-foot-long CVS® receipt. For a $35 order, you'd have to give up an hour of your life. Thanks to Amazon® for their turn-key search, recommendation engine, and checkout, they've mastered the sub $50 dollar sale. Just add to cart, pay, and move on with your day. Items are delivered either the same day or tomorrow with Amazon Prime®. No parking, no lines, just a frictionless customer experience.

Want a cup of coffee but have to stop at the ATM to get $20 to spend $3.50? Thank Apple Pay®. By just waving your iPhone® you've paid for that cup of coffee. No driving to an ATM, no withdrawing more cash than needed, no more clinking of change in your pocket post purchase. ATM-less, change-less, friction-less.

While many argue these aforementioned experiences are displaying technological breakthroughs, which I agree they are, their products all boil down to one metric that seems to go overlooked in the media but means everything to the customer — an *ultra* fast, frictionless checkout experience.

These companies are not asking themselves "How can we make the next coolest widget?" or "How can we offer a lower priced product over our competitor?" Their teams are asking a higher-level question, "How *fast* can we take the customer from pain to solution?"

The faster we get out of our customer's way, the faster they win and enjoy the experience. The by-products are more transactions, increased gross merchandise values, enhanced trust in the shopping experience, repeat sales and increased virality (as more customers use the service, they promote the brand for free to their networks). Increase the speed, lower the friction, and help your customers win faster.

**Founders must focus on three areas at different times to grow —
Activities within the business unit (day-to-day), activities on the
business (managerial), and activities outside of the business
(external). Prioritize what matters when.**

Monday morning would roll around, I'd park my car, walk up the
steps from the parking garage below the WML office, and Tom
would be waiting for me promptly at 9:00am, holding his laptop in
one hand and an oversized coffee thermos in the other. After opening
the office door, and settling in, he would look at me as if waiting for
his daily marching orders. I had no plan. "Think!" I'd shout at
myself under my breath, "Don't just *not* say anything, he is costing
me $280 per day, time is money, and we don't have a moment to
spare!" "Um…." I let out in a hesitant tone. "Where did we leave off
on the white page of death bug? Did MidPhase (our hosting
company) give us increased memory execution time limits so that the
PHP had time to complete the database query?" Tom's eyes lit up. "I
solved it yesterday actually!" "Wow, Tom! Awesome," I exclaimed
with a smile on my face. Tom was good about that. When a problem
existed, he never let a weekend get in the way of solving it —
weekends to Tom were just another workday. He loved solving hard
coding problems, each with their unique backstory of how they came
to exist. What he loved even more, was showing me *how* he solved
them. I enjoyed listening as it gave him a sense of ownership in
moving us forward — he'd walk me through the symptom, his
original hypothesis and diagnosis, and his final prescription to
restore the code to health.

Quickly thinking of the next action item I needed him to get
done, I asked, "Why don't you move onto the next bug on the bug
list?" "Alrighty, sounds like a plan", Tom replied. A few moments
would pass, I'd open my laptop, and think about where I left off on
Friday. "Oh yeah, I e-mailed my investor deck to that Angel but he
didn't write back…maybe a 2nd request e-mail is in order," I'd ask
myself, "Or, maybe I should start entering the invoices into
Quickbooks®, and tomorrow I can e-mail that Angel…I don't want
to appear too hungry on a Monday by following up from my last e-
mail on Friday otherwise he'll think we're *too* hungry."

Knowing what to work on when, is at the crux of successful business. Well, no one ever told me that starting a business can be broken down into three distinct areas and by categorizing them, you can keep your head on straight and accomplish more, faster. Every day seemed like it would fly by in a whirlwind of an experience, and it was virtually impossible to figure out what activity drove what, and when it would yield an output for what part of our startup. But over time, I figured out that you must visualize your startup activities as three distinct areas.

A) **Daily Activities <u>within</u> the Business** — the work that you need to do day in and day out to accomplish technical and operational goals — build the product, pay employees, manage customers, sell the product, market the product, rinse and repeat.

B) **Weekly Activities <u>on</u> the Business** — the work that you need to do on a weekly basis to set 30,000 ft. view strategic goals — reiterate the North Star mission to everyone, financially plan for cash flow, delegate tasks, review product(s) for value creation, learn from customers to deploy findings back into the product, and ignite renewed passion within your team for growth.

C) **Monthly Activities <u>outside</u> of the Business** — the work you need to do on a monthly basis that sets you up to scale — pitching investors, raising capital, managing suppliers, forging new business deals, networking with prospective employees, pitching media, handling speaking engagements and outreach, and most importantly, learning from other successful entrepreneurs to fuel unique insights to drive your company to the next level.

Figure 15.1 outlines an example of the activities that you will need to accomplish in a month. The trick is to not just write out some long laundry list of stuff, but rather be mindful of what tier the activity falls into, and how much time on a daily, weekly, or monthly basis you think it will take you. Then, track how much time it actually takes you over a one-month period so you will start to see the difference between what you anticipated, and what it actually took to complete.

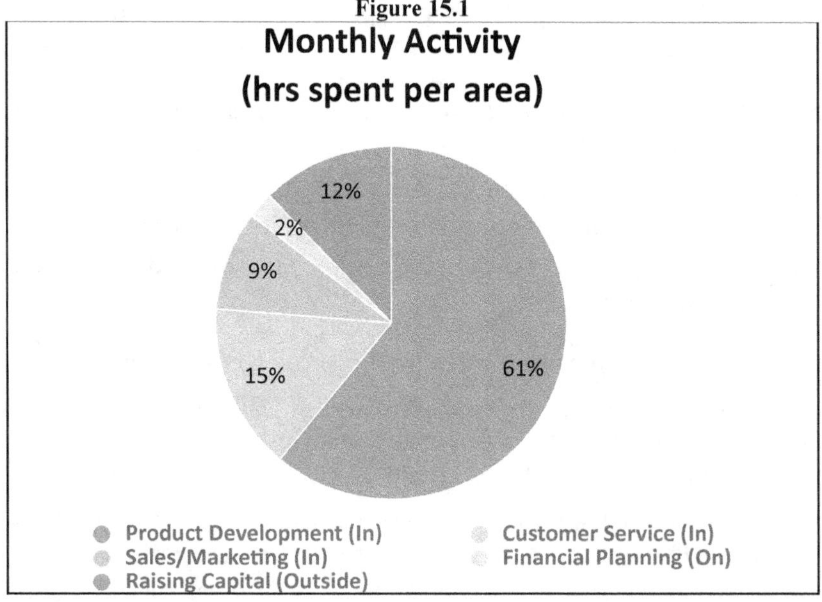

For example, you might say that finding software bugs in the Beta should take you two hours every day from Monday through Friday for a total of ten hours per week. However, when you actually tracked how long you spent on bug finding and regression testing your Beta, it really took you four hours on Monday, three hours on Tuesday, six hours on Wednesday, three hours on Thursday and five hours on Friday, for a total of twenty-one hours, more than two-times what you anticipated. Therefore, you had less time to cold call new customers, finish the pitch deck, and get back to your investors with an update.

Step 1: While there are many time management software programs today, you can simply use Numbers® or Excel® to create a series of columns titled "Work On" in column one, "Work In" in column two, and "Work Outside" in column three.

Step 2: Next, create various rows for each activity that you will need to accomplish, such as "Graphic Design", "Legal Filings", "Beta Testing", "Re-Ordering Supplies", "Investor Presentations to Angels", "Reach out to Newspapers for PR", etc. Then put an *expected* number of hours each task will take to accomplish each week in each cell. At the bottom, sum up the totals. You will see the total number of hours per activity type — Work On, Work In, and Work Outside.

Step 3: Duplicate the set of rows below to create an *actual* time required section. The top rows are what you anticipate, and the bottom are what it actually took. After one week, you will be able to see exactly how long (over or under your projection) each task took you. If you are visual, you can select all of the cells and make a pie chart from the data.

An activity pie chart will visually show you the percentage of time each task took you to complete and will better drive time management for your startup. For the first few months, especially if you're a first-time founder, you will under-estimate how long tasks will take you to complete. The goal of logging your time to task ratio is not solely to see if you are over or under performing in each category, but rather to get a 30,000 ft. view of what sucks most of your time and if it's *actually* moving your business ahead or not.

As figure 15.2 points out, the key to time management is not to just spend the actual time that you originally anticipated per task, it is to also understand what *outcome* each task drives in your business, what activity fuels the most growth, and when to do each. If you are spending hours and hours fixing a bug but leaving customer support tickets by the wayside, you may find that when that bug is actually fixed, no one cares, because that's not what's important to them — they all walked away while you were spending time fixing the U/X while they were ignored.

DATE	TIME ALLOTTED (HRS)	ACTUAL TIME (HRS)	TIME OVER/ UNDER (HRS)	ACTIVITY
4/1/18	10h	5h	-5h	RE-DESIGN U/X
4/3/18	4h	3h	-1h	BUILD PROFORMA STATEMENT
4/10/18	1h	4h	4h	RECONCILE BANK STATEMENTS
4/12/18	3h	2h	-2h	MANAGE PR CAMPAIGN
4/14/18	2h	4h	2h	INVOICING CUSTOMERS
4/16/18	10h	20h	10h	INTERVIEWING NEW HIRES
4/18/18	10h	15h	5h	EDITING BUSINESS PLAN
4/21/18	5h	10h	5h	TALKING WITH USERS
4/23/18	7h	12h	5h	SALES PHONE CALLS
4/25/18	5h	3h	-2h	MISC.
TOTAL	57h	78h	21h	

Figure 15.2

Raising capital is a full-time job that requires 100% focus and takes 3-12 months to accomplish.

"We've got $25,000 left in the bank, which is about three months of runway," I explained to my Board of Directors. "I've already made a list of prospective investors, VCs, you name it, and have color coded them here in red for rejected, yellow for pending, and green for possibly interested." The list was mainly yellow, a few reds, and a few greens. "Do we all agree with Howard's (our attorney) equity dilution from the revised capitalization table he proposed this week?" They nodded in accordance with my request. "So we're raising $1 million as a convertible note, that will discount by 20% in one year's time if it converts to equity, and will have a 6% interest kicker on it, sound good?" They nodded with agreement once more. "This should eliminate the conversation around valuation, and I have to say, I don't think we can command much right now because we aren't live with our first stable version, so this should help get us to our Series-A round, which based on my projections, should be in six to eight months," I concluded. It was agreed — the meeting minutes were signed, the letter for the note was drafted, and we began our hunt for the capital we needed to pull us out of Beta and into version 1.0.

As we broke from our shareholder meeting, I got into my car, and drove down the road. As I stared out the front window, a thought began to emerge — we were now raising a big time round of financing. I knew it would take a different mask, one that oozed complete and utter confidence, an unwavering resolve to manifest my vision, and a compelling narrative fully supported by convincing financials and backed by conservative assumptions. We were in the beginning of the Great 2008 Recession, and things were tightening up. I knew investors were looking for calmer, more predictable waters to tie their capital up in, and a startup in the Music Industry run by a 22-year-old wouldn't be their first choice. We were what we were, and we could only control what we could control. The rest was up to fate.

Over the next few months, while simultaneously managing Tom, helping on-board new users, trying to garner publicity, and keep my head on straight, I beat down the trail of Silicon Valley's Sand Hill Road, and blew up the inboxes of VCs, Angels and Music Executives who I thought might be interested in investing. I cold e-mailed the Manager of Alice Cooper, who had escaped the L.A. music scene for palm tree lined shores of Hawaii. An awkward conversation later, it was a "No". I pinged one of the legends of Silicon Valley, a hard-drive entrepreneur of the 1980s and a millionaire to boot, who had retired in sunny Palm Springs, and whose son I grew up with locally. I mailed out my PowerPoint®

deck on a burned CD along with my executive summary. After a few phone calls and back and forth e-mails, it was a "No". I got a warm intro from one of our Music Industry advisors to the former Manager of the Dave Matthews Band®, set up a telcon, pitched my heart out, and it was a "No". I set up an in-person meeting with a millionaire Angel investor who made his fortunes to the tune of $280 million selling his produce procurement company to a Fortune 500 player, walked on in expecting a one-on-one and was greeted by two other staffers, assumedly to play Devil's advocate — so he could see how I handled the tough questions from all sides, all while selectively sitting at the head of the conference room table at a distance. It was a "No". Onwards, I persevered, one "No" after another. With each rejection I got stronger, smarter, and more fluid in my rebuttals. The hard questions that left me dumbfounded before, began to repeat, and next time I told myself, "I'll have an answer."

The "Noes" came in many forms — the Hard No — "No thanks", "Not for us", "Not interested". The Soft No — "Not sure if this is a fit, I'll get back to you," "We *may* be interested, I'll check with my partners," "Thanks for your e-mail, we'll get back to you if there's interest." And finally, the Silent No — no response. The Silent No was the worst, it was the one that kept me up at night, it was the one that prevented me from marking it red in my spreadsheet, but rather, just leaving it yellow as pending — a false lighthouse in the distant storm.

If there's one thing that burns about being a founder or a salesperson, it's the silent treatment. They say silence is deafening, I say it can kill you slowly over time, unless you learn to consider silence a "No". That's the key — only a "Yes" is a "Yes"; everything else is a "No". I had to be careful not to overtly ask for money, as that was a violation of SEC rules back then but make a presentation of our startup in a discrete and polite manner that created an air of excitement and ephemerality of the opportunity to join our momentum.

Raising money is more than just asking for a check. You need to meet with your Board of Directors to create a financial plan, plan with your lawyer and possibly your accountant, you need to determine your OOC (out of cash) scenario, monthly burn rates, projected revenue sources and uses of the cash for the next 12-24 months, create a killer executive summary and slide-deck, and start networking to line up dates to pitch Angel Investors, VCs, Business Plan Competitions, Incubators, Banks, and even Landlords and Suppliers (pitching them to get more favorable terms). It's more than a full-time job, and takes six to twelve months (pre-traction), two to four months (with traction). Raising money is like a full-time job within another full-time job — here are some of the key phases along the journey:

Education — determining what financial instrument is what and how it can help or hurt your startup, learning term sheets, finding industry benchmarks (comps of other financing rounds) in your space, and making an investor lead list to contact.

Strategy — determining what amount you're raising, how you hope to structure the round (debt/equity/terms), where the funds will get you next, and making a financial plan with an attorney to raise that amount.

Networking/Courting — going to events, handing out business cards, cold e-mailing, warm e-mailing for introductions, and lining up meetings.

Pitching — meeting Angels, VC Associates, and hopefully Partners or Managing Directors at VC firms (the ones who can actually cut a check), pitching your slide deck, following up by e-mail, submitting documents (Executive Summary, Capitalization Table, Projections, Balance Sheet, Customer Referral Lists, etc.)

Negotiating/Closing the Deal — getting a term sheet (the offer) from a VC or negotiating by e-mail, phone, or in person with an investor over covenants, getting the lawyers involved to negotiate on your behalf and close the round, signing off on the paperwork, issuing stock certificates, updating your Cap table, setting new reporting requirements for quarterly/monthly updates and follow-on Board of Directors meetings.

Allocating Funds/Planning — this is where you get the check/wire transfer, begin allocating the funds towards specific capital investments or expenditures that will take you to the next level, and start planning your new burn rates based on new hires and added expenses that you now have so you can plan for the next round of financing or conducting a break-even analysis to when you will be profitable.

For many startups, the cycle of fundraising never ends, but your goal should be to do the *minimum* amount of external financing possible to get you the furthest along towards profitability. This not only will save you equity which should be worth a lot later if all things go well or lower your debt levels, but it also allows you to focus more time and energy on just growing your startup faster.

Brad Feld, Venture Partner at Foundry Group and co-author of <u>Venture Deals</u>[45], has a prescient quote for entrepreneurs when raising capital:

> When we meet people who say they are "trying to raise money," "testing the waters," or "exploring different options," this not only is a turnoff but also often shows they've not had much success. Start with an attitude of presuming success. If you don't, investors will smell this uncertainty on you; it'll permeate your words and actions. Not all entrepreneurs will succeed when they go out to raise a financing. Failure is a key part of entrepreneurship, but, as with all things in life, attitude impacts outcome and this is one of those cases.

It's hard to focus on the one or two things to do today that truly move the needle, but you must do so vigilantly.

It's easy to be excited when you're in the trenches of a new startup — the fresh office paint, the new sign hanging outside of your office door, the stack of résumés seeking a slice of the dream and equity, and the creation of that beautiful logo. Everywhere you turn, there's something to do, and less hands than required to do it. By the time you get started, a million other things are auditioning for your attention. Imagine being on a runner's high but being forced to sit still to write a fifty-page business plan, review bugs with an engineer, reconcile a bank statement, draft a meeting minute synopsis for your Board of Directors, and pitch your dream to an endless batch of reporters, investors, employees and customers. Who has time for lunch? Focus is the name of the game.

Where you focus, determines what moves and what doesn't. Everything is important, but not everything all at once, only one thing at a time — but which what? That's the secret.

I learned to ask myself a simple question every time I would start thinking about a new thing to do, or start acting on it — "Is this *the* most important thing I need to do today to move us ahead for tomorrow? If this doesn't get done today, how will it impact us in the morning? If only one thing gets done today, is *this* the most important thing?"

If the answer was "Well, this is a nice thing to get out of the way today, but it's not vital to our survival," then I would move it down my list of action items from Vital (Do Now), to Important (Do Tomorrow), to finally Do (Very Soon). Things that are on the Do (Very Soon) list likely don't matter and will resurface someday when they become vitals. People who demonstrate a militaristic style of execution often yield the most consistent results. Founders who vacillate on what to do, when to do it, how to do it best, and who delay doing the vital things that must be done, fail the fastest. I should know, I have been both types of people. Something done now is better than something done perfectly tomorrow.

Finding Product-Model-Market Fit (PMMF):

Every business has a model. A circle of life if you will, from customer acquisition, to engagement, to sale, to follow-up, to either repeat purchase or attrition. For a special event like a music concert, it may start on Facebook with a targeted local ad that yields a click to a website that results in the purchase of a ticket, that then lands attendance of the guest with an up-sell of nachos, beer and a t-shirt with the band name on it. From eyeballs, to attendee, to consumption to evangelist. That's one rotation through that lifecycle.

WorldMusicLink was supposed to be built around a subscription model (monthly, quarterly or annual fees). We offered a discount if the musician or the industry professional bought the quarterly or annual package, and also offered a freemium version that allowed them to try it out for thirty days, risk free, and then upgrade to keep the professional features on their respective account.

The first problem with our original model was that we were trying to monetize both sides of the platform. Typically, in a marketplace model, you choose one or the other to charge either on a subscription or transactional basis. Why? Because it helps you grow one side faster — the side that you may need more of in order to attract the side that wants *access* to them more. For example, you need less suppliers but more buyers so therefore you charge suppliers and grow the number of active buyers.

The second problem we didn't realize until later on was that we were pitching a musician on the goal of getting discovered by the music business without first proving that we could deliver on that promise. A thirty-day trial likely wasn't enough time to get qualified, real interest from Industry Pros seeking the next act to sign, so it left musicians wondering if the site would even do what we were hoping it would do for them. From our perspective, we still had ongoing costs to run the site, pay the developer, pay rent, etc., so waiting around for a musician to cough up $15 after a trial was like watching grass grow. We would give the site away for free, watch them fill out their profiles, upload their music, videos, pictures, and copy, and then nothing. A month might roll around, and some bands got contacted, and most didn't, so they decided to just leave their free profile billboard up there, and not pay. The one commonality among all of the musicians was they thought "If I build it, they will come," (a Field of Dreams® movie reference). Meaning, if they filled out their profile once and left it there, record labels and booking agents would be breaking down the door to sign and book them. This isn't how the industry works. What we *could* offer them was just an opportunity to be seen, a foot in the door, and the tools to improve their odds of being discovered without having to be based in the major music markets: L.A., New York or Nashville.

The third problem that resulted from the aforementioned, was that for us, having thousands of ghost musician accounts (that were not paying for the real estate) was okay, because it gave us the appearance that our site was popular, and that activity was happening. This in turn, helped to attract more user signups, but I never felt like we had been able to *guarantee* a relationship or an outcome, and I didn't like that. We had built the system, gave them the tools, but the users were just not communicating as much as we had hoped they would. It was hard to quantify how a musician became successful from the platform. Was it when a Music Pro reached out to them and sent them a message? Was it when a Pro selected from the drop-down subject line that "I'm interested in booking your band"? Was that a quantifiable benchmark of a successful outcome? The model that we built was simply not measurable, and therefore, not as predictable as we had originally thought at highlighting a user's success. The results we were hoping for were not accurately linked to the business model that we were offering. An upgraded subscription did not guarantee an outcome; it guaranteed a better shot at an outcome — a much harder value proposition to convince users to keep paying for.

So, what do you do when you can't see the financial results you want? You do what every startup back then did — you add ads! So, we set up banner advertising and Google AdSense® to monetize the site in the interim while we figured out the business model. But, without high enough site traffic, we couldn't attract sizable sponsors to buy ads, so we used an affiliate program (CommissionJunction®) that would pay us pennies per click but gave us the appearance that we had negotiated ad deals with larger music companies like Gibson® Guitars (which never happened). I was able to ink a short-lived partnership with Guitar Center's subsidiary, Musician's Friend® — the largest music equipment retail catalog supplier in the industry which drove some traffic to our site but yielded little in conversions. Ads rarely work for startups, and it was like throwing whip-cream on a shitty business model that just wasn't right for our users.

As I mentioned before in our business plan, we estimated how many free users would convert to subscribers, how many would stop subscribing, and the costs to support and store all user and data files (free and paid), but we failed to realize that we could not guarantee success for users on the platform, which was the suggested promise of our marketing. We underestimated how many musicians would give the free trial a shot and then leave the site waiting for someone to discover them, without having to do any work against it. We thought, if you build the platform, give them the tools, access and reach, then they will succeed. We were wrong.

For your business, it's always better to have a few models in mind, map them out, and then test them vigorously. Give model number one ninety days to work, and then quickly adapt and switch to the next business model. Don't be scared to change. If it is not working, and you keep holding onto that model, you fail. You need to be ready to say, "Screw it, that last model didn't work, let's adjust the model and test some new things out, and see what happens."

So, what does the correct blend look like of the right product that solves customer pain point(s), the right business model that works for them and you, and the right group of customers?

A great product alone (think the Microsoft Zune® music player or the Segway® transportation system) might *not* be sufficient enough to attract customers and create a scalable business. Additionally, an innovative business model (like on-demand marketplace D-apps — decentralized apps that use blockchain technology) that has never been deployed previously might also be of little value without the right product or market to play (use case). And lastly, a new, emerging market (like Virtual Reality, Augmented Reality, Cryptocurrency, Robotics) might today be of low importance to consumers unless they are blended with the right product experience and in an economic manner in which they create true value. Tomorrow, they could all win.

PMMF — build the right product, launch into the right market, and offer the right business model (figure 15.3).

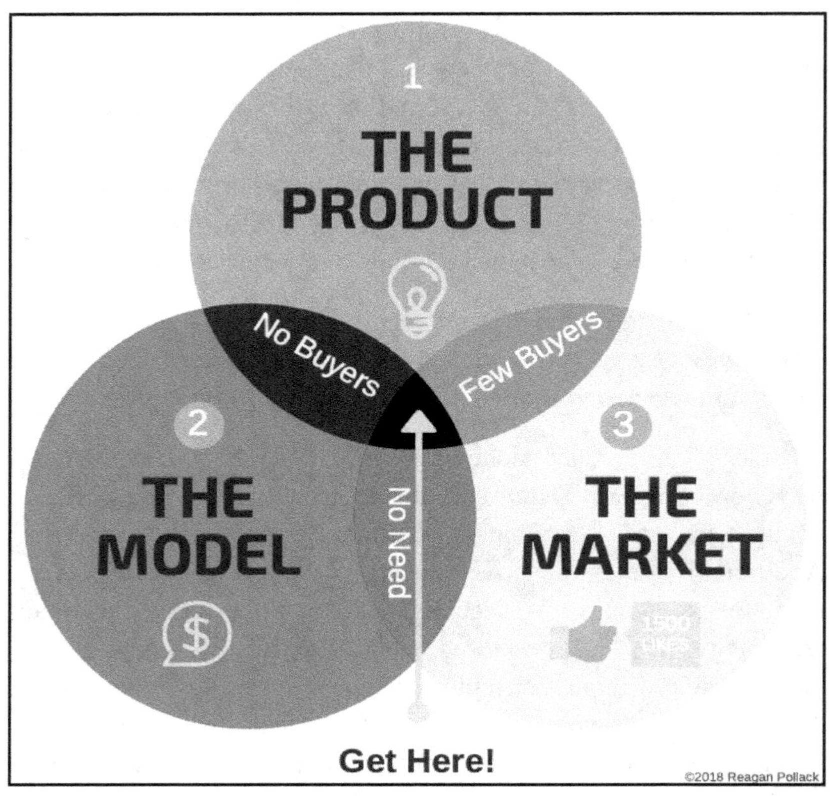

Figure 15.3

Reach this destination, and your customers should love your product or service, and want to boast about it to their peers. The business should have scalable potential and sufficient revenue prospects.

When Product-Market-Model Fit Doesn't Work:

Failure #1: Fighting to Win the Wrong Market

• Right Product

• Right Business Model

• Wrong Market

If you have built a truly great product with an acceptable business model attached, but deploy into the wrong market, you will not gain customer adoption and will burn precious cash trying to convert the unconvertible as they do not value your intended value proposition.

Think selling lemonade outside of a supermarket. They have lemonade and a million other beverages inside, so why do they need you? What you need is to move your operation to a better location where there is no competition.

Failure #2: Deploying the Wrong Business Model

- Right Product
- Wrong Business Model
- Right Market

If you build a great product and deploy into the correct market, after research and testing, but are forcing a business model like advertising, subscriptions, high pricing, heavy up-front switching costs, etc., then you will create friction with the right customers and will turn off many of them. Only a small portion will adopt, but it will be hard for them to persuade others to join the movement due to the barriers to entry.

Think selling lemonade on a hot summer day at the beach, but asking people to pay for an annual subscription model instead of a one-time payment per cup. What you may need, is to price the lemonade by the cup in a single use model.

Failure #3: Launching an Undifferentiated Product

- Wrong Product
- Right Business Model
- Right Market

If you have designed an ingenious new business model that can stand to make customers delighted and also make you wealthy, and have found a new, growing market, but have designed either a "Copy Cat" product (one that lacks differentiation) or the product fails to deliver on its intended promises, then you will have high customer acquisition, but will have an even higher churn or defection rate, as customers will quickly bad mouth you on social media, in reviews, and will likely not promote the company to their friends (low Net Promotor Score, NPS®).

Think on-demand lemonade delivered right to your office from a slick mobile app for a flat rate of $10 per month (all your team can drink), but when it arrives, it's warm, tastes bad, and doesn't match the food that people bring from home to eat on their breaks. What you might need is to deliver a different product, say cookies (regular and gluten free) for dessert that pairs well with meals people bring from home. The model and market are right, but the product does not have a fit.

Getting to Product-Market-Model-Fit Faster:

Bob Caspe used to implore me when I was in the field chatting with prospective customers to ask them, "So, I've showed you how my product solves your pain, right? If it were available, would you buy it?" Now, most people out of courtesy will say "Sure". Most people won't say "No". It's at that very moment, that you say, "Well it's your *lucky* day, because it's available for only twenty bucks!" and ask for the sale. If everyone tells you, "Sure I would buy it" and they don't, then you've got a dud on your hands, and need to get back to the drawing board. If they say "Yes", then you've got your first or second sale. If they say "No", you must ask them "Why not?"

It's just as imperative that you figure out what the objection point is, as to what the acceptance point may be. Was it just that you did not address their pain enough, and articulate how your widget will solve it? Or possibly was it the price? Was it that you didn't listen to their pain more carefully and see if it is a fit with them?

There are hundreds of possibilities of why people say "Yes" or "No" but asking for the sale when they say they would likely buy, is rule number one for generating revenue, regardless of your product, model, or market fit. It is so rudimentary, but it deserves highlighting, as so many founders simply forget to ask for the sale, and keep going on and on about the product, the service, the bells and the whistles, and never ask them to buy today. Ask for the sale every time you talk with customers and you'll know if you've discovered PMMF, if not, and most importantly, *why*.

CHAPTER 16:
LA DOLCE DEAL

My second venture (LaDolceDeal.com — which translates to 'The Sweet Deal'), was founded when I was twenty-six years old, a GroupOn® style discounted deal site regionalized to the Monterey Peninsula (50–75-mile radius). The concept was simple — a website and mobile app would feature local merchant deals — restaurants, hotels, retail shops, special events — to visiting tourists and locals, while providing substantial discounts, often north of forty percent.

Why did I launch this business? Because my area has historically been a highly trafficked touristic hot spot, however many tourists complained about the affordability of the experiences. By lowering the cost of admission, we could drive more traffic to local merchants, boost our local economy, and enable millions of tourists to have access to great meals and events, even on a tight budget.

When tourists would flock back to their cities in the off season, LaDolceDeal could continue to drive locals in to offset the seasonality. Everybody, even folks with more means, enjoy saving when they can, and getting high-end experiences for a fraction of the cost is often a hidden highlight of the week. At the time, GroupOn® and LivingSocial®, the two major players in the national arena hadn't yet penetrated into our market, rather they were focused on winning the major cities such as Chicago, L.A., and New York.

After proving out the model locally, my vision was to then seek other similar regional markets to expand the offering into. Well, at least that was my original plan until things didn't go as planned.

Selling B-2-B is harder than it looks:

Starting LaDolceDeal seemed pretty straightforward — connect a large number of eyeballs on one side of the platform with a curated list of amazing deals on the other. So I began e-mailing local merchants to see if I could schedule some meetings to discuss the opportunity that I was building.

I secured a meeting with the Director and Restaurant Manager of a reputable, international hotel chain that had a location in the next city over for a luncheon. After the initial pleasantries, I dove right in. I only got through about three minutes of my pitch when the Restaurant Manager proceeded to grill me on how our platform didn't have any eyeballs yet — "So, how are you going to guarantee us exposure if you don't have any traffic yet?" Crickets. Great question, for which I really didn't have a smart answer to.

I had to convince them that if we could *just* feature a deal from their restaurant, the traffic would assuredly come. I felt like Kevin Costner in the baseball movie *Field of Dreams*, who hears the voice whispering from the cornfields, "If you build it, they will come," urging him to build the baseball field in the middle of his corn field on blind faith that legendary baseball ghosts from eons past will miraculously show up to play ball. The restaurant manager continued to grill me like a steak, "How are you going to get all of these tourists and locals to, all of a sudden, join your website when they've never heard of it before? How is your marketing going to be any different from what we do today?" My face turned bright red as sweat began to form on my brow. I quickly replied without even thinking about what I was about to say next, "Because, Millennials don't read newspapers, they use the Internet, and our company focuses on the future, not dying media outlets no one reads!" I could see a glimmer of light — the deal was turning around.

As the luncheon drew to a close, I asked for the deal, however that day the managers didn't give me the deal I was seeking, but they gave me something one-thousand times more valuable — a key lesson in the art of salesmanship.

Merchants, like all consumers, get used to what they get used to. Anything new that warrants them to change — even if it can 10X their sales, significantly decrease their costs, or improve customer satisfaction — creates an illusion of fear. Our job as entrepreneurs is to lower the level of *perceived* risk to the point where the perception of a transaction dissolves and where risk-averse buyers feel comfortable enough to give it a shot. Imagine pulling a rope between your startup and the customer, in the middle, is the deal. The harder you pull, the more they resist — fighting tooth and nail to defend their position of prior products and suppliers that they previously decided to work with. By changing, you and your business represents a new choice that makes their prior choices inferior or obsolete. Naturally then, they feel the intrinsic need to either defend their former decisions, ignore your new offering, or agree to accept your offer. By agreeing, they in a way feel they must change, as they now must let go of their prior "smart" choices.

How can you more easily get the prospect over to your side?

This can be done in a myriad of ways — by reducing all on-boarding friction, lowering or eliminating the cost of admission, showing third party testimonials (power of the crowd), displaying awards or achievements, or offering no-risk trials. By sliding over, buyers have to feel like they are winning by choosing your company. The emotion that they must have is that they get to win by choosing you, even if this means that you, the supplier loses a little. Often times in B2B, buyers will negotiate ancillary components of the deal to feel like they got the upper hand — further justification that they made a smart decision. Sometimes they "win" increased payment terms from net 30 to 60 days, other times they score a deeper discount, sometimes they got you to throw in free shipping — all of which are *small wins* but that make them feel they won. This sounds backwards, but buyers don't necessarily want to see their suppliers make a killing on the first transaction, *they* want to win first. If you succeed later on, after they've received an abundance of value then that's fine, but so long as *they* get to win the first round of the game.

Truth was, that Restaurant Manager was right — it's the perennial marketplace question — getting critical mass on one side of the platform is vital to drive sufficient value on the other. Virtually all marketplace-style companies have had to figure this out — Ebay®, Amazon®, GroupOn®, UpWork®, Facebook® — you name it, LaDolceDeal was no different. I realized, after getting shut out of a deal that day, that I needed to re-structure the conversation with merchants from the start to say that we *would* be launching by a certain date, and that we were giving them an exclusive, early opportunity to sign up pre-launch! This way, I discovered, I could build up a sufficient number of merchants on one side of the site, without having to repeat that awkward chicken-or-egg conversation ever again.

Often times it's easier to sell the vision of the future that your product holds, than sell something that's live today.

For the next month, I ran around town, walked cold into establishments, and asked to speak to the owner or manager. I would hand them my business card, tell them my pre-launch spiel, and sign them up — restaurants, clothing retailers, spas, wineries, special events — as many as I could. In the beginning, we signed a great steakhouse, a Caribbean restaurant, a high-end Italian restaurant, a women's clothing boutique, a perfumery, a burger joint, and a wine tasting room. I'd later learn to focus in on only the verticals such as food and wine that were converting the best and skip the ones that put up too much of a fight to close — retailers and hotels.

As I signed up one, I'd use their name as leverage to get another to on-board, and again and again, until I had a dozen or more deals in the pipeline. As more signed up my sales pitch improved dramatically, the perceived risk lowered substantially, and more early adopters joined LaDolceDeal.

Now, for my next problem — go get the damn eyeballs I promised everyone was coming! I heavily leveraged social media — Facebook®, Google Plus®, Twitter® — to get the word out. I created a weekly e-mail that subscribers could share with family and friends.

LaDolceDeal went on to produce thousands of dollars of sales in its first year in business and was profitable from the first few deals. By year two, it was costing me *way* too many hours running around town pleading restaurant owners to give me a deal so that I could go share it online with our four thousand subscribers we had amassed by then. I built a mobile app and featured merchants and their deals to thousands of tourists on the go. Despite having done the hard part — build, launch, and amass businesses and consumers to complete the product — I still had merchants who would open our e-mails dozens and dozens of times a day and kept telling me they wanted to feature a deal, but who would always never do.

Trying to convert the unconvertible is a waste of time. It's easier to convert those that are actually interested, instead of trying to crack open the nuts that lead you on for months.

After two years of meeting after meeting, call after call, e-mail after e-mail with small business owners trying to convince them to see the new sales benefits of joining, I was running out of patience and time. Some of the owners were simply not convinced that lowering their prices for a LaDolceDeal could be made up by volume purchasers. Others would strike a deal with us, and then refuse to pay me the $99 bucks that we were owed after we promoted their deal! Trying to beg a multimillion-dollar Restauranteur to pay a $99 dollar past due invoice was one of the most frustratingly, low points of my days in the group buying business. Only two years into the company, I decided to close it down before I pulled out all of my hair!

Key Lessons Learned from La Dolce Deal:

Marketplaces have two sides (Buyers & Sellers). The experience is 100% different for each. You must devote ample time to understand the distinctive needs and cater to each group. A one-size-fits-all experience doesn't work to attract, convert, retain, and monetize a marketplace.

"What do you mean you can't *print* out the deal?" I retorted. One of my customers on LaDolceDeal, my family's lawyer it turned out, became a huge fan of our Oyster & Champagne deal. We had partnered with a local hotel in downtown Monterey to offer an oyster and champagne special for 50% off. "Who the hell wants to slurp down raw oysters and then wash it down with a glass of bubbly?" I thought to myself. Well, a deal is a deal. At twenty-six, this wasn't for me. Well, it turns out quite a few people loved that deal. Taste preferences aside, I had a technical glitch that a user needed help with — he had paid for the deal online, but every time he tried to print out the deal page to bring into the restaurant, it wasn't working. "I thought we solved this the other week?" I told Roy. "Reagan, I put my credit card in, pressed pay now, and then nothing," in his matter-of-fact Bostonian tone. I was exhausted from trying to recreate the bug, but I had to resolve it for him, he was my family's personal attorney, and I knew I would never hear the end of it if I took his money and didn't fix the issue right away.

The site was just not intuitive enough for the buyer. After staring at the customer experience for months, I knew where everything was and how to do it. Problem was, for first-time users, they didn't realize that the system was e-mailing them the printable deal, whereas they were thinking that they have to download and print it out right then and there on the same page. In my rush to launch the site, I forgot to put instructions on the "payment completed" page that explained that we would be e-mailing them a copy of the receipt along with the downloadable offer that they could print out and bring to the merchant. It was a User Experience rookie mistake — I had forgotten to walk through the actual buying process of a deal, as if I were a real customer, otherwise, I would have caught this and could have corrected it. "I'm sorry Roy, let me do it myself and pay for it out of my pocket and I'll e-mail you the receipt and you can just take mine to the restaurant — no need to pay me back." "*Really?*" he replied in disbelief, more so that I was running a website that wasn't working properly than at my graciousness. "Yes," I replied.

User design and User Experience (U/X) are the most critical elements of nailing a winning product or service. In my haste to build out the product, I spent most of my time addressing the needs of the merchants, the side that I truly needed first to capture the deals and build a draw for our product. I failed to look at each side as unique user experiences, having different goals, problems, and solutions, to be gained (G.P.S. System discussed earlier).

A key problem that we faced was that we first had to sign up merchants to get the deals, *then* market the deals to attract new subscribers. But merchants wanted to know there were going to be eyeballs seeing their deals first, otherwise they wouldn't advertise, so how do you get eyeballs before you have the deals? A Catch-22.

It takes at least twelve months to understand the ins and outs of a new business — the model, the customer journey, and how your solution integrates into that experience.

I think of a business as a machine — it has components that work independently of each other, but all must come together to work in synchronicity to convert inputs (people, talent, ideas, materials) into outputs (products, services, and value) for the customer. Knowing how and why the machine runs — what the inputs are for growth and why those deliver results — should become the focus of the CEO to increase sales, improve margins, and grow marketshare.

But you've got to spend time figuring out what those key levers are that drive traffic, conversions, and growth, and what they are that increase your margins, so that you have working capital to invest for expansion. At LaDolceDeal, I knew that we needed new deal flow in the pipeline from merchants, and a hungry audience on the other end waiting for them. What we didn't plan for, was how damn long it would take to persuade merchants to work with us, and how many deals they would, on average, be willing to give to us.

Great businesses are well oiled machines; know what levers to push/pull at the right time to unlock growth.

Just like any Formula 1® race car, performing at a peak state requires thoughtful planning, design and maintenance. When we fail to address even a few of the underlying parts, the system as a whole begins to atrophy and fail. Your business is no different. It requires key people and key resources, and in turn, creates an output (sales, profits, growth and customer retention). It's not good enough to just turn the car on and hope it runs perfectly every day, nor is it good enough to just show up to the office, open the door, and wait for customers to arrive.

We need to be mindful of the levers that we must push and pull within our organization that makes the business complete a cycle — that cycle may be hiring a new employee, training them sufficiently, and managing them so well that they in turn can lead others and repeat the cycle. Or, it may be launching a new marketing campaign, monitoring the results, getting an order from a customer from that campaign, processing it, shipping it, updating the customer with tracking info, and following up a week later to get feedback from them for improvement. These are cycles, each requiring comprehension.

Time is Money:

Solicit the deal, set up a meeting with the merchant, get paid, create the deal online, publicize the deal, rinse and repeat — this was one cycle at LaDolceDeal. In the beginning, the lever barely moved us forward. No matter how hard I pushed — we had no merchants, therefore no deals, thus no value for our subscribers. As more merchants came aboard, it became far easier to sell the platform's value, collect their deals, and offer new coupons to users.

For the first twenty to thirty deals, the machine would demand around twenty hours of my time in hunting for offers and would output around one deal accordingly — a 20 hour:1 deal ratio. At that slow pace, I'd have to pound the pavement for months just to get a few dozen deals aboard — far too slow of an output to keep our subscribers interested in our site.

As the months rolled on, my sales presentation improved — traction built, and the ratio improved by half the time to 10 hours:1 deal. If I were to spend ten hours e-mailing and running around town, pitching merchants, I knew I would get at least one deal out of it. I thus developed a keen understanding of how my time correlated to the company's key growth metric — deals — that drove the machine.

As my closing ratio kept improving, I learned to simplify the explanation of how the site created value for the business. I thew out the technical jargon and closed more deals even faster. I pushed the lever further, trying to squeeze every bit of return out of my hours out "in the field", getting merchants to sign up for three to six months instead of just offering us one deal for this month. This maximized my time further. Identify the mini cycles in your company — they are directly proportional to growth.

Deals take 2X-3X longer to close with Business-to-Business sales than you anticipate. Prepare for the delay and have more in the pipeline than required. Track your conversions.

So here you are, you've worked so hard to pitch a new firm on becoming a client, you've done the research, the cold calling, the selling, the presentations, the quoting, the follow-up, and the waiting. And more waiting, and more waiting. This is what happens in sales — it's hurry up, quote, and wait. The challenge with long sales cycle times is that it puts pressure on the sales team to hit quotas, deliver realistic projections, and outperform last quarter's results. You nor I can predict what clients will buy, and more chillingly, when they will opt to. That is why VCs know projections are based on best-case scenarios.

I realized, during my first two startups, that deals — no matter how good they appear to be shaping up — take 2X-3X longer than you anticipated. This in turn, causes ancillary problems downstream for your organization — it puts executive leadership in a blind position when it comes to decision making to plan inventory purchases or CapEx (capital expenditure) investments. It puts a strain on cash reserves to float the company for longer to cover operating expenses for sales that haven't materialized, and it can suck the momentum of your sales team when the "high" from a great sales call or presentation begins to fade.

At both WML and LaDolceDeal, we failed to fully calculate the time required of our sales cycles. In hindsight, we should have tracked over a 30-day period, from beginning to close, the average time each cycle took. Then, use that metric in our projections to see how the model shakes out. For LaDolceDeal, we likely would have then been able to pivot our advertising packages to say booking each merchant on a minimum of a six-month package worth a dozen or so promoted deals (2-4 deals per month). If it took me two months to close each merchant from initial touchpoint to an inked contract, we could then better plan for our sales, and make it up by locking in longer deal contracts to give us a longer runway to promote their content without having to hunt so quickly for the next one.

Knowing When It's Time to Pivot:

For LaDolceDeal, the model was supposed to be simple: Find a deal with a local business, then publicize that deal by e-mail and via our website and mobile app to our subscribers. We planned for the merchant to revenue split with us (80/20), and we would list the deal for free. Now at that time, TravelZoo® was taking thirty percent of hotel deals, Groupon® was taking fifty percent of all deals, and both were asking merchants to lower their prices down to nothing, leaving them with very little profit at the end of the day, hoping to make it up in volume. Yes, they got the foot-traffic, but they didn't make much in the end result, they confessed. We felt letting merchants set the deal price, terms, and package, and get to keep eighty percent of each transaction was a fair bargain.

Here's what really happened. Most merchants didn't want to share any revenue with us, even though the deal consultation with me and publicity on our site was given to them for free. We had marketing costs to reach the business, then time in running across town to meet with them to explain the business model and show them example deals. Next, I had to build the deal on our site, promote it across social media, publish it on our app, and create an e-blast for our Deals of the Week newsletter. It was a ton of work, and businesses just were not getting that there was no up-front cost (or maybe they did, but our model looked too good to be true); they just didn't want to revenue share with LaDolceDeal.

Oddly enough, the businesses felt more accustomed to paying for advertising, which meant that we would make a coupon and promote it online to our subscribers after they paid. It turned out, they were used to this print-media advertising model, and not comfortable in waiting for us to cut them a commission check. I learned this on the fly, and decided to pivot our business model to do what they wanted.

We changed our model from the 80/20 revenue split, to selling a one-month, three-month and six-month advertising package. The business would come up with the offer, send it over, I would design the coupon, get approval, and publish it. We were paid up-front (I used Square® to swipe cards in my meetings on my iPhone or would e-mail them an invoice by PayPal®), and they would count the coupons as customers came in to redeem the deal. This was beginning to work.

As I got more businesses to join with a direct advertising model, I promoted the fact that I had other paying merchants seeing results, and it instilled more trust in LaDolceDeal. I would track how many users clicked and downloaded each coupon, and share that engagement report free of charge with the business to prove it was working. We call this type of referral traffic, third-party proof. Businesses assume that if their competitor is now using your service, then they might be winning more customers, so they decided to join.

Here's the issue with that model. It took me too much time to collect, negotiate, design the deals, and then promote them. I couldn't come out with enough deals fast enough for our subscribers.

Plus, the amount of revenue that I could bring in from a few deals wasn't enough to make all that effort worth it. The model was flawed, it required me to do *everything*, and the moment I stopped running after the next deal, the site's value ceased, subscribers forgot about us, and we looked like we didn't have fresh content to offer. An unintended chain reaction that I didn't anticipate.

Could you have predicted this? Oddly enough my mother, a savvy business executive, predicted this might happen before I launched LaDolceDeal. She thought that there was a market need, but that it would require a lot of running around to close the deals, so I might be better off with a street team to close the deals for me. She was right, but in the early stages, a founder must do the pitching to learn the objection points and learn how their own business works first. I never felt comfortable launching the business with a crew of sales reps who didn't know the business, let alone how to sell it. Plus, after I priced out the ad rates, we didn't have enough margin to split a deal with the reps without outpricing the service. Needless to say, I swallowed my entrepreneurial pride, and closed up shop on LaDolceDeal. Don't worry, I don't miss the deals space.

One thing you'll learn from having a few startups — closing them when they don't work gets easier each time — it's like pulling off a Band-Aid®; better to do it quickly than slowly over years.

Walking Away to Win the Sale:

Closing sales in your early days is tough and time consuming. Without a history of traction behind you and key customer references, you're selling thin air. If you can predict that out of one-hundred sales, ninety-nine percent will not buy, then you won't care so much about closing each one, and in turn, will act less desperate to the prospects you are pitching. When you make a presentation, present your solutions, and then walk away, ironically, in so doing, buyers counterintuitively then want to work with you. By doing such, you regain the strength that you need to move towards the next prospective deal. Conversely, when you obsessively follow-up with a client, ponder with anguish as to why they haven't responded to your offer, you emotionally sell from desperation. The less emotion you attach to a sales opportunity, the faster you close. Walk away to win.

Set a sales challenge with yourself to reach one hundred prospects, get twenty to take a call, get ten to review a quote, get five to close. If you can get 5% to buy, that's a great baseline to scale. Increase that rate by one more lead per week.

Content is dead the moment it's published. For us, the newest deal was old once it went live. Consumers demand consistency and frequency of unique content that serves them in greater proportion to what they paid.

How many times today have you checked Instagram, Facebook, Snap, LinkedIn, Google News, Reddit, TechCrunch or any other app that features content? Come on, be honest with yourself. I bet more than once per site. Every time you pull down on your phone to refresh the page, you *demand* a fresh dose of compelling content. God forbid if the app fails to refresh.

Consumers and businesses want unique, fresh content that speaks to them, then disappears, with a fresh dose to replace it. It used to be that you could create a beautiful piece of content, and people would admire it and want to go back and see it over and over again. Boy, have times changed! We want to turn on Spotify® and hear a new track, we want to flip through our newsfeed and see fresh gossip, we want to swipe through dating apps and see fresh faces, we want to browse new books and see newly released titles — the demand for new is now *never* satisfied, and neither are your customers.

If your company creates content for a living — and all business must now be great storytellers and content creators — you must continuously create, share, and refresh your content, or else, you lose relevancy through content expiry.

Our newest deals would only be relevant the moment the e-mail hit the four thousand inboxes — after that, it was as old as last week's bagels. Our newest product sale was only timely over a holiday weekend, and then, it was stale. Our newest featured artist for WorldMusicLink was cool for a day, and then would fade out tomorrow. Treat your content like fresh fish — it's good for no more than two to three days.

Virality is not a business plan. Virality takes users to want to share. You can't just create it with a few posts. You must design for sharable content.

Virality, as we covered before, is the willingness for a market of consumers to *want* to share your content, brand, or products to their respective networks without your incentivization. But, as I have learned, vitality takes more than a mention of "Hey, like us on Facebook®" and most assuredly, is no substitute for a business plan. I used to think — if you post it, they will share. Boy, was I wrong. In actuality, people now covet their networks, whether that network is a few e-mail addresses of their close family members, colleagues, or friends. Getting someone to voluntarily share your content or endorse your brand is harder than it appears. If you consistently beat a follower over the head with a big neon buy button all the time, they're gonna think you don't value them.

The old adage — good things travel slow, bad things travel fast — doesn't hold true for startups. I would revise that — emotionally impactful, uniquely valuable, and hilariously funny content travels fast; everything else is simply ignored.

Customers show you that they're hopeful your product will help them by buying from you once. Repeat customers confirm that they valued your product previously. Don't sell people what you think they want, show them solutions and let them confirm the value in it for themselves.

When you get a customer to buy from you the first time, your marketing worked. But that's it. When they come back again after using your product and buy again, pay for their recurring subscription, increasing their order size on their next order, or writing a positive review — you've jumped from marketing in the abstract, to creating value in the concrete.

With coupons at LaDolceDeal, I chose to launch a business that required little educational curve for the consumer. They saw the deal, confirmed the value of it themselves, added it to the cart, and received it by e-mail. While everyone else is trying to build the next Uber®, Airbnb® and marketplace, I realized that people shop and eat every day of the year, and that by buying online, they could avoid overpaying at a local retail shop or restaurant and gain a new level of access to an historically expensive area. With new web platforms, new mobile apps, new services that require an educational curve, that curve takes time, money, and effort, and usually ends up yielding low on-boarding in the startup days as you spend so much time convincing people that your new product is a better mousetrap than before. Too many first-time founders are dazzled by the headlines that herald a twenty-five-year-old in flip-flops who just walked right into a VC's office, raises $100 million bucks, and turns it into a Unicorn IPO. For most of us, this never happens. For your first startup, you want to learn how to run a profitable shop, scale it to $100k or $1 million in sales, and then you'll be really prepared to raise that $100 million and 100X it if you so choose.

Startups have different growing pains at different phases. Knowing how you'll feel running a startup is impossible if you've never been there before. It feels like running a race blindfolded, following the cheers to find the right direction to run in, to miraculously looking back to relish where you started and how the heck you got there.

I realized that scaling a startup both operationally and financially has its own learning curve. So, to help you better understand this, I've broken the phases down in parts so you can better understand what each might feel like before you reach them.

Pre-Revenue:

Literally, you're just trying to figure out if this wacky idea has legs. You're building the prototype, talking with anyone who returns your call, and understanding the market demand. This is the fun, creative phase where everything is possible, no idea is a bad idea, every glimmer of a smile from someone you talk to about your idea is hope that you're onto something big. You also spend a copious amount of time at Philz® coffee shop. I recommend the Tesora or Greater Alarm.

Zero — $10,000 Revenue:

You're just trying to get the first few folks to show you attention and whip out their wallets. Many businesses get to this point, think they have product-model-market fit, and then fail because they can't scale past the first one-hundred customers who tried the beta. They assume everyone will buy (which they don't) and spend what little money they usually have on the things that don't matter. Being here is like dancing in the dark and bumping into everyone, trying to find the damn light-switch! You know it's there, somewhere, but where?

$10,000—$100,000 Revenue:

Now, you feel like you're moving forward, as you've built a startup from idea to its first $100,000 in sales. While this is impressive, and depending on how fast you got there, it can be a real proving ground for scalability. The question becomes next is, are you profitable, or are you running a loss and getting customers to buy from you because you're either low balling an existing item in the market, found a niche with a limited market, or are a one-trick product pony? Maybe that's all there is, or maybe this thing has real legs to run for years.

$100,000—$500,000 Revenue:

This is where the startup halo fades, and when the real management begins. You're now operating as a business owner who pays taxes and pays yourself (at least something), have recurring customers, know your model, and know what channels are performing the best. You've even got customers on speed dial and know certain ones by their voice when they call your office looking to re-order. You're tracking your KPIs (key performance indicators) and doubling down on the marketing campaigns and distribution channels that are yielding results. You're also likely managing a small team and might be able to hire a few more. Congrats! Most people never get here. You also start to see a few gray hairs. Don't worry, more will show up.

$500,000—$1,000,000 Revenue:

Now you're really focused on growth. You're looking at the bigger picture, asking yourself how big this thing can get, and what else you will need to amplify sales — Investors? Partnerships? Channels? Products? Retail Stores? Trade Shows? You're saying to yourself, "If we have a strong six to seven figure business, what's stopping us from turning this into a strong seven to eight figure business?"

$1,000,000—$10,000,000 Revenue:

This is an elite club of small business owners. You have sufficient cash flow to pay yourself a nice salary, hire most specialists you need to grow your operations, virtually test most marketing channels that may help you 2X or 3X the business without freaking out about losing $5,000, and you're asking yourself questions like, "Are we salable?", "Can we expand internationally and when?", "Am I building a business that will endure for years?" This is a fun time because you have optionality — you can maintain, grow, or sell for a multiple.

$10,000,000+ Revenue:

High fives around Rockstar. Most likely retirement is coming into the picture, or if you're having fun, finding a replacement for you to handle the day-to-day operations as you handle the visionary stuff, speaking engagements, Angel investing, golfing, and oh yeah, Mai Tais baby. If you're totally a Type-A and want to run the world vis-a-vis your company, an IPO might enter the picture, or at the very least an acquisition for possibly 3X-10X EBITDA depending on your business, market, and the M&A climate. If you've raised VC, they're either thinking about a larger round to scale to an IPO in a year or two, or possibly a sizable buy-out.

$100,000,000 Revenue:

Flattered you are reading my book, thank you! When I get here, I'll let you know.

> **Testing variations shows you what works and what doesn't. By improving one hundred tiny things just one percent, your company grows at an incredible, compounding rate.**

I began to pay closer attention to the small tests that were working, and others that weren't, and focused on amplifying the things that were working effortlessly and creating results. For example, when you launch an online ad campaign, you essentially have no idea what keywords are going to be the ones that trigger both clicks as well as conversions. Over time, you analyze the data, and can set up campaigns that yield the highest conversions. By moving more of your budget into campaigns that resonate most for your segments, not just the keywords that you guess they are searching for, you drive faster and more profitable returns. If your product is called the CurlyCue BBQ Set, but no one types in "curlycue barbecue tools" but, instead, they search for "best barbecue tools", you'll never get results. Think how your user might begin their search for a solution to their problem, not how you the founder want your product to appear.

Other small variations like adjusting the user experience of your website to be 10 times simpler can have dramatic results on conversions. People are busy and most are not tech aficionados, so when it comes to shopping online, there is still trepidation and confusion as to where to find something, how to add it to the cart, how to check out, and what to expect next. This may sound rudimentary, but you have to understand that most buyers have never seen your brand, your website, nor have any idea where anything is located.

The Eight/Eighty-Year-Old U/X Test:

I recommend designing the user experience as if an eight-year-old and an eighty-year-old are trying to buy from you. If they both can figure it out, then you've got a winner. Founders often put too many friction points in the way of the customer's path to purchase. Less is *always* more.

Micro-management kills scalability.

In addition to driving sales, becoming more familiar with the stage I was in and what might come next, and designing the site for both an eight and eighty-year-old, I also had to simplify the customer experience (the user interface, the search, the checkout, and automate the follow-up). I decided that in order to scale faster, I should also stop trying to convince customers and fight their rejections and indecision, and just give them the tools to sell themselves online, thus, removing me from the equation. In order to scale, you have to remove yourself from the machine, so it can run itself.

My father used to have this phrase that really stuck well with me. He would say, "Son, when you start your own business, you work for it. The goal is, someday, it will work for you." Pops was right. In the beginning you have to design the system to simply work. Over time, you figure out how to optimize the machine so that eventually, you can put that baby on autopilot. Now, you might disagree with me, and say, "Well hold on just a second, I love it when the owner of my favorite restaurant greets me at the door, comes over and sits down with us at our table, takes our order, and delivers it." One of the leading, and often not talked about, causes of small business death is by micro-management.

The whole point of building an autonomous company is to take an idea that solves a problem and find ways to eliminate the need to micro-manage every operational element. If you are always the greeter, the salesman, the chef, the accountant, and the manager, you can never truly grow. How can you open a second location if you have to be the cook in both? You can't. How can you run an East Coast and West Coast office? You can't. How can you comfortably take a vacation if you always have to be the one on duty? You can't.

Through thoughtful hiring and designing, we can set ourselves up for both scale and lifestyle. By designing a system to be semi or fully automatic, we eliminate functions that suck our time on duty. By hiring well, we pass the responsibility so others can take the reins if we are sick or need a few days off. If a business is so reliant on one operator to make it all work, it should be a red flag for the owner.

There's something beautiful about a profitable startup. No one questions if the idea will work or not. The question then becomes how fast can it scale?

After WML, I had an epiphany. I decided once and for all to stop trying to raise investor capital and become a mega corporation before I reached month over month profitability, despite what all of my business books advised me I should do. This forced me to focus on the only thing that truly mattered — serving the customer, and not on building more features, finding new employees, or gaining publicity. I shifted my mindset from securing outside capital to finding product-market-model fit and proving the model out first. Raising money can be a tremendous distraction for founders, and I implore all founders to try their hardest to reach profitability, or at the very least, sustainable revenue month over month before considering a fundraise.

Seeing the Bigger Picture:

Even with the little traction that these early ventures achieved, they failed to scale to multi-million-dollar companies. And that's all right by me. For being just a twenty something year old entrepreneur, these ventures were successful. Now, hold on just a minute, I know what you're saying. This guy can't do math — he never raised big VC round or IPO'ed! I'll explain later how success can be reframed, but the goal here is to help you understand that there are multiple lenses through which you must judge your business and your life. If you only look at the P&L, the Balance Sheet, and the Cash Flow Statement, that will only tell you one side of the startup story. True, you can't pay bills with Betas, but there are millions of dollars' worth of value in the lessons of each startup if you just look carefully enough. Over time, you get good at spotting early land minds and getting further faster.

Lastly, I asked myself some deeper questions, *"Why* do I want to build a big business, and what is it that I am seeking to feel and gain, from that?"

How Big is Big Enough?

Through reflection, I realized that what I wanted was not to run a big business or a one-thousand-person staff, or go public, but rather the ability to have three little things every day: financial opportunity, flexibility, and enjoyment. Financial security would give me the proper base from which to test new ideas out and not feel so pressured to make them work. Flexibility would give me the opportunity to stretch my legs, travel when I wanted to, and not feel the requirement of always being on duty. Enjoyment, well that should be self-explanatory, but fun is key part of the journey. Fun can be providing value for people who need it. Fun can be giving people the tools that they yearn for but don't know were to look for them. Fun can be sharing laughs with co-workers, suppliers, and customers. For all of the hours that you spend working on a startup, fun must be part of the net benefit.

I hope that over the preceding chapters, you've learned from my un-sugarcoated, real life startup experiences, and gained from my realizations, so that you too, can attain those three little things for yourself. This is up to you to decide what your own personal three take aways will become — this is, after all, *your* startup. You deserve to grant yourself the opportunity to have what you desire. In the beginning, it may not come as fast as you'd hoped, but if you set your intention correctly, it will come eventually. Furthermore, it will be up to you to decide how far you want to push your company, and just how big you may want to become. To each, her own. Building a bigger business isn't always a better life choice. Appearances from the outside can look a lot different than what's on the inside.

Take a moment now to write down your top three takeaways for your own business below. If you could really step back, and highlight three elements that your startup will give you, what might they be?

1. ____

2. ____

3. ____

CHAPTER 17:
BATTLESCARS

At the core of any business, regardless of its type — C-Corporation, S-Corporation, Limited Liability Corporation (LLC), Limited Liability Partnership (LLP) — is that it is its own separate entity that must be governed ethically, and follow state and federal requirements for conducting business, hiring employees, issuing stock, and reporting taxes. I strongly recommend that you interview a number of corporate attorneys and select one who has deep experience with startups; he/she will be able to guide you in entity formation, shareholder, employment and stock option agreements, and more.

When I was nineteen, I met a successful Stanford business professor by luck it turned out. We had a great conversation about my new startup idea for WorldMusicLink, and she referred me to a prestigious law firm in Boston where I was attending school. Howard, the firm's leading Partner, guided me through everything — incorporation, charter creation, stock issuances, capitalization tables, Delaware and California filings, private placement memorandums and more. Working with a seasoned business attorney puts your mind at ease when you're a first-time founder and sets a high standard for how you should conduct business right from the start.

With Howard's firm, we were introduced to our $750 per hour invoices, which hit me in the face like a sack of bricks. None the less, I felt I was doing things the professional way right from the start. Maybe I was playing entrepreneur, or maybe I was scared to make an early mistake, but choosing his prestigious firm was ultimately a wise decision. Was there a time when we simply didn't have the money to pay their invoices? All the time. I recall we had something like a $3,000 invoice that we simply couldn't afford when we were tight on cash and between a fundraise. In good faith, I'd make installment payments — mailing my $100 check every week to his firm until I finally paid it off in full. Howard was completely understanding, and even waived some of his billable hours, instead billing us at his paralegal's lower rate; still unaffordable for us at the time.

Long story short, hire a great startup attorney at a reputable firm. Yes, they are expensive, but it's far better and cheaper to do things well once, then have to go back and re-do your company's legal documents later on. If you intend to raise venture capital, as we had, be sure to partner with a firm that has completed many successful venture capital financings, especially with the VC firms that you may wish to raise capital from as they will be on good terms with the partners. The last thing you want is to hire some small-town lawyer to screw up your term sheet and start arguing for clauses with the VCs that may never really matter and could cost you your term sheet. You often pay for what you get, and when it comes to experienced counsel, it's been my experience that this adage holds. If you want to raise VC, I've been told to form a C-Corporation, given the flexible nature of the ability to modify voting rights and preferred shares, which many VCs prefer to have access to. Always discuss your own startup with an experienced attorney to ensure you are getting the best counsel on what entity to choose, and how to structure all of your agreements.

Wait, this wasn't in my Business Law class:

It's ironic that at B-school, they have you take Business Law, but never really talk about lawsuits (frivolous or legitimate) or how anyone — for almost any reason — can file suit with another company even if they didn't do anything wrong. To answer a suit, you must lawyer-up and spend tens of thousands, if not hundreds of thousands, and often years defending your position. A total time and money drain.

In just the last ten years, I've nearly seen it all — from contractual breaches, to erroneous trade dress infringement suits, to copyright theft, to competitors with falsified patents, to Federal Court lawsuits, to interrogating depositions, to the Court of Appeals, to even fighting one case that went up to the Supreme Court. All legal battles are a financial drain, an emotional rollercoaster, and a derailment of your company's focus. If you can avoid a legal battle, it's often the wiser. However, sometimes you have to fight to protect the integrity of your company, of if you've been unjustly bullied.

Law classes typically cover the basics — contractual law, torts, liability, entity formation, and indemnity — but they unfortunately don't touch on trademark or patent law that much and in the business world, intellectual property law comes up over and over again.

Another area that is not covered typically in B-School is Human Resource law (HR), which is more than just hiring and releasing, it covers ESOPs (employee share option plans), workplace diversity, employment agreements, and more. Whenever you hire someone, you need to follow both the federal and state law to comply with proper hiring questioning, interviewing, and provide a fair and equal process. Also, when you need to let someone go, you must do so in the proper way — with fair notice and be able to articulate why they are being relieved of their duties.

When starting out, typically startups don't have much capital to pay for salaries and benefits. One option is to use Independent Contractors to assist with the initial development of your project. One way is to hire Independent Contractors yourself and manage the relationship. Another way is to hire a professional HR staffing company to handle it all for you — the recruitment, placement, and dismissal of temp, temp to full-time, or full-time employees.

At WML, we worked with Independent Contractors directly and it worked well — they could come and go when they pleased, work on their own laptops, and produce code at their own pace. I also hired eight Account Executives to handle sales on a commission basis. Given that we couldn't afford to pay the engineers large salaries, we would pay a competitive hourly wage for the project, and in so doing, were not required to pay payroll taxes on top of salaries as they were not technically our employees, but contractors. When we owed them more than $600 (the limit at the time), we would issue them a 1099-MISC form so they could file their own taxes and expense their deductions. I kept a time sheet for them to fill out each week, so we both could keep track of their billable hours.

Today, sites like TaskRabbit®, UpWork®, and Fivvr® are all labor marketplaces that could assist your startup in locating on-demand talent who have specialized skills in engineering, website development, sales, marketing, graphic design and more. You can pay an hourly wage or on a per project basis, and they can keep you abreast on their progress on a daily basis to reach your outlined deliverables.

Trademarks:

When we filed our logo for trademark protection seeking to obtain the status of a registered mark (™ to ®), it took about two years to get approval. The first stage was determining what classes our mark was going to be filed under. There are many different classes, and each have their own governing declaration or domain — hats, t-shirts, logos, etc. Our IP attorney walked us through what two classes he felt were the initial ones we should file the mark under. It was my, albeit novice, understanding of trademark law, that a mark is technically only defensible if it has coverage under the specific class(es) in question. Always discuss your own filings, classes, and potential defensibility of such properties with an experienced trademark attorney or firm. When a mark is in use, it is typically used under the "™" designation as it is pending registration from the United States Patent and Trademark Office (USPTO). Once an examining attorney at the USPTO clears the mark, then it is awarded a registration number which denotes the "®" symbol for a period of time. Earning that registered mark for WorldMusicLink's logo was a highlight in my startup journey. I flew the WML logo high and proud on our website, across our t-shirts, on our business cards, and in my heart.

There was a point during WML where I had departed from our office space after our two-year rental agreement ended, where our web developer had left us given our lack of capital to continue to retain him, and we were no longer operational. About a year had gone by, when I received an e-mail from a guy claiming that our registered trademark design was infringing on his. At that point, WML was barely alive. How could *we* be infringing? I thought we had a Registered Trademark! Doesn't that protect you? I mean, part of the process to obtain that status *is* a full background search across the TESS database of the USPTO by both your IP attorney and the Examining Trademark Officer to ensure your mark is in the clear and that any requested classes were clear and uncontested. When I researched that company, I realized that they were basically a team of lawyers who had done this before — reach out to companies to threaten them into acquiescing into remission or settlement payouts. Talk about an attack from left field! Without any desire to battle when all we had was a broken Beta website and no funding left, I decided that I would give in. I would take our trademarked logo and change it on our website and social media pages to remove our brand to just leave our company's name. After making the changes, I realized that I was just bullied into submission by someone who thought we had funding and would pay up.

Where does this come from? Well, I realized, the world is full of all kinds of individuals with all kinds of scruples, who at a moment's notice, can feel threatened by your success — or appearance of success in our case. It leads them to go on the attack and puts you in a precarious position to fight or flight. I chose, in that battle, to fly higher. Was our logo worth a ludicrous fight that would cost me time, money, and angst? Not for what the upside was. This is the point that I want you to see — know when the fight is worth it.

There are always opportunities to fight for things in your startup. Ask yourself, "If I do win, what is the *true* upside?"

Will I gain something greater or just go back to my company's previous status before it happened? For us, fighting for a trademark and winning would be fruitless — we would be no better off or closer to our goals if we win. There are opportunities that I believe you should and must fight for that are at the core of your principles.

Throughout the last ten years in business, I've witnessed more unscrupulous professionals than I'd like to admit (both domestically and abroad). I've even had Chinese companies steal our company's copyright protected images, crop out our logo, and put them up on their website to sell their own knock-off products.

**There will always be battles vying for your attention.
Engage only when you must and do so wisely.**

Non-Disclosure Agreements:

During the course of my early salesman days cold calling, I once made a presentation to a well-known restaurant chain with around three hundred and fifty stores in the U.S. I introduced them to new program that would literally save their stores millions annually on one of their supply items just by switching to our alternative (a renewable option). After phone calls, e-mails, and presentations with the lead Buyer, I was inconspicuously e-mailed an NDA (Non-Disclosure Agreement) to sign, a Trojan horse if you will, disguised as a letter of intent to move forward with the deal with us for the program. Being the rookie, eager salesman I was, I quickly initialed the agreement, and e-mailed it back. After a follow-up, I was advised that they were proceeding with the program, our original idea, but not with us. The nerve! To pitch a game changing, multi-million-dollar idea, then have it stolen from us and muzzled. Despite my efforts to shine light on the crime to their Chief Marketing Officer with CC to the deceitful buyer, I was met with silence. There I was, stolen from, lied to, and gagged for three years. Strike One.

There was another major chain of stationary goods (I won't say the name), and they sought to work with us to develop some new items for the U.S. market. After a series of e-mails and phone calls back and forth, samples and quotes, we received another NDA to sign, suggesting that in order for us to "move forward", we would need to sign off. Having learned our lesson before, we were hesitant. We had spent weeks sharing critical insights from our industry, helping their Innovation Director and team learn key product improvements, and then all of a sudden, they wanted us to sign off and fax back an NDA? You've gotta be kidding. I decided to call the Director. The guy answers and tells me that he just landed in China (China of all places!), and that he just needed us to sign off on that NDA as he was going to be meeting with factories to move forward. Of course, this guy was on his way to take our smart ideas and go manufacture the new product line for themselves at a low-cost factory in China. Strike Two.

I've had numerous examples where people ask you to sign off on an NDA in order to simply discuss their idea or to "move forward" (red flag) — be wary of signing off on anything of the sort.

Typically, a request such as this is a wolf in sheep's clothing who could possibly take your good ideas and go-to-market themselves without you. Other times, those who ask for an NDA, just aren't the kind of honest folks you should be partnering with anyways. Good-natured, reputable, and trustworthy people don't force others to sign off on NDAs, unless what they're proposing is of such secretive, stealthy nature that it simply has to be. 95% of the time, they can usually explain the general idea without divulging the details or proprietary nature of the concept. Should there be mutual interest to continue the discussion further, then you can consider engaging in an equitable NDA. First, seek counsel from an experienced business attorney before engaging in any NDAs.

Being the small guy in business does have two key advantages — endless "good ideas" and the nimbleness to execute them immediately on the fly. Large companies, stifled by corporate bureaucracy, long approval processes, and limited flexibility, often love to learn about what creative ideas the little guys are working on, and should they be compelling enough, they then love to try and find a way to seize the opportunity themselves. Often times, corporate innovation thinking goes as follows — replicate clever ideas and strategies when possible, acquire fast-growing niche players if necessary, and preserve our market dominance no matter what. I've worked with a lot of large, public companies, and there are a plethora of incredibly talented and ethical executives out there. But as a new startup, just be aware of who you're talking with, what you divulge, and when possible, have a working agreement in place before you show them everything under the hood.

VCs don't sign NDAs:

When I went out to roadshow WML to Venture Capitalists in Silicon Valley, I tried to protect my idea by e-mailing a few VCs a Non-Disclosure Agreement along with the Executive Summary of the business plan. The kind ones actually replied and told me that they didn't sign NDAs because of the sheer volume of pitches they receive. Of the ones that didn't reply, I presume they just thought I was some green thumb founder who probably should have known better. I learned that lesson rather quickly — VCs don't sign NDAs — and realized that if there *was* something proprietary in our documentation, that I should remove it to give us an opportunity at a deal. I kept a spreadsheet of who I mailed what to — keeping track of the investor's name, company, date of submittal, response, and follow-ups. On the cover of the Executive Summary, I ensured I put their name and company, so that they would realize it was directed just to them. In hindsight, fifteen years ago, the Executive Summary and brief P&L proforma was enough to get you a shot. Today, due to the sheer volume of startups and overall noise in the market, it appears that a warm introduction from either a portfolio company founder, a former colleague, or another investor who is respected by the VC that you're seeking to get airtime with, is the optimal path in the front door.

Staying focused when things don't go your way:

The best way to beat the competition, as popular Venture Capitalist and marketing guru Guy Kawasaki puts it in his outstanding book (and one of my favorites to this day) <u>The Art of the Start</u>[46], is to simply win customers and not focus on beating your competition. "The best way to drive your competition crazy is not to do anything to it. Rather, the best way is for you to succeed because your success, more than any action, will drive your competition crazy. And the way you become successful is not by figuring out what you can do to the competition but for the customer."

The secret to entrepreneurship, I've discovered, is that your unique journey is actually the reward in disguise. Not that one thing at the end of the startup rainbow you think will be the reward. You may not realize this just yet, but as Tony Robbins often says, "If you're not learning, setting new goals, living in the moment and progressing, you're dying." Be present, be mindful, know what standards you believe in and when to fight to the bone for something with upside that's actually worth it. When you win those battles, remember that you are not alone. Other entrepreneurs have been there and traveled through the Valley of Startup Death. They have been cut down from their highs, they have had mud thrown in their faces, they have been sued and defamed, but they have not given up! They persevered, and lasted, and so can you. You have tremendous untapped power and strength within you to overcome every roadblock, but you just haven't met that person yet. Just know that when the going gets tough — and it will — find mentors who have battled through the trenches and who can guide you safely to the other side.

The darkest moments of our lives shape our resolve. Without the darkness, we don't appreciate the light.

CHAPTER 18:
PERSEVERANCE

So, I've told you startups are hard. I've proven statistically that most companies simply fail. I've even shown you what you're up against from competitors, markets, and frankly, assholes. And you still want to become a founder? Good.

There's just one more lesson that I've saved for last for you. For your final lesson, we must turn inwards, to master our psychology, before we understand how to effectively lead others, sell others, and create material wealth vis a vis our businesses.

Business, if you explained it to a third grader, is quite simple — you buy or build something for a cost (A), sell it to someone for a price (B), and keep the difference, profit (C). Everything else just gets in the way, right? What's harder to explain is everything in between.

Let's start with you — our daring, take-the-world-by-the-horns, ambitious founder. We all come from different walks of life, a blend of different socio-economic backgrounds, a mix of experiences — joyous moments, challenging moments, and everything else in between — and a myriad of education relative to people, business, sectors, markets, psychology, and history. Deep down, everyone has a different set of beliefs in themselves (some motivating and some limiting), that control what they feel is possible to achieve in their lifetimes.

You are both your biggest competitor, and your biggest cheerleader. Choose your inner muse wisely.

As a founder, there are days where you will be on top of the world, confident and duly motivated, ready to bust open a new market and take the industry by storm. There will also be days where you will be totally depressed for no reason, confused as to what to do next, doubtful of your ability to pull it off, lonely, scared shitless, or totally wanting to call it quits. Founders live between both worlds — confidence and doubt — and we must learn to reconcile the two.

The key is to find yourself more often than not on the better side of that psychological spectrum, so that you don't get sucked down the rabbit hole where doubt, indecision, and over-analysis plagues our existence.

Startups are not only the biggest test of our abilities to execute on an idea, but more deeply, test the limitations of our minds. They fully test everything we think we know about ourselves — from our deepest fears to our highest hopes — revealing everything in between.

Most startups fail in the mind before they fail in the market. If you can prepare your mind first for resiliency, you can prepare your business to follow, and then get your team to follow your lead. So how do we prepare our minds to be ironclad? I'll show you what has worked for me. While it may be different from what might work for you, I can only speak from my own experiences.

Visualization:

Visualizing is the key to creating the outcomes you desire. I have had to battle my own mind to just calm down enough in the past to be able to focus on visualizing what I wanted to build — as wild ideas would run, and then my next knee-jerk reaction would be to counter with a self-doubting narrative in my head that that idea was great but might never work.

I'd doubt my skills, my resources, my timing, my team, you name it. In my first startup, this internal battle led me to indecision for weeks on end sometimes, and eventually, dissolution. Glenn Kaplus, my former Board of Advisor used to counsel me, "Thoughts drive actions, actions drive outputs, outputs drive results." We have to dream it, feel it, and believe it, so that we may build it for others to use it.

Gaining Clarity:

There will be countless times where something goes wrong that throws you emotionally off course, or when things don't go as planned, that stymie you with indecision and anxiety. There will also be nights where the thoughts of the day simply keep you up no matter what you do. Here's what works for me to regain my clarity anytime I need it.

Step One:

Start by putting on some relaxing meditation music, deep study music, or a guided meditation from any app like InsightTimer®, CALM®, Headspace® or even white noise (available free on YouTube®). Then, take ten deep breaths — inhaling slowly for three seconds, exhaling slowly for three seconds. In so doing, you will have a lot of thoughts bouncing around in your head. Your job is not to remove the thoughts, but rather focus on one word — "Relax." By focusing on this one word, the thoughts will begin to subside over the next few minutes, and your body will be overcome by a sense of peace and clarity. If the word "Relax" doesn't do it for you, simply think of another word that does — "I am at Peace" (phrase), "I am calm" (phrase), etc., — just keep repeating that word or phrase over and over again for a few moments all while continuing to breathe deeply with intention.

Step Two:

After you have calmed down at least fifty percent, I want you to set an intention and ask yourself a question. This can be whatever you need to focus on at the moment but have been having a hard time doing so. For example — "What is the one thing I should be aware of right now?" "Who is the customer I should call next?" "What is the best business model for us?" "What is the next thing I should do?" "Who should I hire?" Whatever plagues you, turn it into a question and ask your higher self for guidance.

Step Three:

As you focus in on this question, clarity will come to you. Sometimes it will be in the form of an image, a feature, a memory, or even a person. Other times, it will be in the form of an idea, a phrase, or a specific thing you should follow up on. Whatever it is, don't judge it, don't question it, don't even think about how it can work or how you can meet that person or even why you are thinking about it. Open your eyes, write it down, and don't think about it. After twenty-four hours, go back to your notes, and see what you wrote down. Sometimes the clues are encrypted messages that only we can decipher later on, and other times, they become clearer with time as we step away gaining perspective.

There have been countless times as a founder where I would be confused as to what feature to design next. So, I would follow the above three steps, close my eyes, and visualize being one of our customers flying through our website. I would walk through the entire experience from the first click, to feeling what they would feel, to deciding if I should buy or not, to going through the checkout, to closing my computer and waiting a few days to see how the item arrived. I would then get clues as to where the friction points would be for the customer journey, and these clues would unlock these little magical insights that we could build to more astutely service our customers and delight them. The more you practice gaining clarity even when you're deep in the startup storm, the easier it becomes to get into the flow to see where you should sail next and why.

Motivation:

Business, as in life, takes motivation to move forward. We must be compelled just to get started in anything we do. However, motivating yourself in business on a recurring daily basis, ebbs and flows — some days you got it, while other days you don't.

In the beginning, no one is rooting for you except yourself.

Your friends may think you're onto a good idea. They may even be envious that you are bold enough to attempt building it. God knows, it might just work. What happens if you pull it off and become more successful than them? Your family loves you, but sometimes their motivation and encouragement wanes — some days they are there to listen and support you, and other days they aren't. It's not that your friends and family don't care about you, it's just that they're human, busy, and/or fear change. If you change, and improve your life and your status, wealth, connections and knowledge, then what happens to them? Will you still be friends with them? Will you be less available to see everyone? Will they develop an inferiority complex around you?

Startups Equal Change. Change Equals Fear.

You need to understand and accept that your friends and family, who you think should *always* be in your corner, may sometimes not be. This does not mean you should drop them as friends or stop loving them as family members, but you should simply prepare yourself for receiving their adoration, support, and praise in measured, sometimes infrequent doses. If you luck out and get consistently supportive friends and family members like I've been blessed to have, then that's fantastic. But there will always be a few who just can't handle the thought of you going after something bigger than yourself, and actually creating something that humanity might just fall in love with.

Check Your Ego:

If you're the type of person like I was in my twenties, who was seeking encouragement from others to continually reinforce your ideas, beliefs and path, get ready to get shook up when you start a company. Encouragement comes and goes, and there will often be times where you will ask people for their opinion on your business idea, next steps, website/app design, product functionality, service offering, restaurant food, etc., and they'll flat-out criticize it. I used to take this like a dagger to the heart — fully defending my position, idea, and product, and causing a fight with that person to prove that I was right, and that they didn't know a damn thing they were talking about.

Once I hit thirty, I learned criticism in business is not personal. If one person thinks a certain way, you can be assured that at least some group out there might share that same thought, so it's in your entrepreneurial best interests to understand why they have that viewpoint, and how to handle or react to it. When you really listen to what others are saying, you realize that they have an initial viewpoint, and although it may be different from yours, often times it is worth at least taking a look at, even though it is uncomfortable to listen to. Viewpoints change, and most viewpoints are initially established with limited information. If you don't listen deeply to the viewpoints of others, and you just want to be right all the time, you lose out on key lessons that will only make your business even stronger.

Entrepreneurs love to be right and prove the world wrong. But the best entrepreneurs come from a place where they think they could be right, but are open to feedback so they can create the best possible solution(s), not just the first draft they originally came up with.

Now, I know a lot of you have this idea that the best entrepreneurs are the rebels with this contrarian viewpoint that just no one believes will come to pass, and they just persevere and stick it out for years and years until finally it IPOs and becomes the next Google®. Reality check — that's not how Google was created. Great companies have smart minds all working together to make it the best possible solution for a segment of humanity. Research, feedback, and countless iterations are vital to create what people need and desire.

It's hard to hear negative feedback from people right when they give it to you. My tip: write it down, walk away, come back to the feedback when you're not emotionally attached to the outcome of being right and proving them wrong, and ask what motivated them to say that? Getting to the *why* behind the *what* is the secret to mastering feedback so that it doesn't personally offend you.

Perfectionism:

The first startup you launch will essentially feel like studying all night for four years at college with more material to learn than time allows. All the while, you're constantly building something you don't even know will work and are plagued by a never-ending feeling that it's never quite "good" enough. Listen. Your startup will never be perfect. So, embrace the imperfection! The slide deck for your investor — never perfect. The warm intro letter from someone — never perfect. The Beta you painstakingly built over the last six months — never perfect. The new employee you just brought aboard — never perfect. That's how it is — entrepreneurs are constantly striving for perfection in an imperfect art form. If you get tangled up, and demand perfection at all costs, you will likely spend too much time, effort, and capital and will miss the opportunity.

My suggestion is to give 100% effort but allow for a buffer. So what, the colors don't match on the checkout button and on the logo. So what, your pitch deck is in Helvetica when it shouldn't be. So what, the new developer you hired showed up fifteen minutes late to your office. Imperfection *is* the playing field — your job is not to be perfect. Your job is to survive. Know what game you need to be play and play it.

I fought, and continue to fight, my perfectionist tendencies. I hate to blame my early schooling for this, but you sometimes need to point a finger. If you don't write your name, class number, date, assignment number in the upper right-hand corner perfectly, you get docked five points. If you don't turn something in with a laminated cover letter, you get marked down. If you don't write five pages when the assignment tells you to write up to five pages, and you can get it all done perfectly in three, so you end up writing five pages of fluff, you get the picture. Perfectionism yields good grades, and good grades yields upward mobility and a safe career. Ah, the American Dream, right? A pension, a thirty-year mortgage, and a Cadillac® in the driveway.

Throw that out the window before you start your company. There are a few exceptions for when you should not stand for imperfection — but for the most part, you're embarking on a journey with so many unknowns, that it's nearly impossible to try to control it all.

You can only control a few things that matter — the caliber of the people you hire, what you focus on and when, what opportunities you turn down to focus on the ones that matter, what you say, what principles you decide your company stands for, and what values you strive to uphold in the world. Everything else is either dumb luck, fate, accident, or based on other people's reactions to the few things you think you control.

Scheduling:

I, by no means, am the most organized person in the world. I do write a to do list, use sticky notes for ideas and action items, and write my goals down in a journal.

The single most important task of a founder every day is to decide what to focus on, and why it moves the needle.

It's so easy to focus on the wrong things at the right time, and the right things at the wrong time, it should be the theme song of every startup. "Hello logo my old friend, I've come to talk with you again," instead of the Sound of Silence song, "Hello darkness my old friend, I've come to talk with you again."

When you're just ideating and coming up with a hypothesis for what your company could be, it's easy to jump down the rabbit hole to create the logo, print the t-shirts, design the awning out front, create the business cards, decorate an office space — all the "stuff" that you think *should* be done first. If you're stuck in wire framing mode — as I was for nine months — because you're too nervous to launch the product, then you're doing it wrong. You should be out talking to prospective customers and learning about their key pain points are, not re affirming what you think the market may want.

Find a way to schedule what matters most at each phase. Set a weekly list of goals that will truly move your company forward, and then what mini steps you can break it into to accomplish those goals. Founding teams must dream month-to-month, plan week-to-week, and act day-to-day to achieve their goals. Don't think in terms of quarters as you're not a public company reporting your earnings. Know where you are in the process, and what's required of you when as I've outlined in earlier chapters. Survival at all costs, not shareholder dividends.

Coincidences:

I've said that being a perfectionist is the antithesis of being an entrepreneur. Sure, you can be obsessively detailed oriented and strive for greatness as Steve Jobs did, but if you hold on to being a perfectionist, more often than not, you *will* fail.

Furthermore, what I have realized is that life has this very interesting and beautiful windy road that zigs and zags which takes you to and fro along your path. You will encounter new people, new experiences, and new challenges, and with each step you make a decision about you add to the culmination of millions of tiny decisions that set you on a different course. It's funny, as I look back on the last decade of my startup experiences, I could really only see about a quarter of what was in front of me at any given time if that. The rest was purely coincidental.

The easiest way to see what I mean is to look outside of entrepreneurship at your own life. Possibly, to see how you met the love of your life, or decided what school to attend for college, or decided what job to take — they all have elements that are connected by a series of randomized dots (decisions that led to events) that came just before you made a decision.

For a serendipitous example, how did I learn how to become an entrepreneur? One might say I grew up around other entrepreneurs, so by osmosis I inherited the desire to be entrepreneurial, but the formal education came from schooling, assuredly by Babson College. Where did I hear about Babson you might inquire? My sister was dating a pathology doctor, and on a total lark, I met him at a dinner in Palo Alto. He inquired as to what schools I was considering applying to, and I told him I had no idea, but that I wanted to study business (I thought it sounded smart). So, Brad gives me this book on the Best U.S. Colleges as ranked by students and tells me that I should check out this tiny, but powerful school in Massachusetts called Babson College. I had to ask him to spell the name because I swear, I thought he said Boston College, but he didn't. I earmarked that page and never thought twice about it until a few months later, when I was at community college taking a class and met a guy named Anthony. Anthony was a bit older and a lot more into seizing life by the horns and taking chances than I was back then, and when he asked me what colleges I was looking at, I said in passing that I was thinking maybe something in Boston. He exclaimed, "We're going!" I was like, "Um, really?" Literally that night he pulls out his credit card, books us two tickets to Boston, and I e-mail the school to set up a college tour.

I later fell in love with the school after visiting, and after making the challenging decision to just muster up the courage to go back East, I went. Looking back — if it wasn't for Brad's referral (the Doctor), Anthony's wild go-getter attitude (the college friend), the amazing admissions team at Babson (Anne Vozella, Brian Duggan, Katherine Price) — I never would have learned what I have learned, never would have even started my first business, and I assuredly never would have written the words in this book to help you. Pretty cool series of randomized events, right?

Life gives you coincidental opportunities — seize them, be open to taking the leap of faith, because they usually lead you to the right places you need to go.

In the course of your startup, you will encounter people that will introduce you to other people, that will then open your mind up to re-shaping how your business can do things differently, which will then bring someone else into your company because you're now doing something that attracts their eye, and so on. These coincidental events are contagious, if you follow them. If we fight them, we close ourselves off to all kinds of amazing developments both personally and professionally.

When you fly on a plane, chat with the person next to you, exchange cards — you never know where it will lead. When you have a chance to bring up your startup idea — bring it up to new folks and ask for direct feedback — you never know what radical new ideas they might share with you. Often times they might say something like, "Wow, that's a great idea— it sounds like you're the Matchmaker of X" — a totally new way of thinking might just be the phrase that lands you a meeting with an investor, attracts a new hire, or snags a new client.

Enjoying the Ride:

There are fewer things in life more enjoyable than to dream up an idea, build it, launch it, and reap the rewards. You ever wonder why entrepreneurs who take a company public or who get acquired often come back for more and keep starting companies and want to invest in new ones and give back? Even the relentless founders who close up shop on an idea want to roll the dice just once more. The journey is intoxicating, eye-opening, and most rewarding on a multitude of levels.

Startups are a bittersweet video game — you go through a struggle for months on end to launch something you hope might work, to then rise up to the next level in the game to then refine it so it does work, to then rise up again to an even higher level to scale it to work for more people. The journey is simply the best part. If you fail too early and give up, you never really get to experience the best parts of it. If you launch and give up because of low usage or a lack of sales, you never experience the joy of having thousands of people use something that you built with your mind and heart — a deeply gratifying feeling that is near impossible to describe with words.

If you only listen to this one piece of advice from this book, listen to this — regardless of your startup's outcome, enjoy every day you work on it with the people around you. Relish the journey. And, no matter what level you get to in the game, know that you can always start over and win on the next go-round.

Entrepreneurship is for Everyone:

My father, son of an immigrant Russian, Jewish pharmacist, is a self-made entrepreneur and a true American Dream story come to life. He grew up in poverty-stricken Brooklyn, New York in the 1930s and 40s, shoveling snow off of driveways in the winter, bussing tables upstate in the Catskill Mountains in the summer, and slept in a one-bedroom apartment with his parents. He came from a lineage of pharmacists. His grandfather served in the Russian army in Poland during WWI as a medic helping fallen soldiers defeat the invading Nazis. He was later hung by the Nazis and put-on display in the square of Bialystok in 1940. My grandfather, who had immigrated to Brooklyn, discovered his own father's death by happenstance; just reading the morning newspaper.

Brooklyn, in the 30s and 40s was nothing like the posh, Hipster-chic place with organic themed restaurants it has morphed into today. "It was tough, kids routinely brought knives to school. We called it Stinkin' Lincoln High School," he would recount to me. A few startups under his belt, and about fifty years later, sitting on the beautiful coastline in Central California, my father recounts his tough street days from Brooklyn. It's both deeply inspiring and gratefully satisfying for me to see a real-life American Dream story told right in front of my eyes. He explains that after spending time in the U.S. Army, and a few gigs here and there to make ends meet, he got into the book publishing industry. Over the years he worked his way up the ladder by selling encyclopedias door-to-door in the country's toughest neighborhoods — from Harlem, New York to Watts, California — and met every kind of person, of every race, creed and color, from every kind of background along the way. Today, he knows America better than most. If you ask him to name an area code, he can cite off virtually any one from his decades on the road and on the phone.

But life wasn't always so easy. He had to shake off the stutter that plagued him for years prior just to regurgitate the fifteen second pitch he needed to say to get a family to open the door to let him in for a few moments to share the value of the encyclopedia series to educate their children. "Today's Web entrepreneurs have it easy, the world is at your fingertips," he explains. Sales didn't come easy, but he learned to connect with every American because life demanded it from him. He eventually found his stride and worked his way up from door-to-door sales, to territory sales manager, to eventually founding his own firm, Presidential Publishers. Think about that for a moment. From poverty in the 1930s, to President in the 1960s. The entrepreneurial dream was possible then and is still alive and well today.

In the 1960s the U.S. was racially divided, and tensions were high. To counter this and spread peace through education, he purchased the rights to an inspiring single volume history series called In Black America[47]. He met with African American pastors, civil rights leaders, government officials, and businessmen and women throughout the country, and formed deep relationships and goals aimed at educating and inspiring African Americans, to pave the way for a brighter future together. The 1960s hurried on, and the massive racial divide grew wider, and more violent. All the while, his company's vision remained steadfast to eliminate the bigotry rooted in miseducation and bring both sides together through knowledge and appreciation of the often-untold African American heritage, outlined throughout the books. While schools only taught a few

African American stories from Booker T. Washington and a few notables, the series shed a beautiful new light on the forgotten past that led up to the racial divide — the forgotten yet incredible African American inventors, athletes, civil rights leaders, and peaceful protestors — and planted hope for a better future built on mutual respect for all Americans, regardless of the color of their skin.

In 1965, the Watts Riots hit Los Angeles, and sparked an even deeper chasm in our country. While his startup battled on to fight ignorance through knowledge, over the years, the laws changed preventing his sales team from going door-to-door. In a pre-Internet era, door-to-door conversations were the main means to reach families, and the road became impassable to move forward. Looking ahead, my father wanted to be a part of something that everyone could instantaneously love. Something that didn't require a formal education to appreciate — enter, Balloons.

In 1973, he founded a party balloon company, Creative Balloons Manufacturing, and over the next forty-eight years, put smiles on millions of peoples' faces around the globe, and was a part of many of life's most precious celebrations — birthdays, Quinceañeras, anniversaries, baby showers, weddings, and even at the bedside in hospitals, encouraging the sick to "Get Well Soon!" With balloons, his company helped families welcome newborns, support companies to celebrate their own grand openings, and put ambitious entrepreneurs into business with their own balloon startups nationally.

Millions of smiles later, when people ask him what his golf handicap is — because they assume he spends his days on the golf course as most successful entrepreneurs do — he says in his Brooklyn accent, "Oh me? I was a three, now I'm down to a two." They reply, "Wow, you must be a great golfer!" He says, "Listen, you asked me what my handicap was, right? Well, I don't play golf." As they stand with a confused look on their faces, he says, "I'll explain — I'm a high school drop-out from Brooklyn, I'm left-handed, and I used to have a terrible stutter that prevented me from talking to anyone...so I'm now a two handicap. If you can overcome all of that, you can overcome anything!"

My father's entrepreneurial story is one I certainly admire. Today, he loves helping small business owners hit their own stride, as do I, and he finds pleasure in life's simple moments — scrambled eggs with onions, a cup of coffee and a newspaper, sitting in the sunshine overlooking ocean and woods with his dog by his side. His strength in life grew out of his struggles, his setbacks turned into opportunities, and his creative vision to continually build a brighter future for all around the world. The pleasure he derives from owning his own small business is deeper than any financial return he has ever received from it. When he opens the office door before anyone else, it's the dawn of a new day, one more shot to "be a servant of the people" he proclaims and to enjoy the journey past, present, and future.

Never let your age, lack of education, gender, scarcity of resources, or any other setback define what you can and cannot do in life or in business. The magic of owning your own business is that anything is possible, so long as you dream and will it to be.

CHAPTER 19:
EPILOGUE

We've come so far together, but the journey starts now for you. We've covered ideation by looking at deep emotions within humanity as the Insightrepreneur does, to unlock unique insights that lead us to solve micro and macro problems. I've coached you through new product development, what it really takes to launch, how to raise venture capital by flipping the power paradigm, and how to think partner to win. I've highlighted techniques that I've successfully used in my companies to determine the best marketing initiatives that lead to the highest return on investments, and how to optimize and align your brand, messaging, and platform to solve pain, increase life's pleasures, or prevent something from happening in the future for others — the pain killer, the ice cream cone, and the vitamin. I've demonstrated that to motivate and lead others well, we ourselves must know ourselves and must be decidedly clear of our North Star. And, lastly, I taught you how to quiet and tame the inner mind, get total clarity on your milestones, and address your own personal limitations so you can reach your dreams, whatever they may be.

We've covered startup failure at an up close and personal level, and learned to push ourselves through it to reach success on the other side. In chapter one, I've shown you that entrepreneurial failure isn't such a bad thing after all, conversely, it is a required rite of passage to grow and succeed in business. It's near impossible to launch your first company and make all of the right decisions at every step of the way — only sensationalized stories, case studies, and books falsely lead us to believe that it's possible. Overcoming our own internal fear of failure is critical to succeeding, but ironically, fear of failure is only extinguished if we actually fail and get back up and fight again. Otherwise, fear plagues us and our ability to lead purposefully forever. The "successful" entrepreneurs are actually members of the same club; they have at least a few failures in their lockers. We've erased the allure in our minds of becoming the next 'Overnight Entrepreneur' — a mirage that lures us into thinking that we're either missing out by not replicating someone else's startup path, or, by preventing us from even starting the journey in the first place out of a sense that we either don't have great ideas ourselves, or that we could never execute like a Bezos, Edison, Hoffman, or Musk. By way of my own startup tales, I've demonstrated that you should leverage your ephemeral youth and inexperience in a market and turn them both into your key strengths early on — helping you to see where incumbent companies fail to deliver and innovating at lightning speed with youthful exuberance and a make it happen now attitude. Inexperience comes with no prior blueprints on what's possible or not, and from that place, innovation, creativity, and radical new solutions can flourish.

I've taught you to *not* sell product features, but to sell results, as proven results instill trust with customers, increases sales, and unlocks compounding growth potential. We've thrown out the old adage to "Find your passion" and learned to replace it with "Find Profit". Moreover, we've broken the shackles of our own limitations that we must be passionate first before we have any chance to turn an idea into a successful business for ourselves. In establishing this new mindset, we open ourselves up to experimentation, exploration, and ultimately, clarity to build what people truly want or need, not what solely fulfills us.

I've implored you to throw out the fifty-page business plan with five-year pro formas and replace it with the Turnkey Plan — a more realistic twelve-to-twenty-four-month roadmap with key assumptions, actual costs to launch, and clearly defined milestones to achieve in a limited horizon. I later taught you that you must decide where to play in a market and how to effectively price your product, service, or experience to win. We've learned that most customers return to the median price, and by avoiding No Man's Land pricing, we set ourselves up to win a quadrant of the market and differentiate our offering from other competitors.

Additionally, I introduced you to the Four Players when it comes to pricing to win:

- The Low-Cost Leader

- The Premium Player

- The Customizing Specialist

- The Superb Value Creator

In so doing, we showed you that your positioning in the market drives your overall pricing strategy, marketing, and customer segment focus. Choose a quadrant to win or perish in No Man's Land.

I introduced you to Maslow's Hierarchy of Needs, and outlined the critically important connection between consumer psychology, brand positioning, and market adoption. Additionally, I illustrated the three types of startups:

- The Ice Cream Cone

- The Vitamin

- The Pain Killer

By understanding the three types of startups, I pushed you to truly determine what archetype you are intent on being and why you should focus all of your messaging around that claim and never stray.

In later chapters, I taught you about Media Ratio, how to effectively measure advertising spend across different types of marketing channels and advertising mediums, and how to calculate which has the best ROI/ROAS. In addition, we outlined how A/B testing will help you to optimize your ads and marketing collateral so that you better connect with buyers in your markets and increase the likelihood of signup, engagement, and conversion to purchase.

In The Launch, I debunked the myth that startups are still expensive to start, and illustrated how my first startup in 2007 cost nearly $100,000 just to launch a Beta version. Today, entrepreneurs can ideate, launch, and test for pennies on the dollar compared to what it used to be. There are many excuses not to launch a startup but cost to launch to prove market demand in today's time should not be the main part of the equation anymore.

Additionally, I taught you about the customer, and showed that savvy entrepreneurs deliver an overabundant amount of value for them on their initial touchpoint with their brand, filling up emotional debt, spurring goodwill, and subsequent transactional reciprocity. We introduced you to the art of the gift with our story of the baklava, and demonstrated that the best entrepreneurs, regardless of industry, design to delight, deliver a surprise, and treat customers like family. I later pointed out that you can't always please every customer, and that customer complaints are bound to crop up. However, when you fail to deliver, there's a stark difference between a monumental failure and a non-monumental failure. Knowing the difference can help keep you on track moving forward. Admitting mistakes and quickly resolving them can defuse just about any situation with irate customers, and we have now learned how to turn the lemons into pitchers of lemonade.

Furthermore, I showed you with the G.P.S. Rank system, how to effectively compare and rank your entire customer experience — pre, during and post-purchase — against the competition, so that you can improve the underlying areas that support the overall experience. In so doing, we learn deeper insights about the customer, and discover ways to reduce friction points in the customer research phase, signup, transaction, and post purchase. G.P.S. Rank unlocks a new metric that we can use to gauge the experience from our customer's vantage point and helps us differentiate in the building blocks that define engagement with our companies.

Up next, we learned about the power of crafting stories. It is the story that defines the speed and bearing of our journey; the companies that set their compass on a powerful heading, not only reach their destination quicker, but also build unwavering support along the way. To reach our destinations, we must garner the support of suppliers, partners, and customers, so that we unlock a new approach to thinking about these relationships. Instead of thinking solely about what we want to get out of them, we put ourselves in the position of the other side, and think about serving them first, building longstanding relationships, and ultimately, getting what we may wish. And when we get what we want, we learned that humility and a heartfelt "thank you" goes miles above and beyond a payment to a supplier or partner. After all, we are all human and driven by shared emotional currents.

Then, I taught you that rejection is the key to unlocking sales. We learned that we must come to understand the polar difference between having a business concept or a product rejected on the basis of something — price, timing, feature set, etc. — versus that of personal rejection. Otherwise, we will *always* feel personally attacked as an individual when we are rejected and will be plagued by a fear of rejection from others in the future. We learned that the sales process is an exercise, not a finished method. It is a continual journey that gets us closer to getting what we want, but it will never be a guaranteed system with a guaranteed outcome. And we showed you that it is actually *through* rejection — by way of The Rule of 100 Rejections — that ultimately, we hone our pitches and realize financial gains.

In a later chapter, we learned that all startups share similar phases, and that instead of getting lost in our own mazes, we can plan on being in the different phases before we even launch. We were introduced to the four different startup growth patterns:

- The Hockey Stick Curve

- The S-Curve

- The Heartbeat

- The Zombie

By seeing the different types of startup growths, we can better prepare for the financial cash flow requirements and emotional ups and downs that await us. We also learned that we must stop thinking about pro forma statements and start being a performer that delivers real results. In startups, we must live day by day, plan month by month, and dream year by year. We also learned about the importance of cash flow with our Love Birds dating app example and saw the connection between PMMF (product-market-model fit), cash on hand, and traction (over the first twenty-four months of a startup).

Moreover, when you're trying to scale and things just aren't moving, we introduced you to bottlenecks, and specifically the four different bottlenecks that can stunt our growth:

- Emotional bottlenecks

- Intellectual bottlenecks

- Financial bottlenecks

- Social bottlenecks

We learned to self-assess our own lives and our resources, so that we can determine what's truly holding us back today, and what our startups need to grow tomorrow. With financial bottlenecks, we highlighted the importance of access to capital for unplanned situations that can deplete your balance sheet in an instant and explained that The 5% Contingency Rule can help you better weather any financial storm that may hit you when you least expect it.

To win in the market, we must win the mind. So, we delved deep within ourselves, and learned that our startups are simply a reflection of our internal narratives. We tapped into our own motivating forces and our internal narratives that define what we can and cannot do. We learned that anything is possible, but we must get very clear on what we truly want, otherwise "more sales" doesn't represent a financial figure, "faster to market" doesn't illicit a timeline, and "successful" is an amorphous delusion — what does happiness truly look like for you? We learned that what we need are absolute specifics when it comes to manifesting what we truly want — regardless if it is a $350,000 condo, a $4 million dollar yacht in the Mediterranean Sea, or something else. In business, we must always pick a target, as this ensures that everyone and everything is aimed at hitting the mark. Otherwise, any tailwind will get us "somewhere".

I've taught you to think like the Insightrepreneur who finds opportunity through actively listening to users, observing without prejudice, and asking probing questions to unlock pain and friction points, that ultimately unlock new solutions. We also met the four Forgotten Insights:

- An undiscovered, yet more often, just overlooked market

- A shared human experience (psychological or emotional)

- An evolving, rapidly expansive trend (or future ecosystem)

- A deep situational or circumstantial insight

As we delved deeper, we learned about the harsh reality of time on a startup — our most pernicious enemy. We showed you that time to market launch accounts for a large number of failed startup ideas, that either took too long perfecting, too long testing, or too long researching before delivering anything of value. Moreover, we explained that raising capital — through venture capital rounds, angel financings, or other means — is buying you time, not delivering an outcome — more time to experiment and more time to iterate.

Then, I introduced you to the thought process behind VC funding, and how investors like to invest *just* before a startup has a breakout moment. As you recall, breakout moments vary from startup to startup, industry to industry, and most importantly, what an entrepreneur defines as an inflection point, is often times different from what an investor defines as the same thing. Being on the same page yields greater results should your startup be seeking an outside round. Ultimately, most all venture funding decisions devolve to a basic equation centered around traction. We learned about Brad Feld's "Rule of 40", and how, should you be interested in putting your startup in the best possible position to raise a financing, your team should be aimed on hitting one of the three combinations of 40% growth.

Additionally, I have suggested to you that I think you should only raise capital when you are in the strongest possible position to negotiate. The job of an entrepreneur is to flip the power paradigm to make investors jump to fund you. The only way to do that is with proven traction demonstrated over a short time horizon. And I pointed out that an inverse relationship must be planted in your mind when raising capital; the investor is the supplier, and your startup is the customer — they are selling capital, and you are buying it by selling stock. Not the other way around.

In later chapters we covered marketing and learned about the importance of truly knowing your customer acquisition costs (CAC) and lifetime value of your customer (CLV). We learned that value creation for your firm, and ultimately long-term profitability and scale comes from increasing the spread between the ratio of LTV:CAC, by having more lifetime value from recurring payments and cheaper customer acquisition costs through more effective (targeted) marketing campaigns. As a heuristic, most VCs prefer to invest in companies that have a ratio of 3:1, whereby every $1 invested yields a $3 return on the capital. If your ratio is too little, it signals that the cost of acquiring the nth customer is too high, and if the ratio is too big, you are likely leaving money on the table by not spending enough, thus not acquiring customers fast enough. Knowing your unit economics and CLV:CAC ratios are keys to understanding how the machine operates and can scale rapidly, should that be your goal.

To bring the lessons to life, I introduced you to my first two startups — WorldMusicLink and LaDolceDeal — and pointed out how failure at each successive step ultimately led me to startup success. With WorldMusicLink, we learned that spending too much time perfecting the wireframes and building the product features, prevents you from getting to market and getting vital customer feedback. By turning on monetization too early and forcing customers to convert or defect, we showed how early monetization can stunt your growth and alter your value-creating mindset. And lastly, I demonstrated that every entrepreneur must find the right blend of Product, Model, and Market fit. If we only nail two of the three, we are surely setting ourselves up for short or long-term failure. Additionally, I explained that the role of the entrepreneur is three-fold. Startups have three areas that they must focus on and execute in.

- Activities *within* the business

- Activities *on* the business

- Activities *outside* of the business

With LaDolceDeal, we learned that we must treat our content like fresh fish — good for no more than two or three days — so we must always be creating new content to satisfy the ever-growing needs of today's fickle, socially connected consumers. I highlighted that businesses are evolutionary, and that business models take time to tweak and perfect. Often, the first model and market that you launch with ends up looking very different from who you serve in twelve months down the road. I showed that it's acceptable to be open to pivoting, so long as you make the decision quickly. Lastly, we learned that all great businesses are well-oiled machines; their founders know what levers to push/pull at the right time to unlock growth as needed. We ourselves must determine all of the moving parts in our own businesses in order to accurately steer the ship to where we want to go. When we fail to understand how our business works, and what moves what, we end up going in circles and often failing before we should.

Lastly, we learned that building a startup well requires more than the external, tangible elements, rather, the internal mind of the founding team matters most. I explained that startups are not only the biggest test of our abilities to execute on a market hunch, but more deeply, a test on the limitations of our own minds. They fully test everything we *think* we know about ourselves — from our deepest fears to our highest hopes — and most startups fail in the mind first, and the market second. You are both your biggest competitor, and your biggest cheerleader, and we must choose who we allow into our inner sanctuaries while we are building a new company, as startups thrive on positivity and an attitude that anything is possible with a good idea and perseverance. As Glenn Kaplus, my former Board of Advisor used to guide me, "Thoughts drive action, action drives output, outputs drive results." We have to dream it, so we can build it, before others can use it. We must use visualization techniques, block out the naysayers, manage our time wisely, and be open to coincidental opportunities that may lead us forward.

Above all, I taught you that regardless of your startup's outcome, enjoy every day you work on it with the people around you, relish the journey, and no matter what level you get to in the game, know that you can always start over and win on the next go-round. Thank you for reading. I hope that my journey, and my lessons learned have helped to paint a better picture for entrepreneurship and will help you become a more successful founder and leader.

Dream big where others dream small, act boldly when others doubt, make an impact when one is needed, and leave a legacy that raises the bar for others.

Want more startup tips and strategies to grow your business?

⇒ Subscribe to Reagan's Free Newsletter at: <u>ReaganPollack.com</u>

⇒ Follow me on Facebook: @reagantpollack <u>facebook.com/
reagantpollack</u>

⇒ Follow me on Twitter @reaganpollack: <u>twitter.com/
reaganpollack</u>

⇒ Follow me on Instagram @reagantpollack: <u>instagram.com/
reagantpollack</u>

⇒ Follow me on Clubhouse @reaganpollack: <u>https://
www.joinclubhouse.com</u>

A Heartfelt Thank You:

I am honored that you have spent time out of your life to read this book — it truly is humbling, and I hope that my words shed light on the startup journey and provided you with takeaways that you can implement immediately in your startup. If my book has helped you in any way, I would love to hear from you on social media and would be deeply moved if you would write an honest online review for others to see. Again, thank you for your support. I wish you only the best in this lifetime and in your startup!

ACKNOWLEDGEMENTS:

For my father, mother and sister, you all have supported me in so many ways, most of which you will never truly know the profoundness on my development. I thank you all for always believing in me and encouraging me to pursue my entrepreneurial dreams. A personal thank you goes out to my father, who inspired me from the beginning of my business days at sixteen, by showing me the value of a dollar and imparting a lasting sense of pride in owning one's own company. To my mother, the most creative force I have ever had the pleasure of working with, you inspire me daily to reach for the stars and create win-win partnerships with all of those I work with. And for my sister, for always being an inspirational beacon and believer in the possible.

A thank you goes out to all of the buyers who turned my products and pitches down over the years, the investors that passed on my startups, the partners who gave up on our ideas, the suppliers who weren't there when I needed your support, the friends who doubted my dreams, and the customers who defected — you have taught me so much from those experiences, and without the rejection, pain, and struggle — my success, nor this book, would not have been possible. Thank you!

A thank you goes out to all of my amazing professors from Stevenson, Monterey Peninsula College, Babson College, and Stanford University, mentors, advisors, past employees, investors, editor, and friends. You have always been there to inspire and guide me in the right direction, and your ears and words have provided the constructive support that an entrepreneur only wishes to have.

Thank you so much to all who have contributed quotes, edits, and guidance for this book; your support has meant everything to me throughout my journey.

A special thanks to these individuals who have inspired me to write this book and follow my dream to inspire other entrepreneurs to reach their greatest potential: My parents, Christina, Renata, Eric Yuan, Bob Caspe, Ryan McDonald, Angelo Santinelli, Jen Schuster my fabulous editor, Len Green, Bob Jamieson, Kuljit Dharni, Dr. Joel Shulman, Glenn Kaplus, Joe Fletcher, Ted Grossman, Elizabeth Riley, Tamara Conniff, Howard Rosenblum, Dr. Robert Klevan, Bret Waters, Catherine Howard Lovazzano, Katy Mogal, John Rizzo, Rhonda Byrne, Tony Robbins, Deepak Chopra, Napoleon Hill, Brad Feld, Jason Mendelson, Guy Kawasaki, Paul Graham, Eric Reis, Robert Cialdini, Brian Chesky, Jeff Bezos, Reid Hoffman, Jack Ma, Elon Musk, Tien Tzuo, Steve Jobs, Peter Thiel, Bashar Sneeh, Faisel Nimri, Alfred's Coffee, and Roger Babson.

NOTES:

[1] *"Survival Rates and Firm Age"*, SBA, Office of Advocacy November 1, 2016: https://www.sba.gov/sites/default/files/SurvivalRatesAndFirmAge_ADA_0_0.pdf

[2] Katya Wachtel, *"Peter Thiel's Clarium Has Now Lost 90% Of Its Assets"*, Business Insider, 2011: https://www.businessinsider.com/peter-thiels-clarium-nosedives-90-percent-from-peak-hegde-fund-2011-1

[3] *"Insight"*, Merriam-Webster Dictionary: https://www.merriam-webster.com/dictionary/insight

[4] *"Entrepreneur"*, Merriam-Webster Dictionary: https://www.merriam-webster.com/dictionary/entrepreneur

[5] *"Dropbox vs. Box: Valuation Matchup"*, CBInsights, July 11, 2017; https://www.cbinsights.com/research/dropbox-valuation-bubble-2/

[6] The Secret, Rhonda Byrne, November 1, 2006, Published by Atria Books/Beyond Words: https://www.amazon.com/Secret-Rhonda-Byrne/dp/1582701709

[7] Think and Grow Rich, Napoleon Hill, Arthur R. Pell, August 18, 2005, Published by TarcherPerigree: https://www.amazon.com/Think-Grow-Rich-Landmark-Bestseller/dp/1585424331

[8] Image Credit, SYS International Yacht Sales: http://sarasotayacht.com/co-brokerage-used-yachts-for-sale-101-130-feet/?rPage=/privatelabel/listing/pl_boat_detail_handler.jsp?slim=pp288214&units=Feet&boat_id=2755194&back=/privatelabel/listing/cache/pl_search_results.jsp?slim=pp288214&sm=3&is=All&cit=true&searchtype=buy

[9] Image Credit, Zillow.com: https://www.zillow.com/homes/for_sale/Jackson-WY/pmf,pf_pt/194364525_zpid/12085_rid/globalrelevanceex_sort/44.090544,-109.521332,42.858853,-111.498871_rect/8_zm/

[10] Awaken the Giant Within, Anthony Robbins, Simon & Schuster Inc., 1986.

[11] *Masters of Scale*, Handcrafted podcast episode with Brian Chesky, Co-founder & CEO of Airbnb, Reid Hoffman, May 3, 2017, https://mastersofscale.com/brian-chesky-handcrafted/

[12] *"K-Factor"*, Wikipedia.org: https://en.wikipedia.org/wiki/K-factor_(marketing)

[13] Christopher Mance II, "Viral Coefficient Calculator", Nichvertising, http://nichevertising.com/viral-coefficient-calculator/

[14] Kat Odell, Image Credit, EATER Los Angeles, 2013: https://la.eater.com/2013/1/24/6490869/melrose-has-a-sweet-new-place-to-drink-coffee-alfred

[15] Image Credit, MyLittleCosmo.com, LCosmo, 2017: http://mylittlecosmo.com/alfred-coffee/

[16] *"Heuristic"*, Wikipedia.org: https://en.wikipedia.org/wiki/Heuristic

[17] Image Credit: Saul McLeod, "Maslow's Hierarchy of Needs", SimplyPsychology.org, 2020, https://www.simplypsychology.org/maslow.html

[18] Eric Pfanner, Kristine Owram and Jen Skerritt, *"Corona beer brewer extends pot bet with $3.8Billon investment"*, The Denver Post, August 19, 2018: https://www.denverpost.com/2018/08/19/corona-beer-brewer-marijuana-investment/

[19] Thomas Mitchell, *"The Six Largest Dispensary Chains in Colorado"*, February 4, 2019: https://www.westword.com/marijuana/colorados-six-largest-marijuana-dispensary-chains-9128785

20 "The Six Largest Dispensary Chains in Colorado", Thomas Mitchell, February 4, 2019: https://www.westword.com/marijuana/colorados-six-largest-marijuana-dispensary-chains-9128785

21 J. Clement, "*Online dating in the United States – statistics & facts*", Oct 26, 2020: Statista, https://www.statista.com/topics/2158/online-dating/

22 Bigad Shaban, Robert Campos, Anthony Rutanashoodech, "*Hidden Cameras Reveal Rare View of 'Epidemic' as Car Break-Ins Hit Record High of Nearly 30,000 in San Francisco*", NBC Bay Area, March 12, 2018: https://www.nbcbayarea.com/news/local/Breaking-Point-475109113.html

23 Bernard Marr, "*The Key Definitions of Artificial Intelligence (AI) That Explain Its Importance*", February 14, 2018, Forbes.com: https://www.forbes.com/sites/bernardmarr/2018/02/14/the-key-definitions-of-artificial-intelligence-ai-that-explain-its-importance/#3cf5f14b4f5d

24 "*Artificial Intelligence*", Merriam-Webster: https://www.merriam-webster.com/dictionary/artificial intelligence

25 Adam Barone, Gordon Scott, "Inflection Point", Oct 17, 2020, Investopedia.com: https://www.investopedia.com/terms/i/inflectionpoint.asp

26 "*J-Curve*", Wikipedia.org: https://en.wikipedia.org/wiki/J_curve

27 "*S-shaped Growth Curve*". A Dictionary of Zoology, Encyclopedia.com. September 1, 2018: http://www.encyclopedia.com

28 Tren Griffin, "*12 Things about Product-Market-Fit*", A16Z.com, August 2, 2017: https://a16z.com/2017/02/18/12-things-about-product-market-fit/

29 Product-Market-Fit Analysis of Love Birds Dating App, No Startup Left Behind, Reagan Pollack, January 16, 2021

30 Bob Caspe, "*What Kills Most Start-Ups?*", CaspeGroup.com: http://caspegroup.com/blog/2015/04/what-kills-most-start-ups

31 Subscribed: Why the Subscription Model Will Be Your Company's Future - and What to Do About It, Tien Tzuo, Gabe Weisert, June 5, 2018, Published by Portfolio

32 Brad Feld, "*The Rule of 40% For a Healthy SaaS Company*", FeldThoughts, Feld.com, February 3, 2015: https://feld.com/archives/2015/02/rule-40-healthy-SaaS-company.html

33 Brad Feld & Jason Mendelson, Venture Deals: Be Smarter Than Your Lawyer and Venture Capitalist, Second Edition, December 26, 2012, Published by Wiley: https://www.amazon.com/Venture-Deals-Smarter-Lawyer-Capitalist/dp/1118443616

34 Tony Robbins, https://www.tonyrobbins.com/

35 Deepak Chopra, https://www.deepakchopra.com/

36 Paul Graham, http://www.paulgraham.com/articles.html

37 Peter Thiel and Blake Masters, Zero to One: Notes on Startups, or How to Build the Future, September 16, 2014, Published by Currency: https://www.amazon.com/Zero-One-Notes-Startups-Future/dp/0804139296

38 Guy Kawasaki, The Art of the Start, September 9, 2004, Published by Portfolio: https://www.amazon.com/Art-Start-Time-Tested-Battle-Hardened-Starting/dp/1591840562

39 Robert B. Cialdini, PH.D., Influence: The Psychology of Persuasion, Revised Edition, December 26, 2006, Published by Harper Business: https://www.amazon.com/Influence-Psychology-Persuasion-Robert-Cialdini/dp/006124189X

40 MySpace, Wikipedia.org: https://en.wikipedia.org/wiki/Myspace

41 MySpace, Crunchbase.com: https://www.crunchbase.com/organization/myspace#section-acquisition-details

42 The Lean Startup: How Today's Entrepreneurs Use Continuous Innovation to Create Radically Successful Businesses, Eric Reis, Crown Publishing Group, September 13, 2011.

43 Brian Headd, *"Why Do Businesses Close?"*, May, 2018, SBA.gov: https://www.sba.gov/sites/default/files/Small_Biz_Facts_Why_Do_Businesses_Close_May_2018_0.pdf

44 Blitzscaling: The Lightning-Fast Path to Building Massively Valuable Companies, Reid Hoffman and Chris Yeh, Currency (Crown Publishing Group), October 9, 2018.

45 Brad Feld & Jason Mendelson, Venture Deals: Be Smarter Than Your Lawyer and Venture Capitalist, Second Edition, December 26, 2012, Published by Wiley: https://www.amazon.com/Venture-Deals-Smarter-Lawyer-Capitalist/dp/1118443616

46 The Art of the Start, by Guy Kawasaki, September 9, 2004: https://www.amazon.com/Art-Start-Time-Tested-Battle-Hardened-Starting/dp/1591840562

47 Jules Pollack, In Black America, First Edition, Published by Presidential Publishers, January 1, 1970

Figures:

Figure 4.1: Yacht Image "Ginger". Image Credit, SYS International Yacht Sales: http://sarasotayacht.com/co-brokerage-used-yachts-for-sale-101-130-feet/?rPage=/privatelabel/listing/pl_boat_detail_handler.jsp?slim=pp288214&units=Feet&boat_id=2755194&back=/privatelabel/listing/cache/pl_search_results.jsp?slim=pp288214&sm=3&is=All&cit=true&searchtype=buy

Figure 4.2: Condo/House Image. Image Credit, Zillow.com: https://www.zillow.com/homes/for_sale/Jackson-WY/pmf,pf_pt/194364525_zpid/12085_rid/globalrelevanceex_sort/44.090544,-109.521332,42.858853,-111.498871_rect/8_zm/

Figure 9.1: Alfred's Coffee, "But First, Coffee". Kat Odell, Image Credit, EATER Los Angeles, 2013: https://la.eater.com/2013/1/24/6490869/melrose-has-a-sweet-new-place-to-drink-coffee-alfred

Figure 9.2: Alfred's Coffee, "Interior". Image Credit, LCosmo, MyLittleCosmo.com, 2017: http://mylittlecosmo.com/alfred-coffee/

Figure 9.3: G.P.S. Rank Chart. Image Credit, Reagan Pollack, 2021.

Figure 10.1: Maslow's Hierarchy of Needs Pyramid. Image Credit: Saul McLeod, *"Maslow's Hierarchy of Needs"*, SimplyPsychology.org, 2020, https://www.simplypsychology.org/maslow.html

Figure 11.1: Product Market Fit Love Birds Dating App example. Image Credit, Reagan Pollack, 2021.

Figure 12.1: Bob's Java Customer Acquisition Cost to Lifetime Value example. Image Credit, Reagan Pollack, 2021.

Figure 15.1: Monthly Activity Chart example. Image Credit, Reagan Pollack, 2021.

Figure 15.2: Time Management Graph example. Image Credit, Reagan Pollack, 2021.

Figure 15.3: Product Market Model Fit Venn Diagram. Image Credit, Reagan Pollack, 2021.

9 798218 234874